SUCCESSFUL LYRIC WRITING

SUCCESSFUL LYRIC WRITING

A Step-by-Step Course and Workbook

Sheila Davis

Author of *The Craft of Lyric Writing*

 Cincinnati, Ohio

94 93 92 91   6 5 4 3

Library of Congress Cataloging-in-Publication Data

Davis, Sheila,
　　Successful lyric writing.

　　Bibliography: p.
　　Includes index
　　1. Popular music—Writing and publishing. I. Title.
MT67.D255   1987   784.5'0028   87-28044
ISBN 0-89879-283-5

Design by Sheila Lynch

To my students

The art of making art
Is putting it together
Bit by bit. . . .
  STEPHEN SONDHEIM

ACKNOWLEDGMENT

I want to acknowledge my special thanks to Stephen Sondheim for granting permission to quote from two songs from his Pulitzer Prize musical *Sunday in the Park with George.*

FROM "PUTTING IT TOGETHER":

*The art of making art
Is putting it together
Bit by bit. . . .*

*First of all you need a good foundation,
Otherwise it's risky from the start. . . .*

*Every minor detail
Is a major decision. . . .*

*Putting it together,
That's what counts. . . .*

*Having just the vision's no solution,
Everything depends on execution. . . .*

*Link by link,
Making the connections. . . .
All it takes is time and perseverance
With a little luck along the way. . . .*

FROM "MOVE ON":

*Anything you do,
Let it come from you.
Then it will be new. . . .*

*Move on.
Just keep moving on. . . .*

CONTENTS

INTRODUCTION

Stage One   **How to Build a Sound Structure**
   Step 1   The Essential Lyric Framework   2
   Step 2   The Major Song Forms   20
   Step 3   Managing Viewpoint, Voice, Time Frame, and Setting   46

Stage Two   **How to Make Your Words Work**
   Step 4   Applying the Top-Ten Principles to Avoid the Pitfalls   72
   Step 5   Figuring Out Figurative Language   88
   Step 6   You Got Rhythm   103
   Step 7   A Rundown of Rhyme   113

Stage Three   **How to Put it Together**
   Step 8   Writing with the Whole Brain   123
   Step 9   Finding Your Voice   140
   Step 10   The Moral Dimension   149

Stage Four   **How to Keep the Ideas Coming**
   Step 11   Ten Lyric Writing Assignments   156

Stage Five   **How to Move Onward and Upward**
   Step 12   Starting a Songwriting Workshop   238
   Step 13   A Guided Critique Session   246
   Step 14   Joining the Pros   256

APPENDIX
Song Starter Pages   264
Answers to Practice Critiques and Quizzes   268
A Songwriter's Bibliography   273
Songwriter Organizations   276

INDEX OF SONG TITLES   **285**

SUBJECT INDEX   **289**

INTRODUCTION

Soon after the publication of *The Craft of Lyric Writing,* letters began to arrive that both delighted and surprised me: I was delighted that readers liked the book, and surprised that they wanted more how-to material. Clearly, there was a need to be filled.

Some readers asked for cassette lectures. Some asked for videotaped seminars. Still others wanted a correspondence course. But none of those teaching modes, for one reason or another, struck me as ideal.

I decided that the job would be done best by adapting my Basics Course into book form. So here it is: *Successful Lyric Writing,* a home course and workbook.

Like students in my classes at the New School in New York and in workshops around the country, you will put theory into practice one step at a time: First you'll learn the principles and techniques, then you'll do warmup exercises, and finally you'll write ten full lyrics.

In addition to quizzes on theory and practice critiques with teacher feedback, this book offers guidelines on how to form and conduct a workshop in which your skills can continue to develop through the interplay of the group dynamic.

No one learns lyric writing solely by reading about it. Or by listening to lectures about it. Or by watching videos about it. Those activities can of course be enriching. But the way to learn to write lyrics is to write lyrics.

So let us begin.

How to Build a Sound Structure

First of all you need a good foundation,
Otherwise it's risky from the start. . . .
STEPHEN SONDHEIM

The Essential Lyric Framework

Five elements frame every well-written lyric:
> A Genuine Idea
> A Memorable Title
> A Strong Start
> A Payoff
> The Appropriate Form

A GENUINE IDEA

Your genuine idea should:
> Be about believable people in recognizable situations
> Express a clear attitude or emotion
> Be substantial enough to be set to music
> Strike a common chord
> Put the singer in a favorable light
> Have its "situation" built in
> Make millions of people want to hear it over and over

Every thought you get for a lyric may not pass the screening test as an identifiable idea. For example this one:

TIRED

Morning comes
I don't want to get up
Hide my face in the pillow from the sun
Nothing moves me
My thoughts weigh a ton
Wish the day were over
But it's just begun and I'm

TIRED
Can't keep my eyes open
TIRED
And listlessly hopin'
The day would go back where it came from
I'd gladly give up my place in the sun
I'm so TIRED.

It's the third straight Monday
I've felt this way
For the love of the weekend
Something must pay
Guess I donate my body
When Friday night calls
By the weekday morning
I can barely crawl, I'm so

(repeat Chorus)

© 1985, Student lyric. Used with permission.

Although every potential listener knows what blue Monday feels like, physical fatigue doesn't qualify as AN IDEA. There's no emotion there—unlike the Beatles' "I'm So Tired." Their lyric reflected on the singer's depression after three weeks of sleepless nights thinking about his lover; that emotion is substantial enough to warrant being set to music. The student lyric makes the singer sound wimpy and thereby violates a second essential—putting the singer in a favorable light.

Here's an excerpt from another entry scratched at the starting gate:

FASCINATED BY YOUR FRECKLES
(An Excerpt)

I'm happy to relate, my cares are dissipated
That's because I'm FASCINATED BY YOUR FRECKLES.
I count them one, two, three—on to infinity;
Why you'd be tanned if you should land
A few more freckles.

Eyeing you in the sunshine, watching the pigment spread
You're no mirage, no, you're no figment coming from my head.
My ice cream had no sprinkles, pepper was just a spice.
I never knew the holes in Swiss cheese could be paradise!
Fillet of flounder I do without: I've switched to speckled trout.
My waterspout can shower out a spray of speckles
If I'm a complete wreck, I plead guilty,
And I'm FASCINATED BY YOUR FRECKLES!

© 1984, Student lyric. Used with permission.

The writer has a facility for internal rhyme. But rhymes without substance do not a lyric make. This "idea" flunks an absolute requisite: to be about believable people in recognizable situations. *Fascinated* by freckles? Unbelievable. *Charmed* would even be stretching it. Alluding to a lover's freckles—along with other more noteworthy physical attributes might be worth a few words, but not an entire song. The lyric lacks emotional truth. And lacking that, lacks everything.

Here's another idea aiming for a pop record:

BROADWAY

When I ask my wife where to go
She always says, "A Broadway show."
I don't know why I never learn;
It's just the beginning of a long, slow burn.

BROADWAY! BROADWAY! Wear your finest tweed.
BROADWAY! BROADWAY! Feed producers' greed.
BROADWAY! BROADWAY! I get so aggravated.
BROADWAY! BROADWAY! It's just so overrated.

Yes, it's true I love my wife, though I may soon forsake her,
For every time we walk into Neil Simon's Little Acre,
We dodge nimble street performers and obnoxious mimes,
Passing unconvicted felons pondering their next crimes.

BROADWAY! BROADWAY! Fifty bucks a seat!
BROADWAY! BROADWAY! End up feelin' beat.
BROADWAY! BROADWAY! Get crushed in the lobby.
BROADWAY! BROADWAY! Let's get another hobby.

So next time the little woman wants to see a show
Let her go all by herself, or buddy, you're a schmo!
BROADWAY! Sit there adding up the tab
BROADWAY! And then stampede for a cab
BROADWAY! The critics all cry "Groovy!"
BROADWAY! Better see a movie!

The lyric shows writing talent. It's well-constructed, well-developed and even contains a few laughs. But it's not the stuff that pop songs are made of—because it doesn't speak for most people. It speaks for one character—one highly individuated personality—feisty, lowbrow, and judgmental. Lyrics aiming for the pop marketplace—whether rock, country or R&B—should reflect generic characters.

Although it wasn't the writer's intention, this lyric could work in a different genre. Let's imagine, for example, that "All in the Family" was adapted into a musical. Picture the neighborhood bar. Archie Bunker comes in and complains to his buddies about Edith's nagging him to take her to the theater; he sings "Broadway." The lyric now works because we know the character and we've been given a context. A popular song—unlike a theater song—must create its own built-in context.

Pop Writers Think "Record"

Every time you aim a lyric at the pop marketplace, you must think in terms of writing a record. Consider as you begin: for whom am I writing this song? What recording artist can I imagine in my mind's ear singing these words?

Recording artists seek songs that express emotions with which millions will identify: "Nobody Does It Better," "She Works Hard for the Money," "(I'm a) Material Girl," "Nothing's Gonna Change My Love For You."

When you can give an artist an idea that an audience will want to sing along with, you're off to a good start.

Before Moving On
Exercise #1

Before sending your lyric out into the world, be sure that it reflects a universally shared emotion, or universally understood situation, or universally comprehended meaning. Here are some well-known song titles that illustrate those three qualities. Fill in the blanks with additional universal qualities, giving other songs that illustrate them.

Universally Shared Emotion	*Song Title*
Self-assertion	"I Will Survive"
Hope	"Tie a Yellow Ribbon"
Optimism	"Everything's Coming Up Roses"
_____	_____
_____	_____

Universally Understood Situation	*Song Title*
Anticipation of holidays	"Easter Parade"
Commitment to new love	"We've Only Just Begun"
Irony of bad timing	"Send in the Clowns"
_____	_____
_____	_____

Universally Comprehended Meaning	*Song Title*
Everything changes	"Same Old Lang Syne"
Even a worm will turn	"Coward of the County"
Like father, like son	"Cat's in the Cradle"
_____	_____
_____	_____

A MEMORABLE TITLE

A memorable title:

> Is identifiable after one hearing
> Resounds with one meaning
> Summarizes the essence of the lyric's statement

The title is the name of your product—what the listener asks for at the store. Skillful songwriters know how to make a title both unmistakable and unforgettable. To make it unforgettable, you must put it in the right place and then repeat it often enough. That's easy to do when you're familiar with song forms—which we'll take up soon in detail. To make your title unmistakable, make sure that no secondary phrase competes with your intended title. One heavyweight title is better than two or three middleweight titles. To illustrate the multiple-choice malady to my Basics Class, I read the following lyric aloud and ask them to identify the title. I suggest that you read it aloud too, so that the competitive phrases will bombard your ear. (If someone is handy to read it to you, so much the better.)

It's reprinted here without separating its various sections—the way your ear would hear it. Read it through quickly and immediately jot down on the line below what you think the writer titled the lyric.

_____

(Title?)

I can tell by the smile on your face
Just what he's been saying.
I can tell by the way you behave
The game he's been playing.
There was a time when I loved him too,
But listen, 'cause I'm warning you
He's a criminal of love and
He's dangerous,
So watch what you do.
This man's wanted, dead or alive,
He gets his pleasure from seeing you cry.
He'll steal your heart, it makes him high,
He's a heart thief,
Thief on the run.
He strikes with his charms.
He'll make you feel like a child again.
He'll hold you till the time is right.
You'll place your faith in him, but
As soon as you fall for his con,
I can tell you, girl, he'll be gone.
He's a criminal of love,
He's dangerous,
He's leading you on.
This man's wanted, dead or alive,
He gets his pleasure from seeing you cry.
He'll steal your heart, it makes him high,
He's a heart thief,
Thief on the run.

That's a lyricist with a natural pop style. But her title circuit is overloaded. That lyric contains enough distinctive phrases to title six songs: Criminal of Love; (He's) Dangerous; This Man's Wanted; Wanted Dead or Alive; Heart Thief; Thief on the Run. Whew! The lyricist's intended title, incidentally, was "Heart Thief."

Write Your Title

Even successful professional songwriters sometimes "misdesign" a lyric in which two ideas unintentionally fight each other for attention. The giveaway is the parenthetical title: "Here I Am (Just When I Thought I Was Over You)"; "Mutual Surrender (What a Wonderful World)."

The objective is to make your title complete the phrase: "and that is why I say...." Ira Gershwin—a master of one-of-a-kind titles cautioned lyricists: "A title is vital/Once you've it, prove it."

To prove your title be sure it's what your song is really about. I remember a student lyric called "When Night Time Falls" but her lyric was really about wanting to get back together with someone; the title didn't sum up the plot of the lyric.

Make your title resound with one clear and consistent meaning. Another student lyric titled "Feedback" gave the word three interpretations: negative feedback, positive feedback, and no feedback. Because the title lacked significance, it left no after-image. Ira Gershwin practiced what he preached: "Someone to Watch Over Me," doesn't reflect multiple ideas, such as once I had someone to watch over me; sometimes I don't like someone to watch over me; I may never again have someone to watch over me. It states only, "Oh how I *need* someone to watch over me." The simplicity and consistency of that one thought is what helped make the song a standard. Hearing a title should immediately trigger its meaning: "Body and Soul" . . . "It Was a Very Good Year" . . . "Teach Me Tonight" . . . "I Will Survive". . . .

Ac-cent-tchu-ate The Positive

State your title in positive terms. I remember two student lyrics that illustrate the wisdom of this guideline. One was about a long-lasting love that was titled: "Easy Come, Easy Go"! That's exactly the opposite of the song's content. The chorus began ". . . we're NOT easy come, easy go." The writer didn't write her title; instead she imposed an ill-fitting script on a title she was eager to write. (Given her story line, she would have had an effective song by titling it "Lifetime Lovers," or "Timeless Love.")

The second title was intended to capture the singer's feeling of euphoria: "What in the World Could Be Wrong?" Seeing that title on the top-40 might lead one to think the song dealt with suspicion rather than an emotional high.

Take a tip from manufacturers of household cleaners who name their products for what they do, rather than for what they don't do: Not, "Out with Dirt," but "Spic and Span"; not "Worknomore," but "Easyoff." When it comes to titles, think positive.

Detect "Dead-end" Titles

Be wary of titles you can't "prove." Writers—ever on the lookout for fresh titles—can be easily ensnared by a seductive phrase they overhear, or read, or invent. For example, "It Isn't Even My Life," "If It Comes to Love," "When Was the Last Time It Felt Like the First Time?" These phrases may initially sound like intriguing song starters. They did to three students. But the lyrics that those three titles sparked sounded contrived. In each case the writer's defense was, "But I loved the title!" Loving a title isn't enough; you've got to make it work. A title phrase needs to be rooted in a real life situation or universal emotion. Be sure you can do that before you begin to write.

Save Your Title For Your Title

Your title deserves special treatment. It's what your listeners have been waiting through a verse or two to hear. So *really* make them wait in a way that pays off. A small craft warning: Don't dilute the effectiveness of your title by using any of its words elsewhere in your lyric unless doing so is essential to the title's setup. For example, in the country hit "Nobody," we had to hear the singee claim "nobody" was on his mind before the singer exclaimed, "Well, your nobody called today." On the other hand, our hearing the word "Maniac" in its first verse would have rendered the title less effective when it struck in the chorus.

Before Moving On
Practice Critique #1

Here's a student assignment that grabs the listener with a provocative opening line, features a fresh and memorable title, strikes a common chord, and, on first hearing, appears to be a well-conceived verse/chorus lyric. Yet it has a major flaw. After you read the lyric, review the title guidelines. Then try to pinpoint the problem and how to remove it.

NITPICK

Verse
*Nothing's really wrong
But nothing's quite right.
You've been home ten minutes
And we've started to fight.
I don't know who began it
And I don't care.
All I care about
Is keeping the loving feeling there.*

Chorus
*I don't want to NITPICK anymore.
All we do is NITPICK—what a bore!
We might pick, pick, pick away the love,
All the love we had before.*

Verse
*Put aside the bills.
I'll let the dishes sit.
Turn the TV off and hug me,
It won't hurt a bit.
I'd rather sit and kiss you
And kiss again
Than fight a fight
That neither of us can win.*

(repeat chorus)

Bridge
*"I said. . . ." "You said. . . ."
How'd we get to this?
"You don't. . . ." "I did. . . ."
Baby, how I miss you.*

Chorus *I don't want to NITPICK anymore.*
All we do is NITPICK—what a bore!
We might pick, pick, pick away the love,
All the love we had before.

Your critique: _____

_____

_____

_____

_____

(To compare your critique with mine, turn to page 268.)

Title Techniques

Starting to write a lyric from a title is more likely to produce a cohesive lyric than starting to write without one. "Title first" has been the preferred work method of successful writers from Ira Gershwin to Cynthia Weil. Here are some title categories that traditionally bring home the hits:

Device	Example
Antonyms	I Got It *Bad* and That Ain't *Good*
Alliteration	"The *T*ender *T*rap"
Days/Months	"See You in September"
Colors	"Green Tambourine"
Places	"Moonlight in Vermont"
Colloquialisms	"Too Close for Comfort"
Altering the Adage	"Two *Hearts* Are Better Than One"

When titling your lyric with an idiomatic expression, look it up before you leap. A misused colloquialism can send a lyric into the wastebasket. Here are some common offenders from students: the "eye of the storm" does not refer to the height of the storm, but rather to its calm center; the "tip of the iceberg" does not imply more things to come (in general) or more *good* things to come, but solely more *bad* things to come; "on my own" does not mean alone, in the sense of "without someone else," nor does it mean "lonely"; it means independent—without outside help. Tip: You'll find precise definitions, along with lots of title ideas, in *The Handbook of Commonly Used American Idioms,* edited by Adam Makkai.

Before Moving On

Exercise #2

Invent three song titles that suggest to you an emotion or meaning with which millions will identify; then synopsize the plot you would give each:

1) _____

(An intriguing one-word title such as "Muscles")

Plot synopsis: _____

2) _____

(A place title such as "Do You Know the Way to San Jose?")

Plot synopsis: _____

3) _____

(Substitute the word *love* in an idiomatic expression, for example "*Loving* Beyond My Means")

Plot synopsis: _____

A STRONG START

You need a start that:

> Pulls the listener into the song

> Establishes the Who, What, When, and Where in the first few lines

Like effective advertising copy, a well-wrought lyric grabs the listener's attention and holds it. Your first objective is to pull the audience right into the center of the action. Here are some techniques to hook the ear:

THE QUESTION. "Is this the little girl I carried?" ("Sunrise, Sunset"—Harnick/Bock)

THE GREETING. "Well, hello there, good old friend of mine." ("Come in from the Rain"—Sager/Manchester)

THE REQUEST. "Grab your coat and get your hat." ("On the Sunny Side of the Street"—Fields/McHugh)

THE PROVOCATIVE STATEMENT. "I've been alive forever, and I wrote the very first song." ("I Write the Songs"—Johnston)

THE TIME FRAME. "Wednesday morning at five o'clock." ("She's Leaving Home"—Lennon/McCartney)

THE SITUATION. "We had the right love at the wrong time." ("Somewhere Down the Road"—Weil/Snow)

THE SETTING. "On a train bound for nowhere I met up with a gambler." ("The Gambler"—Schlitz)

THE IMAGE. "Over by the window there's a pack of cigarettes." ("Him"—Holmes)

THE OCCUPATION. "Behind the bar I see some crazy things." ("You Could've Heard a Heart Break"—Rossi)

Try To Upgrade Your Opening

Take a critical look at your first draft to be sure its first two lines compel an audience to stay tuned. Then see if you can find a stronger way to pull your listener into the scene. Here's what I mean:

First draft: "Lately you've been acting different."

The revision: "When did you start reading poetry?"

With its lackluster cliché, the first line tells us nothing. The revision, with its compelling question, tells us the singer is suspicious because the singee (the one sung to or about) is behaving out of character. Now we're intrigued enough to stay tuned.

Before Moving On

Exercise #3

Revise examples 1 and 2 in the manner indicated. Then create three original opening lines for 3, 4, and 5 using one of the techniques discussed on page 10.

1) "Lately I've been thinking we don't talk much anymore."

_____

(Try showing it with a request)

2) "On my daily commute to the city. . . ."

_____

(Show where he is with a Time Frame and Setting)

3) _____

(Show the singer's occupation)

4) In two lines addressed to a particular singee, give an entreaty, a warning, or command:

_____

_____

5) Show the singer is a performer flying home to his lover after being on the road for a while:

_____

_____

_____

_____

A PAYOFF

To build to a payoff:

       Choose your plot type—attitudinal, situational, narrative

       Know what it is you want your audience to feel

       Place elements in ascending order of importance

       Draw some conclusion—either stated or implied

Three Kinds of Plots

A plot is the pattern of events in a story. Most lyrics are not stories as such. Yet, the word *plot* is common songwriter parlance. It refers to a lyric's sequential movement—whether it be narrative or simply emotional. Lyric plots come in three levels of complexity: attitudinal, situational, and narrative—that is, story songs.

    The *Attitudinal Song,* the simplest of the three, is one in which the singer expresses an attitude or emotion about someone or something. For example, "I Can't

Smile Without You," "Endless Love," "Always on My Mind." The majority of pop songs are simply attitudinal.

In the *Situational Song,* the writer has given that attitude or emotion a dramatic framework: the singer is reacting to a particular set of circumstances; for example, in "Somewhere Down the Road," the male lover is saying goodbye to a woman who's going off to do her thing; in "Tie a Yellow Ribbon," an ex-con is traveling on a bus home to his girl. Situational songs are the second most common plot category.

The *Narrative,* or *Story Song,* has a plot in the true sense of the word; it's a linear tale with a beginning, middle, and end. The story song is either the singer's recollection of a personal event, as in "Taxi" and "Ode to Billy Joe," or a tale about someone the singer knows, like "Harper Valley PTA," and "Richard Cory." Lastly, a story can be told by that impersonal camera eye, such as "Eleanor Rigby" and "She's Leaving Home."

The lyricist's job is to take that attitude, or situation, or story, and develop it to a satisfying conclusion—a payoff.

Every well-written song gives the listener a total experience—from something, through something, to something. The emotional profile of a well-developed lyric—even an attitudinal song—looks like this: x————————x——x. A lyric without a point—such as "Tired"—feels more like this x————————————x.

In order for your lyric to make a listener fight back a tear, get up and boogie, or march on the Pentagon, your words must convey one clear, consistent emotion. So first decide the effect you want your song to produce. Knowing your end will lead you to the right means.

Develop—Don't Paraphrase

New writers frequently mistake paraphrasing—saying the same thing in different words—for development. As a case in point, I recall a student who, moved by the accident at Chernobyl, turned his fears for the future into a lyric. The writer reflected that all the inhabitants of the earth shared his concern. He conveyed the idea in the first verse in examples like *from castles to igloos . . . the bag lady and the duchess . . . from the White House to the Kremlin.* But every subsequent verse was composed solely of more such examples: *from the tenement to the penthouse . . . from the private to the general. . . .* Each coupling kept restating the same thought that everyone—regardless of stature or nationality—is equally anxious. The lyric never went anywhere.

Go Somewhere

Starting with a universally understood situation like Chernobyl assures your lyric of that essential quality of familiarity. It's like the *hello* of recognizing an old acquaintance on the street. But you don't just keep saying hello, hello, hello. After hello, comes the brief exchange: "How's-the-family-are-you-still-living-in-Scarsdale?" And then comes the wrapup: "It's-been-good-to-see-you-let's-have-lunch." Hello/conversation/goodbye.

The Chernobyl lyric spent four verses saying hello. In any lyric the listener wants to hear some new thoughts in the middle and an emotional closure at the end. Again: x————————x——x.

Here are the devices to help your lyric say something after it says hello.

Development Techniques

Meaningful Sequence

To create a satisfying conclusion, place the details of your plot—whatever they may be—in ascending order of importance—from small to big.

In addition to lacking a conclusion, the Chernobyl lyric suffered from the willy-nilly order of its couplings. The sets of pairs would have benefited from being grouped, for example, in ascending order—from individuals, to habitats, to nations. Remember the three verses of "First Time Ever I Saw Your Face"? The lyric developed from ". . . saw your face . . . kissed your mouth . . . lay with you."

Keep your eye on your plot's clock and calendar. If your story moves in time—even imagined time—put the hours or days or years in logical order. The singer in "Losing My Mind" thinks about her former lover from her morning coffee, through her afternoon chores, to her sleepless nights. Another good example is Alan Jay Lerner's three seasonal scenes of summer, autumn, winter in "If Ever I Should Leave You."

The concept of meaningful sequence also applies to putting the cause before the effect, the premise before the conclusion, and the action before the reaction or consequence. First comes the banana peel, then comes the pratfall. Not vice versa.

Imagery

An attitudinal lyric can be enriched through word pictures that appeal to the five senses. The country hit, "I'm Going to Hire a Wino to Decorate Our Home" illustrates the wife's threat to renovate with a series of graphic examples: *neon sign, sawdust, aluminum beer cans, pretzels, TV above the bar, Hamm's bear.*

"Gentle on My Mind" has no real situation other than the singer's being at some geographical distance from the singee, but it is made rich in atmosphere through the skillful arrangement of word pictures that slowly progress from far away to up close: *railroad track, wheat fields, clothes lines, dirty hat, gurglin' cauldron . . . cupped hands 'round a tin can. . . .*

The artful imagist will intuitively arrange a lyric's word pictures from distant to close so as to parallel the way our senses perceive: first we hear, then we see, then we touch, then we feel, then we know. (Both "Wino" and "Gentle" are reprinted in *The Craft of Lyric Writing* with a full analysis.)

The Scene Method

Like dramatists, lyricists often present scenes; for example, the sequential vignettes of "By the Time I Get to Phoenix" and "It Was a Very Good Year." Scenic sections can also alternate with or be followed by nonscenic ones as in the concluding verse of "Good Year," which sums up the singer's attitude toward his life.

Reversal

Aristotle defined this technique as "the thrilling turn of luck at the last moment in comedy or tragedy." Like virtually all dramatic devices, it adapts to lyrics.

Reversing the fortune of the singer has been a plot staple in our standards. The introductory verse of many earlier hits bemoaned the singer's lovelessness and the chorus celebrated the miraculous appearance of a lover from "Out of a Clear Blue Sky," or "Out of a Lemon Colored Sky," or "Out of Nowhere." In "Blue Moon" the singer's solitary state was instantly changed when "Quite suddenly appeared before me/The only one my arms could ever hold." (Rodgers/Hart).

Foreshadowing

This technique suggests a plot development before it occurs. One of the most memorable examples is the opening line: "Everyone considered him the coward of the county" (Bowling/Wheeler). That hints that we're going to hear a story that will show that "everyone" was wrong.

Midway through "Class Reunion" (Henry/Morris) a foreshadowing line gives the listener a clue to a possible development in the plot. This artfully written story song (recorded by John Conlee) opens with the singer sorting his mail and finding an invitation to his high school reunion. He muses about the old gang and wonders if a girl who never noticed him might be there. On reunion night, as he enters the school's dark, deserted gym, a familiar-looking woman steps shyly out of the shadows and confesses to having sent him the invitation.

The Question Plot

This device presents a question in the first verse which is not answered until the last line of the lyric. In a song of mine, "What Do I Need?" the singer is asking herself what can she do to make it sink in that the affair is really over; she concludes "I need more than a prayer/Or a new affair can ever do/I need a miracle to get me over you."

In one of the best-known examples of the Question Plot, a wife greets her arriving-home husband with "Guess Who I Saw Today (my dear)?" (Boyd/Grand). She proceeds to tell him that after shopping she stopped in a café to have a bite. In a dark corner she saw a couple "so much in love" that they were oblivious to their surroundings. She finally answers her own question: "Guess who I saw today . . . I saw you." The introductory verse gave the alert listener a hint of the plot to come in the foreshadowing line: "You're so late getting home from the office. . . ."

In "Could I Leave You?" from *Follies,* Stephen Sondheim has designed the quintessential question plot. After aiming a barrage of verbal bullets at her boring husband, the long-suffering wife seems to resolve her question with "yes." But then we're treated to the surprise denouement: "Will I leave you? Guess!"

Note: A song with an opening line question or a question title is usually simply a rhetorical device—and rarely turns into a Question Plot, which is an underused development technique.

The Return

This plot device brings back some key word, phrase, line or even entire section heard at the outset of the lyric. In "Same Old Lang Syne," the winter scene is established by the line ". . . the snow was falling Christmas eve. . . ." In the song's last line, ". . . the snow turned into rain. . . ." The return of the snow motif, by bringing the story full circle, gives the listener the sense of having had a complete experience.

Near the climactic final verse of "I'm Still Here," from *Follies,* Stephen Sondheim returns the first images of the opening verse: "Plush velvet sometimes/Sometimes just pretzels and beer." Hearing the line again reinforces the financial seesaw of the acting profession.

Sometimes a song's opening line returns as the lyric's last line to show the habitualness of the action. For example Mac Davis's "In the Ghetto": "On a cold and grey Chicago morning a baby's born and his mother cries. . . ." Hearing that line echoed at the end of the song reminds us of the vicious circle of poverty and crime. Again, in his tribute to Nashville's songwriters, "16th Avenue," Thom Schuyler returns the opening lines of his first verse to emphasize the ongoing nature of the song's plot.

Some lyrics create emotional closure by the return of the entire first verse: "California Dreamin'," "Do That to Me One More Time," and "Annie's Song."

Conflict

"Baby, It's Cold Outside," "Feelings," and "Separate Lives" all employ the essential element of drama—conflict—an opposition between the singer and some other force.

Sometimes it's the human heart in conflict with itself as in "Coming In and Out of Your Life." Often the conflict is between the singer and singee, such as "What Are We Doing in Love?" Occasionally the singer is at odds with society: "Society's Child."

Surprise

Surprising your listener can be achieved three ways—through *The Turnaround, The Discovery,* and *The Twist.*

The Turnaround is a last-line effect that's often accomplished by reversing a key word in the title with its antonym: "I Got *Lost* in His Arms . . . but look what I *found*" (Berlin); "This Is the *End* of a Beautiful Friendship . . . but just the *beginning* of love" (Kahn/Styne); "I fell *in* love with love . . . but love fell *out* with me." (Rodgers/Hart). Sometimes the turnaround comes from a play on the title as in "Careless" ("You're *careless* in everything you do"); the payoff changes an adjective into a verb—"or do you just *care less* for me?" (Howard/Jurgens/Quading).

One of the several development techniques Stephen Sondheim uses to build to his climax in "I'm Still *Here*" is the turnaround line "Lord knows at least I was *there*. . . ."

The Discovery is the dramatic technique by which the truth of the drama is not revealed until the end. It isn't until the last line of Tom T. Hall's "Harper Valley PTA," for example, that we discover it's the singer's mother who socked it to the PTA.

"Guess Who I Saw Today," in addition to being an example of a question plot (and using foreshadowing) saves identifying the "who"—the truth of the song, that the singer saw "you"—until the last line.

The Twist, in much the same way as the discovery, withholds the truth until the song's end—but with a difference. It jolts us with an unexpected conclusion. In Gilbert O'Sullivan's "Claire," for example, we presume throughout the song that the singer is talking to his troublesome lover; it's only at the end we realize that all along he's been addressing his little niece. Comedy songs often use a form of surprise as a payoff. Here's a student's lyric that evolved from an assignment to make an original statement using Cole Porter's meter and rhyme scheme of "You're the Top." The result successfully employs the Discovery device.

YOU'RE A JERK
You're a mindless turkey
YOU'RE A JERK
And your future's murky
You're a lazy oaf
Who lives to loaf and putz
You're beneath a nerd
(As I've inferred),
A total clutz.
You're a slob
And a hopeless boozer
With no job;
You were born a loser.
And I regret
The worst is yet to say
And that's you're the jerk
My daughter weds today.

© 1985, Noel Cohen. Used with permission.

Most surprise plots result from a writer coming up with a title, devising the last line, and then filling in the lyric from the bottom up. It's an ideal way to work.

Ironic Tension

Songs without either conflict or a surprise can of course sustain our interest. "Send in the Clowns" is a perfect example. Its success rests partially on the tension engendered between the singer's expectation of renewing a romance she had ended and the ironic actuality that it's too late.

Irony results from the clash between what *seems* to be or *ought* to be, and what *is*. For example, in Fran Landesman's plaintive "Spring Can Really Hang You Up the Most," spring, which generally elicits delight, has the singer ironically despondent— "praying for snow to hide the clover."

Before Moving On
Exercise #4
First, write a Turnaround ending. Create a last line that pivots on a word that's opposite to one word in the lyric's title. For example, the song "You Are Not My *First* Love" (Windsor/Howard) concludes, "but maybe you'll be the first to *last*."

_____

(your title)

_____

(your final line)

Now imagine you've got an idea for a situational song about the end of a long-term marriage. The wife has been slowly evolving into a high-powered executive while her husband's career has leveled off. She has just announced she's leaving him. The lyric is the husband's reaction to the news. Write a four-line verse that foreshadows for the listener what's about to happen.

———————————————————————————————————

———————————————————————————————————

———————————————————————————————————

———————————————————————————————————

The Conclusion: To State or Not To State

There are three ways to produce a lyric with a satisfying emotional experience. You can state the meaning of the song, you can imply the meaning, or you can leave its interpretation to your listener. Your lyric concept will direct its own method.

The Stated Conclusion. Many pop songs contain a particular line that says, in effect, "Here's the point of my song":

"You may never want to change partners again." ("Change Partners"—Berlin)

"Until you find the love you've missed, you're nothing." ("Alfie"—Bacharach/David)

"You'd think I could learn how to tell you goodbye." ("You Don't Bring Me Flowers"—Bergmans/Diamond)

The longer you can keep the audience waiting for that wrapup line the better. Ideally, it arrives in the song's final phrases. Two examples come to mind: The rhetorical question "Why Did I Choose You?" (Martin/Leonard) resolves with the lyric's closing words: "If I had to choose again, I would still choose you." "Desperado's" last line warns, "Better let somebody love you before it's too late." (Frey/Henley)

When stating your meaning, the basic technique is to establish the situation, slowly fill in the details, and save the biggest statement for the last.

A verse/chorus song, by its very construction, tends to make its point in the chorus's title—*and that is why I say:* "Papa Don't Preach" or "Everything That Glitters Is Not Gold."

The Implied Message. Stating the conclusion is the direct approach to a payoff, and the most common one. Some songs are more subtle: They let the listener infer what the writer has implied. A simple illustration is Dan Fogelberg's "Same Old Lang Syne"—that chance meeting of two former high school lovers on Christmas eve. After they reminisce in her car, the married singee drives away leaving the (unmarried) recording artist gazing after her. His feelings—obviously wistful—are left unidentified. To one listener the song's meaning might be: life was simple back in high school; to another: every love affair must come to an end; to still another: life is all compromise; to someone else: to gain success we must sometimes forego an intimate relationship. The lyric states none of those things, but implies them all.

The Ambiguous Meaning

In "Blowin' in the Wind" Bob Dylan pricked our conscience on the questions of racial discrimination and war. The *plot* is clear. But his title's meaning was ambiguous. My quizzing of students on what "Blowin' in the Wind" meant to them has prompted such responses as "The wind is blowing seeds of meaning"; "I can harness the wind"; "The wind has blown the answers away"; "The answers are elusive"; "If we tune in to nature, we'll find the answers."

Often, what has not been spelled out can be made more evocative by being unstated.

A Word About Ambiguity

Before leaving the subject of plot development, I want to briefly clarify the term *ambiguity* as it applies to lyric writing. Essentially, there are two kinds: desirable ambiguity and undesirable ambiguity.

As just discussed, leaving the *meaning* of your lyric open to interpretation can enrich the listener's enjoyment. That is desirable ambiguity. Conversely, the *plot* of your lyric—its attitude, or situation, or story—should be clear.

In "Who Will Answer," for example, I presented clear vignettes on divorce, suicide, war, drugs, and the bomb. Similarly to "Blowin' in the Wind," the *meaning* of "Who Will Answer" was left to the listener to interpret: God will answer; no one will answer; we each must answer; there is no answer. The diversity of reactions that arrived in my mailbox ran the gamut from "Your lyric is blasphemous" to "Thank you for your ministry."

What more can a lyricist wish for than to have an audience listen and react—one way or another?

But don't confuse intriguing with baffling. Multiplicity of meaning is one thing, vagueness of plot is another. Any word, or phrase, or line that confuses your listener as the lyric streams by requires clarification. (Both the causes and prevention of verbal ambiguities will be taken up in detail in Steps 3, 4 and 5.)

Avoiding Plot Block

Novice lyricists often experience the frustration of getting stuck midway through a song. Although there may still be a verse or a bridge left to write, the writer has nothing left to say. This syndrome often results from *beginning too big*. In other words, if in the first verse your character's raving with jealousy at his unfaithful lover, where have you left to go except to have him strangle her?

Start small so you can end big—believably.

And beware of coming to a conclusion too soon: a wrapup statement such as "there's nothing left to say except goodbye"—if said in the first verse—shuts down the development process. That creates a plot line that looks like this: x———ˣ—————————x. The writer then begins to think in clichés instead of making fresh responses to the individuality of his character. And it's blah, blah, blah all the way home.

If you ever experience plot block midway through a lyric, look back to see if you've let either an oversized emotion or a premature judgment stem the flow of your ideas.

Shaping Your Lyric

Let's suppose you've got a title you're eager to write and that you've come up with both a strong first line and a twist ending but that you can't decide into which music form to pour all your good ingredients.

Content dictates form. That dictum holds true for every kind of writing.

THE APPROPRIATE FORM

Only the appropriate form will

> Support and enhance the lyric's purpose
> Deliver the desired result

To successfully shape every lyric idea you need an understanding of the key music structures. That's why "The Major Song Forms" rate their own section, which is coming right up.

STEP 1   QUIZ

Without looking back to the text, test yourself on how much you remember about the essential lyric framework.

1) Name the five components of a well-conceived lyric:

   _____

   _____

   _____

   _____

   _____

2) Identify three devices that can create a memorable title:

   _____

   _____

   _____

3) Name three techniques that can give your lyric a strong start:

   _____

   _____

   _____

4) In order of sophistication, list the three types of lyric plots.

   _____

   _____

   _____

5) What development technique does each of the following famous songs employ:
   "It Was a Very Good Year" _____
   "Gentle on My Mind" _____
   "Send in the Clowns" _____
   "In the Ghetto" _____

(You'll find the answers on page 268.)

The Major Song Forms

For some years now the verse/chorus format has dominated popular music. But discerning ears—especially those tuned to country stations—can pick out examples of the two runner-up pop favorites: the AAA and the AABA. So the emphasis throughout this book will be on these three forms.

In my Level I lyric writing course we also restrict the focus to the AAA, AABA and verse/chorus. To master these three forms in ten weeks is challenge enough. But in my mirror image course for composers, I give melody-writing assignments in four more classic forms—ABAB ("Fly Me to the Moon"), ABAC ("Moon River"), Through Composed ("You'll Never Walk Alone") and the 12-bar blues ("Empty Bed Blues").

To consider yourself a true professional, you should have an understanding of these pop music formats: A composer who can write only verse/chorus tunes is as limited as a swimmer who can only do the side stroke. We'll take a brief look, therefore, at these other four song forms so you'll at least be able to identify the structures of such standards as "Tea For Two," "Autumn Leaves," and "White Christmas" the next time you hear them.

THE 12-BAR BLUES

Because the 12-bar blues is a uniquely American song form, it will serve as an introduction to our three most popular forms.

More than anything, the blues is a vocal art, a means of self-expression in which the singer complains about some personal problem, real or imagined. But the blues is never self-pitying. And often it's exuberant and joyous.

The lyric form is essentially a couplet (two rhymed lines with the same meter) that's been stretched to three lines by repeating the first. What we hear is a premise and a consequence in a call/response pattern. The rhymes are sometimes more approximate than perfect:

> *My man don't love me, treats me awful mean (pause)*
> *My man don't love me, treats me awful mean (pause)*
> *He's the lowest man I've ever seen. (pause)*
>
> *When you see me comin' lift your windows high (pause)*
> *When you see me comin' lift your windows high (pause)*
> *When you see me goin' hang your head and cry. (pause)*

Ashes to ashes, dust to dust (pause)
Ashes to ashes, dust to dust (pause)
If the whiskey don' get ya, den de cocaine mus'. (pause)

The 12-Bar Harmonic Pattern

Each line of lyric stretches over four bars of music—but slackly, so that there are usually at least 1½ bars left over for both musical and verbal improvisation. The three primary chords of a major key, the I, IV, and V, create the simple harmony. (In the key of C, the chords would be C, F, and G.) The melody features a predictable chord progression that changes in the fifth, seventh, ninth, and eleventh measures.

The only requirement for a song to be blues is to adhere to the basic I IV I V I progression. Within that, there can be a great deal of chordal variation.

A	I	I	I	I
A	IV	IV	I	I
B	V	V (IV)	I	I

The Blue Note

The distinguishing sound of the blues is created by flatting (lowering) the third, or the fifth, or the seventh of the scale and singing those "blue notes" against a major chord. The main blue note is the third; in the key of C that would be E-flat.

You create this blue note on the piano by changing E (a white key) to E-flat, a black key. The piano can only suggest the vocal bending or slurring between the E and E-flat that blues singers achieve. The pianist's solution is to sound two or three neighboring keys simultaneously thereby making a major/minor sound. That tense minor-mode feeling of the "blue note" is what gives American music its distinctive color.

The second most popular blue note is the flat seventh, and the third is the flat fifth; in C these would be B-flat and G-flat, respectively.

The vocal range of the 12-bar blues rarely exceeds an octave (eight notes) and is often limited to four- or five-note melodies that derive their personality from the lyric rather than from the originality of the melody.

A Blues Example

Here's a student example written for the composer's class in music forms.

SUMMER IN THE CITY BLUES

I got the summer in the city, city in the summer blues
I got the summer in the city, city in the summer blues.
I'd rather be anywhere else than walking on this avenue.

Ain't got money for a train that can take me past the city line
Ain't got money for a train that can take me past the city line
But when these feet start walkin' they ain't stoppin' at no traffic sign.

Don't wanna wear no shoes, don't wanna walk on no concrete.
Don't wanna wear no shoes, don't wanna walk on no concrete.
Wanna get up to the country, feel the grass beneath my feet.

There ain't nothin' like the summer when you're sittin' 'neath a willow tree.
There ain't nothin' like the summer when you're sittin' 'neath a willow tree.
So I'm gonna thumb a ride out on Highway 63.

I got the summer in the city, city in the summer blues
I got the summer in the city, city in the summer blues.
I'd rather be anywhere else than walkin' on this avenue.

© 1986, Words and Music by Carrie Starner. Used with permission.

The lyric captures the style, tone, and simplicity of the 12-bar blues form. The first verse states the problem; the second gives the cause of the trouble; the third adds a detail to support the complaint, and the fourth gives a picture of the singer's solution along with the means of reaching it ("So I'm gonna thumb a ride. . . ."). The writer emphasized the plaint by circling back to the opening statement and repeating the first verse for emotional closure.

As you can see, the blues is basically a moan that starts with a complaint—or a wish. The whole trick is to write nine-beat phrases that will leave seven beats of room where the singer and musicians can let themselves go.

One last thought: If you're going to write the blues, you'd better mean it.

Before Moving On
Exercise #5
Write a concluding statement to these lines:
If I had five dollars and a bottle of cherry wine
If I had five dollars and a bottle of cherry wine
I'd _____.
Now write a follow-up verse, based on the opening.
If I had _____
_____
_____

For Your Study

If the blues particularly interests you, I recommend you search out *Stomping the Blues,* by Albert Murray (Vintage Books), a first-rate illustrated study of this classic American music form.

THE AAA FORM

After the 12-bar blues, the AAA makes the simplest musical statement. This form, identified by music theorists as the one-part song form, is composed of a series of verses—generally sixteen bars in length—without a bridge or a chorus. The number of verses can vary from three (the average) to five or more, depending on how much the lyricist has to say. As a rule the title either begins each verse or ends it.

SOME FIRST LINE TITLES

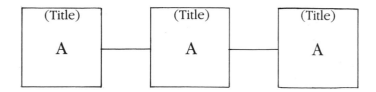

First Time Ever I Saw Your Face
It Was a Very Good Year
By the Time I Get to Phoenix

Do That to Me One more Time
Try to Remember
Puff the Magic Dragon

SOME LAST LINE TITLES

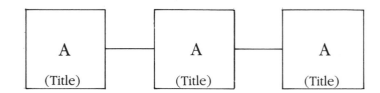

My Cup Runneth Over
The Rose
Ladies of the Canyon
Lawyers in Love

Gentle on My Mind
Crazy in the Night
Cactus Tree
Desolation Row

The Refrain

Frequently the verses of an AAA song end with a two-line lyric statement called a refrain. Its tone is often ironic. In many AAAs the title is built into the refrain, as in "Blowin' in the Wind" and "Taste of Honey" and the Bon Jovi hit, "Wanted Dead or Alive." Other AAAs with refrains take their titles from the lyric's featured character or setting, as "Eleanor Rigby," and "Scarborough Fair." The memory retains a name more readily than an abstract idea like "once she was a true love of mine." As a case in point, John Denver, when titling an AAA ballad, wisely ignored the refrain, "come fill me again" and decided on "Annie's Song."

AAA SONGS WITH REFRAINS

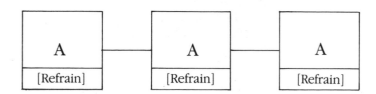

Frankie and Johnny

Blowin' in the Wind

Sunny

I Walk the Line

Reason to Believe

Miss Otis Regrets

Eleanor Rigby

Friendship

Little Boxes

Yesterday's Songs

California Dreamin'

Ode to Billie Joe

Bridge Over Troubled Water

Harper Valley PTA

The Shadow Knows

The Times They Are A'Changin'

Ballad of the Shape of Things

A Taste of Honey

Scarborough Fair

Annie's Song

Big Yellow Taxi

Wanted Dead or Alive

Although the AAA has resounded on Broadway in show tunes by Cole Porter ("Miss Otis Regrets"), Sheldon Harnick ("Ballad of the Shape of Things"), and Stephen Sondheim ("A Bowler Hat"), it's in the simple guitar melodies of folk and country writers that the form is heard the most.

The free-standing structure of its independent verses makes the AAA ideal for creating characters and changing time frames and settings. The form often brings out the social commentator in its lyricist.

A Refrain Is Not A Chorus

Those unfamiliar with the AAA sometimes have trouble understanding what distinguishes a refrain from a chorus: A refrain musically and lyrically resolves the AAA verse and therefore *ends* it. In contrast, a chorus *begins* a distinctively new music section, which is usually at least eight bars long. Any confusion you may feel about the musical aspects of a refrain will vanish if you study recordings of some of the AAA songs listed above.

An AAA Example

Here's a student example:

SUE AND JOHN

A
Sue and John are busy moving
To a cute and cozy nest.
The peeling walls could use improving
And the view is not the best.
But she'll sew a flowered curtain,
Have a baby, and John's certain
Sue will be the perfect wife;

Refrain
There's nothing like the married life.

A	*Sue and John are busy moving*
	To a nice suburban home.
	His office hours need improving:
	They've so little time alone.
	But with three young mouths to feed
	She doesn't dare bring up her needs.
	She tries to be the perfect wife;
Refrain	*There's nothing like the married life.*
A	*Sue and John are busy moving*
	Neither one will say quite where.
	She says her mind could use improving
	He tells her that he doesn't care.
	With the kids now off at college
	Sue will go in search of knowledge,
	John will seek the perfect wife;
Refrain	*There's nothing like the married life,*
	There's nothing like the married life.

© 1985, Marilyn Munder. Used with permission.

That's using the AAA for all it's worth, complete with ironic refrain, and moving settings and time frames. You'll recognize the development technique of the scene method. In choosing *Sue and John* the writer picked the perfect homespun names to imply the "everydayness" of the scenario. As the best lyrics do, it shows us—rather than tells us—a universally acknowledged truth.

In addition to the repetitive element of the refrain, the writer laced her story with word motifs: ". . . are busy moving . . . needs improving . . . perfect wife." That echoing device adds both cohesion and polish to her lyric.

The AAA Payoff

When the AAA shapes a linear story, the payoff, as in any story song, comes near the end of the last stanza, as in "The Ballad of the Shape of Things," and "Miss Otis Regrets," and "Ode to Billie Joe." More generally, in attitudinal and situational AAAs like "A Taste of Honey" and "Sunny," the effect is cumulative.

Write A Strong Tune

Because the AAA form seems to be the special province of the one-person team—one who writes both words and music—I've a cautionary word for the tune-writer side. If your AAA song is written well enough to become a hit record, its tune should be able to spin off additional instrumental recordings. Yet few AAA melodies hold up without their words. Usually it's the lyric's message that makes an AAA a hit, rather than its tune, which often serves merely as a rhythmic motor to keep the words moving. The songwriter—eager to tell a compelling story—often neglects to compose a tune that can stand on its own without a vocal.

The Crux Of The Matter

The problem stems from the tune's lack of development: Many sixteen-bar AAA verses consist solely of one eight-bar phrase repeated with only a slight variation in the final cadence. As a consequence, a four-verse song with such a design asks an audience to be entertained by a succession of eight (almost) identical musical phrases! That's why you hear so few instrumental versions of successful AAA songs.

A side-by-side comparison of the sheet music to two AAA standards, "By the Time I Get to Phoenix" and "Blowin' in the Wind," will illustrate my point. Your eyes alone will show you why the instrumentals of the former far outnumber those of the latter. The moving melodic curve and varied harmonic changes in "Phoenix" make a musically interesting verse; we can therefore be entertained by hearing it—without lyrics—three successive times.

Conversely, each verse of "Blowin' in the Wind," accents one note (the opening -A-) eleven times; thus, in hearing the song played through once we've heard that same -A- note in a stressed position thirty-three times! A little variation in the motif could have reshaped the melody into one that had an instrumental life of its own.

When you conceive your verse music, try to develop your melodic motif in such a way that the listener will look forward to hearing the verse repeated three or four more times.

Before Moving On
Exercise #6

Imagine you've designed an AAA lyric which—like "Sue and John"—illustrates the national statistic that one out of three marriages ends in divorce. Your lyric won't state it, of course, it will show it by means of changing scenes of three different breakups. Now devise a two-line refrain that will make your point as it closes each verse.

As an example of what I mean, your refrain could be a variation on the thought embodied in the country song title "What's Forever For?"

THE AABA FORM

In contrast to the stop-start quality of the AAA (and the verse/chorus form), the AABA flows in an uninterrupted expression of one moment's feeling. This form virtually insists on a lyric designed with a single time frame, a consistent viewpoint, and an unchanging setting.

How It's Shaped

In the fifty years between Fred Astaire's film rendition of "They Can't Take That Away from Me" and Whitney Houston's global hit, "Saving All My Love for You," the AABA has kept its classic shape. It's still often composed of thirty-two bars of music; the opening A section—the main musical idea—traditionally contains eight bars that are immediately repeated. The bridge (B) section, a musical contrast with A, also usually contains eight bars, sometimes constructed of two four-bar phrases. Its last phrase prepares for the return of the final A section.

Some Variations

The 8/8/8/8 framework, although classic, is not mandatory. Ever since Cole Porter expanded the thirty-two bar form to forty-eight bars in 1932 with "Night and Day," no one's keeping count of measures. Here, for example, are the number of measures in some standards: "Yesterday" (7/7/8/7); "Raindrops Keep Fallin' on My Head" (9/9/10/12); "What I Did for Love" (11/12/7/16); "Send in the Clowns" (6/6/9/8). Perhaps you've already noted that those melodies were written by four of our most successful composers: McCartney, Bacharach, Hamlisch, Sondheim; they don't count measures, but rather let their instincts dictate the length of their AABA melodies.

Where The Title Goes

The song's title generally either begins the A section ("Over the Rainbow") or ends it ("Body and Soul"). Even when starting off with a title, fine craftsmen intuitively shape the final A so that the name of the product concludes the song and thereby echoes in the listener's memory.

SOME FAMOUS AABA SONGS

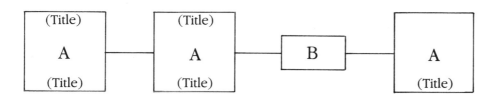

Over the Rainbow	As Time Goes By
Body and Soul	Climb Every Mountain
If I Had You	Three Coins in the Fountain
I'll Be Around	When Sunny Gets Blue
Ain't Misbehavin'	On the Sunny Side of the Street
That's Entertainment	Raindrops Keep Fallin' on My Head
Misty	I Can't Get Started
Yesterday	Alone Again, Naturally
Send in the Clowns	I've Got My Love to Keep Me Warm
Here You Come Again	What the World Needs Now
Cabaret	Just the Way You Are
Michelle	Come in from the Rain
On the Road Again	She's Out of My Life
What I Did for Love	Don't It Make My Brown Eyes Blue
The Man I Love	I'd Rather Leave While I'm in Love

The Extended AABA

Up until the late 60s it was rare for a record to exceed three minutes playing time. Today even four minutes is not unusual. To accommodate the longer contemporary record formats, some AABA's have a second bridge lyric that extends the length of the song and thus gives the AABA more viability in a competitive marketplace. In other contemporary AABAs the bridge lyric repeats, but the final A presents some new, or all new lyrical lines.

SOME EXTENDED AABA SONGS

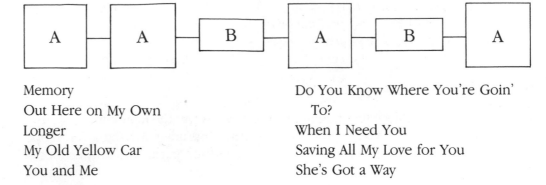

Memory	Do You Know Where You're Goin'
Out Here on My Own	To?
Longer	When I Need You
My Old Yellow Car	Saving All My Love for You
You and Me	She's Got a Way

The Bridge

The main purpose of the bridge (or release) is to serve as a foil for the A sections. To achieve the required contrast, composers use such techniques as harmonic variety, rhythmic contrast, melodic movement, modulation—going to a different tonal center.

Lyricists too have a number of contrast techniques to draw upon. In essence, whatever you've been doing in the first two verses, stop doing, and flip to its opposite in the bridge:

Change Pronouns. If the emphasis has been on *I,* switch to *you,* or vice versa.

Change Time Emphasis. If you've been talking about now, try a flashback to the past, or a flashforward to the future.

Change Focus. If you've been generalizing, then particularize with details, or close analysis, or examples. If you've been particularizing, make general statements.

Some time-tested phrases can help pave your way into the bridge: *so now I . . . but once we . . . I guess you . . . remember when we'd . . . I can tell that . . . I wish you'd . . . if only . . . maybe . . . someday. . . .*

An AABA Example

Here's an AABA lyric designed with a last-line title:

MIDNIGHT MOOD

A   *Turn off the television*
Put down that paper, too.
I've got an indecent proposition
That I'd like to propose to you.
I'm gonna unhook the receiver
As soon as I send out for Chinese food.
Although the sun's still high in a daylight sky
I'm in a MIDNIGHT MOOD.

A   *Put on some Charlie Parker,*
    Pour me some Spanish rosé,
    I can't hold out till it gets any darker,
    What I'm needing I need right away.
    And if you cooperate fully
    Just try to imagine my gratitude.
    Come on and do your part, let's get an early start
    'Cause I'm in a MIDNIGHT MOOD.

B   *I've read all about this in the* Ladies Home Journal
    So you know you're in capable hands
    Dr. Brothers says that love doesn't need to be nocturnal
    I think it's got something to do with the glands. So . . .

A   *Take a short vacation*
    Sample some forbidden fruit.
    I'm gonna shake you to your foundation
    While you're wearing your birthday suit.
    Why don't you wrap your arms around me,
    And keep me from coming unglued.
    I wanna do it all before the shadows fall,
    I'm in a MIDNIGHT MOOD.

That's a fine example of using the scene method to develop a situational plot. The lyric starts strong with an opening line request that pulls us right into the situation: "Turn off the television."

To unify the AABA form, the writer outlines the first two lines of each A section with more requests: *Turn off/Put down, Put on/Pour me, Take a/Sample some.* That's a word designer at work.

In the bridge she produces the requisite contrast: The first two A's emphasize what the singer hopes she and the singee will do; the bridge particularizes with supportive research information on why her proposal is worth accepting.

In addition to being sassy and fun, the lyric has polish. The ear delights not only in the variety of rhymes—one-, two-, and three- syllable ones—but in the freshness of the linkings: *Parker/darker, glands/hands, journal/nocturnal, and (forbidden) fruit/(birthday) suit.*

To fortify her lyric with the ring of the familiar, Maureen Sugden taps a favorite device of good writers, the *allusion*—a direct or implied reference to a well-known person or thing. The specificity of Chinese food, Charlie Parker, Spanish rosé, Dr. Brothers and *Ladies Home Journal* adds to the lyric's memorability.

Every line flows out of the previous one and into the next. And just before we hear the final title, the singer neatly summarizes her proposal: "I wanna do it all before the shadows fall."

The writer, incidentally, found her title in a magazine ad for panty hose, which proves that titles are everywhere—if you're looking for them.

"Midnight Mood" shows off the AABA in what it does best: unify time, place, and action into one moment's feeling.

Before Moving On
Practice Critique #2
You won't need hints to help you detect the obvious flaw in this AABA. Identify the malady and make a recommendation for its cure.

A *As long as there's a song to sing,*
   A daffodil to greet the eager spring,
   While there's a child to laugh upon a swing,
   I'LL BE IN LOVE WITH YOU.

A *As long as there's a hill to climb,*
   A poet who will find the words to rhyme,
   While there's a clock to tick away the time,
   I'LL BE IN LOVE WITH YOU.

B *Whatever fortune holds in store*
   I swear I'll cherish you forevermore
   Though trouble may come knocking at the door
   My love will stay like new.

A *As long as I have eyes to see*
   And arms to hold you close as you can be,
   As long as there's a breath of life in me
   One thing I know is true
   I'LL BE IN LOVE WITH YOU.

© 1965, Solar Systems Music. Used with permission.

Your critique: _____

_____

_____

_____

_____

(To compare your critique with mine, turn to page 268.)

The "stretched" last A of "I'll Be in Love With You" gave it a greater sense of finality. Stretching the final A by two-to-four lyric lines or bars of music is a device commonly used by lyricists and composers alike. Some examples worth study include: "Here You Come Again," "New York, New York," "Saving All My Love For You," and "Somewhere Out There." Take a tip from the pros: Build your last A to a climax.

THE ABAB, ABAC, AND THROUGH COMPOSED FORMS

Back when Berlin, Kern, Gershwin, Porter, and Rodgers were composing their AABA standards, they were also turning out an equal number in the ABAB form. Like the AABA, the ABAB and its variant, the ABAC, usually contain thirty-two bars; but instead of three A's spanned by a bridge, these structures consist of two sixteen-bar sections joined in the middle rather like Siamese twins—identical ones, ABAB, and fraternal ones, ABAC.

The Classic ABAB

The opening eight-bar A section, which embodies the main musical idea, immediately moves into the B section. The B, another eight-bar phrase, may be considered a development of the A. The B's last phrase is designed to prepare for the return of the A; a repeat of the complete AB section completes the song.

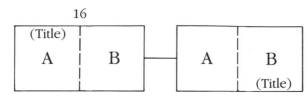

Toyland	I Could Write a Book
Do It Again	But Not for Me
Sometimes I'm Happy	Fly Me to the Moon
Till the Clouds Roll By	Swanee
Odds and Ends of a Beautiful Love Affair	

The ABAB Today

The ABAB still puts songs on the charts. Here's a profile of a 1985 country hit, "To Me." To fill out today's longer record formats, the second B was restated:

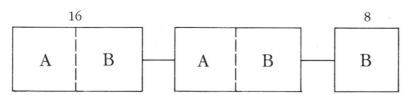

In 1984, Lionel Richie used the ABAB as the blueprint for his No. 1 hit "Hello." To augment the form, he repeated the sixteen-bar segment three times instead of the usual two. In designing his hit record, Richie inserted an instrumental between the first two AB sections; then he stretched the song by restating one more AB, but in a unique way: the sixteen-bar section is broken up into a guitar improvisation for the first six measures, followed by a recap of previously heard lyrics.

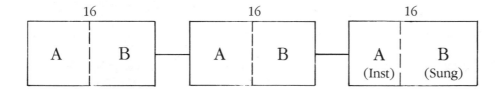

The Classic ABAC

The ABAC frames many of our film and theater standards. Because its final (C) section is heard only once, the ABAC structure is ideal for creating a song whose lyric develops, along with the music, to an emotional payoff.

As in the ABAB, the opening eight-bar A section contains the dominant musical strain, which immediately moves into the B section. The B section (again as in the ABAB) is an eight-bar phrase that may be considered an outgrowth of the A. And again the B's last phrase prepares for the return of the A. Now comes the difference. The final (C) musical section often begins like the first few bars of the B, but it then moves into new material. C sections can also consist wholly of new material. A C section that starts off melodically like the B, may also be termed an "altered" B—and labeled ABAB′ (called B prime). Some composers apply the term ABAC solely to those songs whose C contains all new material.

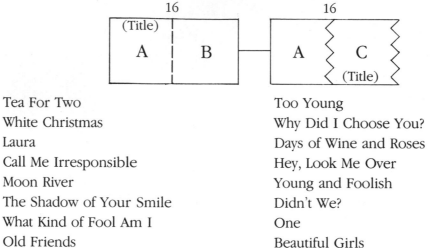

Tea For Two	Too Young
White Christmas	Why Did I Choose You?
Laura	Days of Wine and Roses
Call Me Irresponsible	Hey, Look Me Over
Moon River	Young and Foolish
The Shadow of Your Smile	Didn't We?
What Kind of Fool Am I	One
Old Friends	Beautiful Girls

Where Does The Title Go?

In "Hello," Richie was unconventional with his title placement. The closing line of each AB section was "I love you," sounding, as it hit the traditional title spot, like the natural title. My guess would be that he picked "Hello"—the first word in the seventh bar of the sixteen-bar AB—as the title because it has a fresher and more memorable ring to it. His mega hits "Still," "Lady," and "Truly," make it apparent that Lionel Richie knows the power of one-word titles.

The two logical title spots in both the ABAB and the ABAC remain either the opening or the closing line of each AB or AC section. You unify the song by fusing the song's title to the main musical phrase as in "Sometimes I'm Happy" and "Fly Me To the Moon"; when we hear only the melody of those songs, the words spring to mind.

An ABAC Example

To illustrate the shape of the ABAC, here's a song Herb Martin (words) and I (music) wrote for a musical adaptation for children of the book *The Ballad of the Flim Flam Man.* The tune came first, designed to be called "Partners" and to be sung with different lyrics by various characters throughout the show. This version is sung by Curley, a naive teenager, as he accepts the Flim Flam Man's offer to join him in hoodwinking escapades. Like many classic ABAC melodies such as "My Romance," and "There's a Song in My Heart," this is played in "cut time"—in which there are two counts to the bar. You can get the feel of it by counting ONE, two, ONE, two, ONE,

PARTNERS

A   *I like your free-wheelin' style*
     So I think for a while
     I'll go PARTNERS.
     You've got a real Midas touch
     So we'll con twice as much
     Being PARTNERS.

B   *Altho' I'm still kinda green*
     You have seen I can turn a trick
     And I'm learnin' quick, too.
     Yessir, Mr. Jones,
     I could be very good for you.

A   *You'll find me right at your heels*
     Makin' flim-flammin' deals,
     Really PARTNERS.
     And if and when trouble comes
     We'll be chums
     Who will muddle on through.

C   *I know I'll find the life delicious*
     Hookin' all those greedy bright-eyed "fishious"
     It's a deal. Put 'er there!
     We're a pair!
     I'll be PARTNERS with you.

Look back at the last line of the second A and you'll see and hear how the form starts to move away from the original pattern: the end meter changes from a two-syllable rhythm ("partners") to a one-syllable one ("through"). This was designed to set up a last line in which the title would be dropped in the middle, thereby giving the singer a final note (word) to hold—such as "now," or "me," or "you,"—at the song's end.

The ABAC Today

Because today the verse/chorus and AABA forms scaffold most pop music, the ABAC form would seem to be an uncommercial way to go about shaping a lyric. Yet, given a contemporary rhythmic and harmonic treatment, the ABAC can still elbow itself onto the top-40. The most recent gold-record ABAC (1985) is "When October Goes," a vintage Johnny Mercer lyric set posthumously by Barry Manilow.

Before Moving On
Exercise #7
Here are the ABA sections of a lyric I wrote for an ABAC instrumental. I've left the body of the C section blank for you to draw a conclusion that will flow into a restatement of the title in the song's last line. Remember that the C music differs from the B; in lyric terms, this means that you can vary the accents of your words here from those

in the B section. I've also given you *three* blank lines to allow you to create an extended C section, if you want one. A longer last section is common in this form, which gives more room to build to an emotional climax.

Obviously, you will have to set up a rhyme for *you.*

A   *WHERE WERE YOU*
When my heart was my own?
Where was I
When you still slept alone?

B   *Why couldn't you and I have met*
When we both were fancy free—
Before we each had settled for less
Than love could be?

A   *Here we are*
With our lives upside down—
Torn apart
By the joy we have found

C   _____
_____
_____

Where was I?
WHERE WERE YOU?

© 1982, Solar Systems Music. Used with permission.

If you're not sure how to handle the three lines, here's a suggestion for the rhyme scheme: make the first two rhyme with each other, and the third with *you.*

The Through Composed—or ABCD

The term *through composed* applies to a song whose melody continues to develop from section to section, never returning to its opening phrase. Probably the two best-known examples are "The Star Spangled Banner" and Irving Berlin's "God Bless America." Berlin also found this form appropriate for "The Girl on the Magazine Cover," "Lazy," and his setting of the Statue of Liberty inscription, "Give Me Your Tired, Your Poor."

If you listen analytically to the Broadway classics "You'll Never Walk Alone" *(Carousel)* and "My Time of Day" *(Guys and Dolls)*, you'll discover how the linear nature of their lyrics led inevitably to the through composed form.

In a sub-type of the form, which I call *semi-through composed,* only a bar or two of the melody repeats: for example, "Softly, As I Leave You," "I Have Dreamed," "I Remember (Sky)," and "Not a Day Goes By." A study of the foregoing songs will augment your understanding of the axiom that content dictates form.

Experiment

For those times when you want to affect your audience on a deeper level than the average pop song does, remember the through-composed form. Instead of immediately restating an entire eight-bar section, experiment in stretching your initial motif.

Study how Rodgers and Sondheim went about it. You'll discover that the three basic techniques are to vary your motif harmonically, rhythmically, and/or melodically. The goal is to make a lot out of a little.

To take a melodic motif—such as the initial phrase of "You'll Never Walk Alone"—and to expand it without repeating a single bar takes skill. Once you develop your variation techniques, you can then apply them to any song form—with especial effectiveness to the AAA verse, which needs all the variation it can get.

A Note On The Term "Chorus"

It is not uncommon to hear someone musically untrained refer to the title section of "Hello" or "When October Goes," or "Saving All My Love" or even "Blowin' in the Wind" as "the chorus." On occasion, you may even see such mislabeling in print. Don't let it confuse you. You've seen the facts: no form we've discussed so far has had a chorus.

Now here comes the real thing.

THE VERSE/CHORUS FORM

If you've come up with a title phrase that seems to cry out to be repeated over and over, the ideal form would seem to be the verse/chorus.

A chorus in a verse/chorus song embodies the melody's most memorable phrase and the lyric's title and main message. The verse, musically and lyrically, is an introduction to the central idea.

Some beginning writers—unaware of the classic ABAB song form—refer to the verse/chorus as an ABAB. In the interests of clarity and historical accuracy (and in the hope of standardizing our pop song vocabulary), I will refer to the verse/chorus song solely as the verse/chorus song. As you've seen, the classic ABAB lacks a chorus.

The Setup Verse

You'll remember from Step 1 that your opening verse should establish the Who, What, When, and Where in the first few lines.

Sometimes a story song requires a second or even third verse to prepare for the statement of the chorus, as in "The Gambler." But remember that your listener is eager to find out what your song's all about. As a general guideline, try to limit yourself to one introductory verse. You can't go wrong by following music publishers' favorite advice: *Don't bore us, get to the chorus.*

On the average, a verse contains eight lines. Depending on the length of the line and the inherent rhythmic feel of the words, those lines will translate musically into eight or sixteen measures, which is fine. A verse longer than eight lines tends to lose its forcefulness. The verse's last line prepares for the first line of the chorus—and implies, in effect, "that is why I say": (fill in the title).

Before Moving On
Exercise #8
Here's a double chorus designed for an uptempo dance song. The chorus needs a setup verse that shows the listener who is talking to whom and what has brought the singer to this moment. Devise an emotional background for the relationship that

would lead the singer to make the chorus statement. Remember, the first line of the chorus should sound like the natural consequence of the last line of your verse. Decide before you write whether the singer will be male or female.

Verse _____
_____
_____
_____
_____
_____
_____
_____
_____

Chorus   *Let's GO FOR IT!*
You and me
Here and now
GO FOR IT!
Start a dream
Build a life
GO FOR IT
Baby, what 'd'ya say?
Let's GO FOR IT!
Aiming high
Holding on
GO FOR IT
Staying true
Through it all
GO FOR IT
GO FOR IT all the way. . . .

© 1982, Solar Systems Music. Used with permission.

Note: If you really get involved in writing the setup verse, you may want to develop the idea further; with a new chorus, you'll have a good start on a whole new lyric. Many students have turned these warmup exercises into successful original songs.

Shaping The Song

After writing the first verse of "Go For It!" you may wonder what the ultimate shape of the song might be. Should it have a second verse? A bridge? A climb?

The verse/chorus form has three basic variations: the simple verse/chorus, the verse/chorus/bridge, and the verse/climb/chorus/(bridge). Whether you add a climb or a bridge or an extra payoff section are matters for you to decide as you write. There is no right or wrong number of sections. Each song has a life of its own and will virtually dictate its shape to you. The more you write, the better instinctive choices you'll make.

The Simple Verse/Chorus

Although the majority of today's hit verse/chorus songs include a bridge, the simple verse/chorus format still makes for a viable record—especially if there are three sets of verses and choruses. Songs augmented by sixteen-bar double choruses, such as "Through the Years," are often bridgeless.

Putting your title at the top of the chorus unquestionably creates a song with the greatest impact—and staying power.

SOME FIRST-LINE TITLES

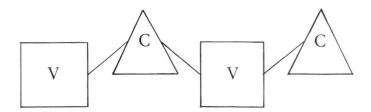

Tie a Yellow Ribbon

You Decorated My Life

I'll Never Love This Way Again

Don't Cry Out Loud

Have You Never Been Mellow?

Material Girl

Nobody

Nobody Does It Better

Leaving on a Jet Plane

She Believes in Me

Sunrise, Sunset

On the Other Hand

More Than Just the Two of Us

I Wanna Dance With Somebody

A second option, though clearly a weaker choice, places the title at the end of the chorus. Although last-line chorus titles can produce hits, a writer's asking a lot from an audience to make it wait that long to find out what the song's all about. Verse/chorus songs with last-line titles often give the impression that they've evolved more by default than design. And they rarely generate cover records (any record after the initial one).

SOME LAST-LINE TITLES

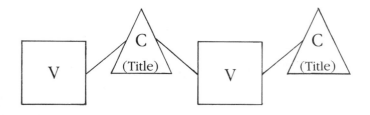

The Search Is Over

What's Forever For?

100% Chance of Rain

Somewhere Down The Line

Separate Lives

Try Getting Over You

Every Little Kiss

Everything That Glitters

Before Moving On
Exercise #9
In the following verse a woman confronts a man with her suspicions of his extramarital activity. Write a chorus whose top-line title is the direct result of the thought, "and that is why I say. . . ." Space is provided for eight lines; you might find that four are enough.

Verse

Lately you've been whistling while you're shaving
And you're wearing an expensive new cologne—
I think I've figured out
Why you're so tired ev'ry night
And not acting like the man I've known . . .

Chorus

_____
_____
_____
_____
_____
_____
_____
_____
_____

© 1980, Solar Systems Music. Used with permission.

The Verse/Chorus/Bridge

Many verse/chorus songs feature a bridge that arrives after the second chorus and leads back into a third chorus statement.

You'll remember that the bridge of an AABA is essential to the structure of that form. The verse/chorus bridge, however, is more like a salad course after your entrée—pleasant but unnecessary.

Because it functions basically as a diversion before the return of the final chorus, the bridge is often only half the length of the verses.

As in the AABA's bridge, the verse/chorus bridge should also offer the ear some musical contrast—harmonic, rhythmic, or melodic—to what's gone before. Similarly, the lyric should vary in some way. All the devices that bring freshness in an AABA bridge apply as well to the verse/chorus bridge. (See page 28.)

Occasionally in a verse/chorus, the lyric pays off in the bridge, leading to a climactic restatement of the last chorus.

SOME VERSE/CHORUS/BRIDGE SONGS

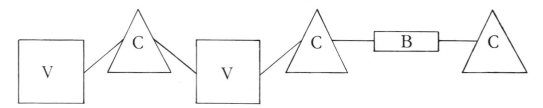

Touch Me in the Morning
Just Once
Somewhere Down the Road
Sometimes When We Touch

Private Dancer
Up Where We Belong
Stranger in My House
Our Love Is on the Faultline

A Verse/Chorus/Bridge Example

Here's a class assignment that turned into the writer's first record.

TELL YOUR STORY WALKIN'

Verse
You worked late at the office—
Well, the office must have moved,
'Cause you were seen doin' business
At a downtown saloon.
You had your arms wrapped around her,
She was holding you real tight,
And I know what kind of business
You took care of last night, so

Chorus
TELL YOUR STORY WALKIN'
You're not talkin' to a fool.
You know we said that honesty
Would be the only rule.
Don't bother with excuses;
They're worth nothin' anymore—
Just TELL YOUR STORY WALKIN' out the door.

Verse
You get no second chances
When you're foolin' with my heart.
You lied before, you'll lie again—
It's easy once you start.
Overtime is meant for working,
But you made it time for play.
Now you've blown what we had going;
You overstayed your stay. So

Chorus
TELL YOUR STORY WALKIN'
You're not talkin' to a fool.
You know we said that honesty
Would be the only rule.
Don't bother with excuses,
They're worth nothin' anymore.
Just TELL YOUR STORY WALKIN' out the door.

Bridge
There's no way you can have it all,
No matter what you do.
And if one of us has got to cry,
I'd rather it be you.

(repeat chorus)

© 1985, Lyric by Arline Udis/Music by Ron Evans. Coffee and Cream Music.
Used with permission.

"Tell Your Story Walkin' " typifies the commercial verse/chorus lyric: it makes one simple statement that bears repeating—again and again.

The writer followed the theory all the way: set up the situation in the first verse; made her chorus the natural outcome of the verse; developed the second verse with details; said something new in the bridge that led naturally back to a third repeat of the chorus.

The Verse/Chorus/Climb

This variation has a prechorus section—often called *the climb,* which musically and lyrically seems to pull out of the verse and to rise toward the chorus. A climb serves as aural foreplay to extend the song's emotional tension by delaying the arrival of its climactic section.

At its simplest, a climb is a couplet—two rhymed lines in the same meter. A case in point is Amanda McBroom's ballad "From Time to Time." After its eight-bar introductory verse, a couplet keeps the listener eagerly awaiting the title line of the chorus:

> *"I've heard it said when love is real,*
> *You never lose the way you feel. . . ."*

A Verse/Chorus/Climb Example

For dramatic purposes a climb may extend to as many as eight lines. In my own duet "We're Ready," a six-bar climb melodically moves into a new key as it lyrically identifies the symptoms of the lovers' "readiness." Here's the first verse, climb, and chorus:

WE'RE READY

Verse
You've been playin' it cool,
I've been playin' it safe,
Neither one comin' on strong.
Well, we've both been burned
By past mistakes
When a love that looked right went wrong.

Climb
But lately I've been wond'ring
How your movin' in would be.
And lately you've been usin' words
Like "us" and "we."
Got a feelin' tonight—
And if I'm readin' us right, then

Chorus
WE'RE READY
To lay our hearts on the line—
READY to make our lovelight shine
As steady and bright as a star.
Baby, WE'RE READY
I really believe we are.

© 1983, Solar Systems Music. Used with permission.

Both because of the extended length of the climb in "We're Ready" and its melodic, rhythmic, and harmonic contrast to the verse and chorus sections, the song needs no bridge for more contrast. Some songs with a tame couplet climb may need that extra punch of a fresh bridge section. Let your intuition tell you.

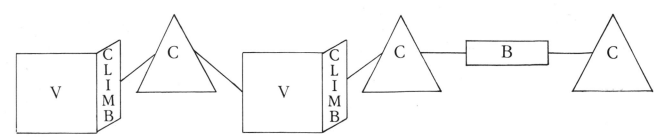

Come What May

Heartbreaker

One Man Woman

Solid (As a Rock)

Open Your Heart

You've Lost That Lovin' Feelin'

I Made it Through the Rain

If Ever You're in My Arms Again

How Am I Supposed to Live Without
   You?

There Is Nothin' Like a Dame

Touch Me in the Morning

Before Moving On
Exercise #10

The first verse and chorus of this lyric work pretty well. But a two-line climb will unquestionably add to the lyric's momentum. Design a climb in the form of a couplet—two lines with the same meter and rhyme—to propel the singer into the chorus.

Verse   *I think we oughta take a break from each other*
I think we need time off and more space
There's an edge in your voice when you talk to me now
And I seldom find a smile on your face.

Climb   _____

              _____

Chorus   *BURNOUT*
We're headin' for
BURNOUT
A case of
BURNOUT
Not a trace of flaming love
We're close to
BURNOUT
Before we
BURNOUT
Let's take a break in the name of love.

© 1983, Solar Systems Music. Used with permission.

The Hook Chorus

In songwriting terms, a "hook" is that part of a song that grabs (hooks) the listener's attention and stays in the memory after one hearing. More often than not, a song's title is its hook. A secondary kind of hook may be an instrumental riff, or the record's compelling rhythmic groove.

If your radio dial is usually set to a top-40 station, you already know that the hook chorus—a kind of musical mantra—is the mainstay of contemporary pop music. The chorus design of "Go for It" in which the title repeats seven times, and "Burnout," with its five title repeats, are typical hook choruses.

In many dance records, or those designed for aerobic exercises, a single repeated phrase may comprise the entire chorus. Sometimes a slight change in emphasis makes it even hookier:

> *I want your LOVE*
> *I WAAAAAAAANT your love.*
> *I want your LOVE*
> *I WAAAAAAAANT your love.*

Something as simple as that one-phrase hook can spin itself right onto the charts. Such a lyric has been purposefully designed as a one-shot *record*—rather than as a *song*. The fully developed chorus of "Tell Your Story Walkin'," on the other hand, was designed for the long-distance potential of cover records. "Walkin' " is still "hooky," but there's more meat on the hook. How fully you develop your chorus depends on your lyric's purpose.

Watch The Chronology Of Your Verse/Chorus Plot

After finishing your first draft, double check that your chorus statement still holds up after the second (or third) verse. Sometimes writers develop the story past the point where the words of the chorus still apply. For example, a student lyric about a highway flirtation featured this chorus:

> *BUMPER TO BUMPER she's got me in her sight.*
> *Shoulder to shoulder I passed her on the right.*
> *The traffic is slow but my heart's beatin' fast.*
> *I wish BUMPER TO BUMPER would last.*

© 1987, Student Lyric. Used with permission.

In the song's second verse, the singee speeds out of sight. Although the writer then repeated the chorus, the plot has advanced past the point where the chorus factually holds up. Actually, the chorus didn't work after its second line: How could they be bumper to bumper if he'd *passed* her on the right"? In fact, the only way that "bumper to bumper" could work as a title would be if the singer/singee encounter stayed in that parallel position for the entire lyric: A chorus could then express the singer's frustration at being trapped in emotional gridlock.

A guideline: use your verses (and bridge) for plot details including one-time actions; reserve your chorus for a summing-up kind of statement as in "Sunrise, Sunset," "Somewhere Down the Road," "Up Where We Belong."

Chorus Words Can Vary

There is no law that proclaims that the words of a chorus must never vary. Occasionally, you may want to use the chorus to continue the story as in the Beatles' "She's

Leaving Home" and Rupert Holmes' "Escape (The Piña Colada Song)." If, in order to advance your plot, you need to change the words in a subsequent chorus or two, then change them. For a look at how the last chorus can contain the payoff, check "Sly Like a Fox" (page 206) and "It's All Over but the Leaving" (page 143).

Before Moving On
Exercise #11
Sometimes a simple verse/chorus lyric could be greatly enhanced by the addition of a two-to-four-line bridge. Here's such a case.

THANK GOD FOR MUSIC

Verse

When the morning headlines bring me down
And I need some cheering up
I just turn on my radio
And refill my coffee cup.
I spin the dial till I find the sound,
The sound that turns my frown around.
And before I can say top-40,
I'm feeling fine once more.

Chorus

THANK GOD FOR MUSIC
Thank God for a song.
With words that fit my feelings
And a tune I can hum along.
It sure can make my outlook brighter
When things are going wrong.
THANK GOD FOR MUSIC,
For the singer and the song.

Verse

I love to move to rhythm and blues
And I love to rock and roll.
I love those cheatin' country stories:
They got heart and soul.
So I spin the dial till I find the sound,
The sound that turns my frown around.
And before I can say top-40,
I'm feeling fine once more.

(repeat chorus)

Bridge

_____

_____

_____

_____

Chorus

THANK GOD FOR MUSIC
Thank God for a song.
With words that fit my feelings
And a tune I can hum along.
It sure can make my outlook brighter
When things are going wrong.
THANK GOD FOR MUSIC,
For the singer and the song.

The first verse sets up the situation, the chorus sums up the singer's attitude about it, and the second verse presents some new details. It all works fine. But it needs something more. Something that a bridge could offer. Write a two-to-four-line bridge that makes a new statement—perhaps something personal about the singer. Review the contrast devices on page 28. And here's one more requirement: Use new end rhymes that haven't been heard in either the verses or chorus. The bridge's fresh vowel sounds will help to set off the chorus when it hits for the last time.

Pass The Whistle Test

In composing a verse/chorus song, strive for a clear distinction between the verse, chorus, and bridge sections—both musically and lyrically. As in any song form, this distinction can be achieved musically through a rhythmic change in motif, a shift in the harmonic colors, and of course, by changing keys (modulating). Remember that the chorus is the dominant section, and after one hearing should pass the whistle test. A useful rule of thumb: start your verse at a pitch low enough to allow your chorus to begin on a note higher than any accented note in the verse.

A verse/chorus melody that can stand on its own without benefit of lyrics or grooves will pay you dividends in instrumentals and cover records.

A Demo Tip

At demo time bear in mind that sometimes a song is best served by starting off with its chorus instead of (more traditionally) with the first verse. Your choice depends on the effect you seek. Remember the hits "Nobody Does It Better," "Solid (As a Rock)," and "Say You, Say Me" led off with the chorus.

Art dictates no absolutes.

STEP 2   QUIZ

1) Without looking back at the text, identify the form of the following famous songs. Hint: Humming helps.
   a) "White Christmas"   _____
   b) "Annie's Song"   _____
   c) "Fly Me to the Moon"   _____
   d) "Over the Rainbow"   _____
   e) "Sunrise, Sunset"   _____

2) The most common "blue note" is the flatted third; what other two notes of the scale are frequently flatted in a blues song? _____

3) How does a refrain differ from a chorus?

   _____

   _____

   _____

4) In each of the following song forms, identify the strongest places to put your title.
   a) The AAA form _____
   b) The AABA form _____
   c) The verse/chorus form _____

5) How does the bridge in the AABA differ from the bridge in the verse/chorus?
_____

6) a) What is the function of the AABA's bridge?
_____

   b) Give two means by which to accomplish this objective.
_____
_____

7) What's the purpose of a climb? _____
_____

(You'll find the answers on page 269.)

Managing Viewpoint, Voice, Time Frame, and Setting

Early on in the songwriting process you will be making four decisions, consciously or unconsciously, regarding your lyric's Viewpoint, Voice, Time Frame, and Setting:

1. Will the story be told from the angle of first person, second person, or third person? (The Viewpoint)
2. Will the singer be talking to someone or merely thinking out loud? (The Voice)
3. Will the action be set in the past, the present, or the future? (The Time Frame)
4. Will the lyric happen in a specific (or implied) place or simply in the singer's mind? (The Setting)

First-rate lyricists may make these choices unconsciously—but they make them. Viewpoint, Voice, Time Frame, and Setting interconnect to form the spine of your story.

Viewpoint

Voice

Time Frame

Setting

Without each set firmly in place, a plot lacks a backbone. Here are your treatment options:

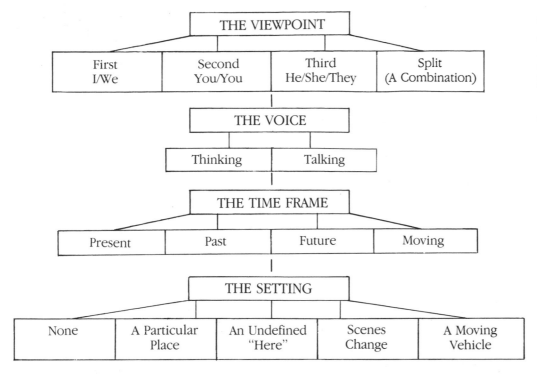

AN OVERVIEW

The diagram illustrates that a lyric's plot can be viewed from three standpoints—first, second, or third person. Because the majority of pop songs are either attitudinal or situational, the predominant viewpoints we hear are first and second person with the emphasis on *I* and *you* respectively. The third person narrates the story song. Generally, lyrics reflect a single viewpoint, but on occasion we hear a purposeful split of two.

The majority of lyrics find the singer in the thinking Voice—either reflecting on an experience or emotional state or mentally addressing some absent person, place, or thing. In the talking Voice the singer is holding a face-to-face conversation with a singee.

Like the Viewpoint and Voice, the Time Frame and Setting aspects usually remain constant throughout the lyric with the exception of story songs, in which changes are not unusual.

Similarly to the vertebrae, Viewpoint and Voice, and Time Frame and Setting are joined together. How you handle one element will affect the others. The goal then is to control each of the four so that they work together to form a unified and coherent lyric. The diagrams refer you to famous songs for study as well as to student examples in the workbook to help you to "get a fix on the VVTS (vits)." You'll find student examples listed by title in the song index.

THE VIEWPOINT

The Viewpoint, or point of view, is the narrative perspective from which the plot is told—the "eyes" of the story. A lyricist can tell that story from the inside (first and second person), or stand outside the narrative (third person). Each Viewpoint requires special handling.

FIRST PERSON (With the emphasis on "I" or "We")			
SINGULAR		**PLURAL**	
Generic "I"	Persona "I"	We (You & I)	Collective We
Yesterday	Wichita Lineman	Up Where We	We Shall Overcome
I'm All Smiles	Dirty Laundry	Belong	Woodstock
Both Sides Now	Private Dancer	We've Got Tonight	What the World
My Way	Rhinestone Cowboy	Just Once	Needs Now
Satisfaction	King of the Road	Reunited	We Are the World
		Born to Run	
Book Example	*Book Example*	*Book Example*	*Book Example*
Between Men	Kiss Me, Carmen	Partners	Changing, Changing

Write Likable Characters

If you are not a singer with a recording contract, then you must design words that will feel good in someone else's mouth. This is why I stress the universal aspect of a lyric—the need to strike a common chord.

First-person lyrics create the strongest singer-listener identification. By placing the emphasis on "I," you ask the singer to become that character—and by extension, the audience to become that singer. So make your characters likable. No singer will want to "become" someone who is judgmental or who sounds like a bully, or an egotist, or a loser, or a wimp. Recording artists seek lyrics that express sentiments with which they hope millions will identify.

Bear in mind that a listener fuses not only with a first-person "generic" character—such as the singer of "Goin' Out of My Head," but also with the character of a *persona* song.

The Persona Song

In poetry and fiction, the *persona*—the projected speaker or narrator of the work—is a "mask" for the actual author. A persona song is one in which the lyricist gives the singer a particular identity: the TV newscaster of "Dirty Laundry," the performer of "Rhinestone Cowboy," or the blue-collar worker of "Wichita Lineman." Since the vast listening audience lacks identification with these occupations, the lyricist must provide some other kind of listener identification—such as a universal emotion expressed by the singer of "Wichita Lineman" or the universal truth conveyed by the plot of "Dirty Laundry." So when you use this literary strategy to design a persona song, be sure to create a character whose values speak for millions or a plot that reveals some aspect of human nature or society.

First-Person Narrative Perspective

In every first-person story song, the narrator views the events from the inside. Depending upon the narrator's involvement in the events, the singer can play one of three roles: the lead role ("The Piña Colada Song"); a featured, but smaller role ("Ode to Billie Joe"), or the role of an interested onlooker ("You Could've Heard a

Heart Break"). The sensibility of each of these three songs derives largely from the degree of narrator's involvement in the story. To deepen your understanding of the three perspectives available in the first-person narrative, I recommend that you study the three lyrics cited. You might even give yourself an assignment to write a lyric from each perspective.

The "She/You" Glitch

When you begin a personal narrative by referring to the singee in third person as *she* or *he,* be consistent. In a subsequent line or verse make sure you don't slip into second-person and start to refer to the same singee as *you.* Here's an example of what to avoid.

> *When I called to say, Honey, I'm on my way home,*
> *Do you want anything from the store,*
> *I could tell by* her *laugh she was not home alone*
> *And my stomach felt tight, like before.*
> *When I asked* her, *honey, just what's goin' on*
> *She said Maureen had come by for a chat.*
> *I'd like to believe* you *but this time I can't*
> *'Cause I saw Maureen down by the laundromat.*

© 1982, Student lyric. Used with permission.

By the third line, we presume we're hearing a song about a man telling a friend about a past incident, or possibly he's just mulling it over in his mind. We (unconsciously) figure that if we stay tuned, we'll find out which. But in the seventh line, the third-person *she/her* perspective suddenly shifts to the second-person *you.* That last *you,* of course, should have been the word *her* and the verb should have been put in the past tense: *I'd like to have believed her. . . .*

Viewpoint coherence results from maintaining your chosen perspective on the story. First pick your viewpoint and then stick to it.

A Footnote On Our Times

You may have noticed that the song titles under the Collective We column (with the exception of "We Are the World") were written in the socially conscious sixties. Since songs reflect their times, it's not surprising that songwriters appear to have stopped addressing humanity at large in favor of self-reflection. Lacking a student example—since most student lyrics also express concerns that are more personal than cosmic—a lyric of my own will illustrate the viewpoint of the first-person Collective We. This is the second verse and chorus of "Changing, Changing," a chart single for Ed Ames in 1968 that mirrors its time:

> *We are searching, we are searching*
> *In the tea leaves on a spoon*
> *Placing palms upon a table*
> *Charting phases of the moon*
> *Tearing cobwebs from illusions*
> *Spinning new ones in their place*
> *Finding solace in a chalice*
> *Or forgiveness on a face.*

CHANGING, CHANGING, ever changing
Like the waves upon the sand,
Reaching in to find a meaning,
Reaching out to touch a hand.

By choosing the Viewpoint of the First-Person Collective We, the lyricist is asking the world to sing along. A lyric set in this Viewpoint must then express sentiments that are widely shared.

To have a song hit the charts brings a sense of satisfaction to every writer. With "Changing," what gave me even greater pleasure was its being chosen—years after its initial success—by several high school graduating classes as their yearbook theme.

SECOND PERSON (Emphasis on "You")		
SINGULAR Addressed to:		**PLURAL** Addressed to:
An Absent Place, Thing or Named Person	A Singee Who Is with the Singer	The Collective You (An Unseen Audience)
(Thinking)	(Talking)	(Thinking)
Galveston Swanee Willow Weep for Me Snowbird Mona Lisa Mr. Businessman Papa, Can You Hear Me?	Young Girl Hey, Big Spender Come in from the Rain Touch Me in the Morning Claire Papa, Don't Preach	Ac-cent-tchu-ate the Positive Climb Every Mountain Abraham, Martin & John One Hundred Ways You'll Never Walk Alone Try to Remember
Book Example Hello, Paris	*Book Examples* Manhandled Midnight Mood Tell Your Story Walkin'	*Book Example* Have You Seen My Guy?

Watch Your "You"

In a second-person lyric, the emphasis is on one *you*. In other words, if your singer's talking to someone present ("Hey, Big Spender"), or addressing in his or her mind some absent person ("Papa, Can You Hear Me?"), place ("Take Me Home, Country Roads"), or thing ("Good Morning, Heartache"), or speaking to the world at large ("You're Gonna Hear from Me"), the person or thing addressed becomes the *you* of the lyric—for the whole lyric. So whichever of the "yous" you picked, stay with it. Don't let any other *you* intrude to confuse your listener.

Here's an excerpt from a student's song addressed to the city of Paris. In this second-person-singular lyric, Paris is the sole *you* throughout the lyric—as it should be.

Hello, Paris! Bonjour, Paree!
Are you getting ready for me?
I'm feeling ripe and romantic
And my jet's just halfway 'cross the Atlantic.

Avoid the *You/You* Confusion

In conversation we use such colloquial expressions as *what can you do?, it depends on how you look at it, look before you leap.* That use of *you* of course means *anyone,* or, more formally *one: what can one do?* In a second-person lyric be careful not to let a colloquial *you* set up a conflict in your listener's ear with your singee *you.* Here's an example of what to avoid:

Last night you said that a year ago
You'd fallen for someone new
And you'd been meeting her secretly all this time;
Well, what you don't know can't hurt you.
That was your excuse. . . .

The first three lines are easy to follow: a singer is addressing her lover and recounting her shock at discovering him unfaithful. After hearing the first two *yous,* which both refer to the singee, we've been set up to expect that subsequent *yous* will do the same. So when the fourth line hits, the listener anticipates a meaning more like: "Well, what you don't know—is I've had a lover too." Instead, we get the singer quoting the singee's thoughts. Remember, the ear can't hear the implied quotation marks, so the unexpected colloquial *you* confuses the listener. Be alert to avoid the *you/you* conflict.

When You Pick Second Person, Decide The Voice

In second person, viewpoint and voice are flip sides of each other. An effective second-person depends on your deciding if your singer is thinking the words to the song or saying them to someone. Look back at the diagram and you'll see that two-thirds of second person lyrics are written in the thinking voice—those in the end columns. The talking lyrics in the middle column are songs in which the singer is having a conversation with someone present. (We'll take up this special aspect of second person when we get to the Voice.)

A Second Person Caveat

It's not uncommon for writers to want to set the world to rights. This can result in lyrics that send preachy messages to the second-person Collective You:

If you live in the here and now
You'll become master of your fate.

Look in the mirror and put on a smile
And you will find that life is worthwhile.

If you have an impulse to give the world advice, or even worse, to scold—"put your anger and hate away"—I urge you to resist it. Audiences want to be entertained, not sermonized. Such preachments put the singer in an "I'm-okay-you're-not-okay" stance. But if you're bursting with a message you've got to deliver, then take a tip from "That's What Friends Are For," and use the second-person *singular* Viewpoint. The singer then addresses a singee instead of the world. That way the audience is over-hearing the advice instead of getting it. (You'll find a well-executed example of second-person advice in "Follow Your Heart" on page 135.)

THIRD PERSON (Emphasis on He, She, or They)		
Camera-Eye View		Personal View
Illustrates a Universal Truth	Characterizes a Type, Group, or Famous Person	With a Singer-Singee Connection
Eleanor Rigby Sam Stone In the Ghetto She's Leaving Home Johnny Can't Read Jack & Diane *Book Examples* Sue and John Dying on the Vine Dirty Little Secret	Valley Girl Bad, Bad Leroy Brown Old Hippie 16th Avenue Willie, Mickey, and the Duke *Book Example* Heart Hunter	Mr. Bojangles Coward of the County Richard Cory *Book Example* Man Who Walked on the Water

Create Convincing Characters

As you can see from the examples, the third-person Viewpoint is a favorite with lyri-cal sociologists who create cameo portraits like "Mr. Bojangles" or minidocumentaries such as "Old Hippie," which comment on the human condition. In analyzing these songs you'll find a common denominator: convincing people in believable situations. As the diagram indicates, successful third-person songs break down into two main divisions: the impersonal camera-eye view, and those stories told by a narrator with a connection to the story.

The Impersonal Camera Eye

In the Camera-Eye story the narrator stands outside the events and the characters, rather like the on-the-spot commentator at a television news remote.

This perspective in fiction writing is called third-person omniscient because the story teller assumes the privilege of an all-knowing presence who can move freely about and read the characters' minds.

The Camera-Eye present-tense suggests that the events portrayed reflect a pat-tern that is endlessly repeated and is of some social significance, as exemplified in "Eleanor Rigby" (lonely people) and "Johnny Can't Read" (our high illiteracy rate).

If you pick this objective viewpoint from which to write your lyric, then be sure to focus your lens on characters and situations that fulfill those two conditions. In other words, show us a social condition we recognize. For example, "In the Ghetto" shows us that poverty begets a relentless cycle of crime; similarly, "She's Leaving Home" reminds us of the sad fact that society produces millions of runaways annually.

What A Close-up Requires

Beginning lyricists sometimes focus on idiosyncratic individuals we can't recognize (often someone the writer knows) rather than create an archetype with common characteristics. Such lyrics don't work because they fail to fulfill the third-person camera-view requirement of universal contexts. A listener, for example, who's been given a detailed account of a day in the life of an alcoholic woman may reasonably ask of the writer, why are you telling me all this? What meaning can I infer? But when a camera-eye lyric is written right, like "Harper Valley PTA," the meaning of the story of the miniskirted mother resounds long after the tale is told: People in glass houses shouldn't throw stones.

The Singer-Singee Connection

A third-person close-up that contains no universal truth must then establish a connection between the singee and the singer. For example, we'd be interested in the story of that alcoholic woman if she turned out to be the singer's mother or wife or daughter; then we could draw some conclusion about human nature. But without such an emotional link the lyric will fail to sustain our interest.

First/Second	SPLIT VIEWPOINT		
First/Second	Split-Second	Third/First	Third/Second
Cajun Moon The Portrait Please, Mister, Please	Evening Star Tie a Yellow Ribbon	Sniper She's Leaving Home	Nowhere Man 40-Hour Week
Book Example Museum			*Book Example* Dirty Little Secret

Split Viewpoint Guideline

Songs that feature a split viewpoint are uncommon—especially split second-person and split first- and third, which explains the lack of two student examples.

Should you, however, venture to purposefully shift your lyric's viewpoint, be advised: a split viewpoint requires special handling.

If, for example, you conceive a plot that changes viewpoint from first person to second or from third person to second, you must explicitly show the ear the change. The place to make the shift is at the top of a verse or chorus, as opposed to within it. With the exception of the exceptional lyric, "She's Leaving Home," which embodies both the narrator's viewpoint and those of the parents of the runaway, each of the titles listed above changes viewpoint or voice in the opening line of a stanza.

In "Evening Star," for example, the first verse addresses the collective you—in this case the general male listener who is getting suggestions on the joys of life in the great outdoors; the three choruses switch at the top-line title to address the star, requesting that it shine down on those without dreams. Clear to the ear.

Before Moving On
Practice Critique #3

This lyric's ailment you'll find easy to diagnose. Also give a prescription for its cure.

Verse
She told me it was over
That she'd rather live alone.
She has a need to test her wings
And fly off on her own.
She's longing for adventure
That this small town can't supply.
Changin' times have changed her
And today she said goodbye.

Chorus
You got MID-LOVE CRISIS
Somethin' ev'ry couple goes through
Just MID-LOVE CRISIS
That's all that's ailin' you.

Your critique: _____

_____

_____

_____

_____

(To compare your critique with mine, turn to page 269.)

THE VOICE

Some lyrics make evident to the listener that the singer is holding a face-to-face conversation with someone present—talking. Some lyrics make evident that the singer is alone and having an interior monologue—thinking. I've termed this lyric writing option The Voice.

The diagram on page 55 lists examples of songs that make the distinction between the two Voices—talking or thinking—clear to the ear.

Thinking/Talking Confusion

The first time I heard "Leaving on a Jet Plane," I was baffled: How, I wondered, did a singer who is standing "outside" the door of a sleeping singee in the first verse, get inside that door in the chorus? When did she wake up? And where are they when the singer pleads, "hold me like you'll never let me go"? The lyric always sounded to me

THE VOICE		
THINKING		TALKING
1st Person (Musing)	2nd Person Addressed to Absent Person, Place or Thing	2nd Person A Conversation With Singee Duets
Feelings Private Dancer Material Girl My Old Yellow Car Every Breath You Take	Vincent Luck, Be a Lady Amelia Galveston Climb Every Mountain	I Will Survive Take a Letter, Maria What Are We Doin' in Love? Move Out!
Book Examples Girl's Night Good Morning Goodbye Fool If I Don't	*Book Example* Hello, Paris	*Book Examples* Midnight Mood Manhandled No Reason to Stay

like a split between a thinking verse and a talking chorus.

The cause of the voice discrepancy is obvious: the writer hadn't pictured the scene in his mind or made a decision as to whether the singer was thinking the words or saying them. Quite simply, failure to focus on such structural elements in a situational song—especially on the voice—can cause lyric murkiness—platinum status notwithstanding.

The emotion expressed in "Jet Plane" is clear: the singer feels sad about leaving. But the Voice of its situational plot doesn't stand up on either a talking or a thinking basis: If the singee's asleep and the singer's thinking, then the singer can't be asking her to hold him; if the singee's awake and the singer's talking, he'd never *say* something to her as self-evident as "I'm standing here outside your door. . . ."

To write a coherent situational plot, follow Aristotle's timeless advice: keep the scene before your eyes. And, I add, decide whether the singer is talking or thinking.

The Viewpoint/Voice Relationship

First-person lyrics are musings; the singer is thinking out loud; therefore, first-person lyrics are all thinking lyrics. Simple.

Third-person lyrics are essentially story songs in which the singer tells a tale to the unseen audience. Again, these are also *thought* lyrics because the singer is not talking to a character in the lyric's plot, but rather relating to us what the characters in the story have said. Again, simple.

The second-person Viewpoint presents the lyricist with choices of Voice: two kinds of thinking lyrics and two kinds of talking lyrics. A little less simple.

The Second-Person Choices

The singer of a second-person Viewpoint plot can do one of four things:

1. Address someone present such as in "Hey, Big Spender," "I Will Survive" and "Claire."

2.   Hold a two-sided discussion (a duet) where the listener hears both sides of the matter as in "Let's Call the Whole Thing Off," "Anything You Can Do I Can Do Better" and "Barcelona."
3.   Mentally address some absent person, place, or thing: "I Say a Little Prayer," "Climb Every Mountain," and "Take Me Home, Country Roads."
4.   Hold an interior monologue while someone is present. Here, although the singer and singee are together, the singer is thinking the song. To write a successful lyric of this kind simply requires that you make those two facts clear to the listener. I'll illustrate with a lyric of my own.

FOOL IF I DON'T, FOOL IF I DO

Crazy scene, like a replay of way back when—
Crazy me, thinking twice about you again.
But your eyes are melting me down like a snowman in the sun,
And all my defenses are crumbling one by one,
And I'm thinking—

FOOL IF I DON'T—FOOL IF I DO
Fool, to pass up the chance of making love to you.
Heaven knows you can take me higher
Than anyone since or before;
But will I be sorry I had tonight
When I wake up wanting more?
I'll be a

FOOL IF I DON'T—FOOL IF I DO
A fool to ever believe we could still come shining through;
There's a world of diff'rence between us
We couldn't work out before,
But here I am trembling from head to toe
And I don't want to think anymore.

Oh! why did I ever let this sweet warm feeling begin—
And get in a situation I can't win—
Where I'm a

FOOL IF I DON'T—FOOL IF I DO
A fool, whichever I choose before the night is through.
You're the one great love of my lifetime, and
I'd be crazy to walk away—
But a sensible voice inside me's sayin'
You're out of your mind if you stay!
FOOL IF I DON'T—FOOL IF I DO
FOOL IF I DON'T—FOOL IF I DO (repeat to fade)

"Fool" permits the listener to eavesdrop on the singer's inner conflict. We know the singee is there from the line "your eyes are melting me down . . ." And we know that he or she is thinking because the singer states it.

Similarly, in "She Believes in Me" the audience hears the singer's feelings of gratitude toward his sleeping mate on those nights when he comes home after another small-time gig. Knowing the singer is tip-toeing around the house as she sleeps adds another dimension to his emotion.

How Not To Do It: The Thinking/Talking Blur

When a songwriter neglects to clarify the Voice, a schizoid lyric can result. For instance, this "morning after" song; is the singer talking to her lover or thinking these words?

LET ME PRETEND

Wake up and smell the coffee brewing,
Act as if you've got all day to spend.
Reach out and pull me down beside you—
Later you may disappear
But for now LET ME PRETEND.

Lie still and hold me in the shadows,
Make me think today will never end,
Lean back and share the Sunday paper,
But for now LET ME PRETEND.

Don't give a half-hearted valentine,
What I want is your best shot.
Open up and give me half a chance,
And I'll give you all I've got.

You get up and dash to meet a friend,
You smile and say you'll call tomorrow,
I may never hear from you again.
But for now LET ME PRETEND.

© 1981, Student lyric. Used with permission.

The Viewpoint, the Time Frame, and the Setting are clear, but the lyric doesn't work because the writer hasn't yet learned to discriminate between a thinking and a talking Voice.

We know it's Sunday morning at the singer's place and that last night's lover has dashed out without reading the paper. But we don't *feel* anything because we're unable to identify with either a thinking singer (wistfully wishing he'd linger) or with a talking singer (plying him with cafe au "lay").

In "Let Me Pretend," the singer makes a string of requests: *Wake up/smell/act/ reach out/pull me/lie still/hold me/lean back/share/don't give/open up/give me.* Certainly no one ever spoke such a succession of orders. The lyric is thereby rendered unbelievable as a conversation. Furthermore, a woman who had just said something as poetic as "hold me in the shadows"—if indeed anyone would ever speak those words—would not say in the same breath—"What I want is your best shot"! That's synthetic speech. On the one hand, the writer, by having the singer make all those requests, indicates that she's speaking, but then we hear two successive lines phrased as thoughts: "You get up and dash to meet a friend/You smile and say you'll call tomorrow. . . ."

Is this lyric worth saving? Absolutely, because the situation and emotion are both universally understood. It simply needs to be shaped into either a clear talking voice, or a clear thinking voice. Either treatment, if well executed, could produce a successful lyric.

A Talking-Lyric Guideline

When we want someone to do something, we *speak*. Getting someone to turn up the TV or turn down the covers cannot be accomplished by thinking it: we've got to say it. It follows then that if your singer is asking the singee to *do* something—even if it's abstract like *hang on to your dream*—you should purposefully write a talking lyric. So here's the guideline: If you want to advise, entreat, or command a singee to do something specific, or to behave in a particular manner, put your lyric in a talking Voice— with the singee present. Then make all the lines conversational.

When you choose a talking lyric over a thinking lyric, you automatically place the singer and singee in a setting (unless it's a phone call.) So you'll have to decide where they'll be. (More on this when we get to The Setting.)

Can You Switch Voices?

In a second-person lyric in which the singee is present, as in "Fool If I Don't" and "Let Me Pretend," it is virtually impossible to have the singer switch from thinking to talking or vice versa within the lyric.

Imagine, for example, that your singer is dancing with his lover; how could you show the listening audience that some lines are thought and some are spoken? With words alone, it's difficult to differentiate between the thinking voice and the talking voice.

But with "sound" devices—an echo chamber, reverb, or additional singers—a shift can be made vivid to the ear. In "Sniper," Harry Chapin pulled off multiple characters and a present-tense/flashback plot with filter effects, falsetto voicings, and backup singers—and superb craftsmanship.

The Voice Can "Work" On Two Levels

Some second-person songs work on two levels: they can be interpreted as either a talking *or* a thinking lyric. This comes about when the lyric doesn't explicitly show the singee is present and the language style is totally conversational. For example, "You Don't Bring Me Flowers": one listener may imagine that Barbra Streisand is lying in bed back to back to the singee thinking the whole lyric; another listener may picture her speaking the words to the singee over a pre-dinner drink. Because the lyric doesn't specify that the singee is present and because the diction is conversational, the Voice can be interpreted as either a talking or thinking lyric. It sounds credible on both levels.

Talking Versus Thinking

Certainly a thinking lyric ("Feelings") can be dramatically effective. But if you want to create a song with a greater sense of immediacy, design a face-to-face dialogue. The drama generated by Gloria Gaynor's "I Will Survive" and Diana Ross's "Touch Me in the Morning," was due in great measure to the talking voice: in each case, we *experienced* the emotional encounter of two lovers as it was happening, rather than hearing the singer relive the encounter in her mind.

Before Moving On
Exercise #12
Let's put some theory into practice. You've seen how Viewpoint and Voice are linked together; you can't have one without the other. And you've seen that the downfall of "Let Me Pretend" resulted solely from the writer's inattention to the Voice. Here's a warmup exercise that will increase your skill in controlling the Voice. Rewrite "Let Me Pretend" as either a thinking lyric or a talking lyric. If you're feeling really ambitious, rewrite it both ways.

The thinking guideline: Reread the original to get yourself into the Sunday morning scene and the singer's emotional state. Remember that she's thinking; she can make no direct requests. Her desires could of course be rephrased so that the listener would know she's thinking the line; for example, "I wish you'd wake and smell the coffee . . . if only you'd reach out. . . ."

Before you plunge in, here's something else to consider. You could make it instantly clear to your listener that the singer is thinking by referring to the singee in the third person: "If only *he'd* wake up. . . ." Using the third person would reinforce the emotional distance between the singer and singee.

Consider, too, that you'll need to modify the title to keep it consistent with the thinking Voice. Change lines in any manner you feel will enhance the unity of the lyric. And feel free to throw out any line that doesn't work. Option: Write an original all-thinking or all-talking lyric based on the plot line of "Let Me Pretend."

(New Title)

_____

_____

_____

_____

_____

_____

_____

_____

_____

_____

_____

_____

_____

_____

_____

The talking guideline. This time imagine how the singer would awaken her overnight guest and charm him into spending a leisurely Sunday with her. The objective here is to make the listener know the singer's actually talking to the singee: every word should sound conversational; none of that "in the shadows" stuff.

A small craft warning: You'll remember that the AABA virtually demands that time stand still. "Let Me Pretend," in addition to its Voice problems, also suffered from a moving time frame; considerable time passed—he had got up, dressed, and left. In your talking revision, time should freeze as the singer rhapsodizes about how Sunday would be if he'd stay.

Before you write, decide exactly where your singer is. I had trouble visualizing the action in the A sections. In the first, she may be leaning over the bed gently waking him (after all, she's been up making coffee). The second verse sounds as if she's lying beside him and giving him two (conflicting) commands: make love and read the paper. Only if *you* see the scene clearly can you make your listener see it clearly. Again you may need to adjust the title.

_____

(New Title)

_____
_____
_____
_____

_____
_____
_____
_____

_____
_____
_____
_____

_____
_____
_____
_____

Congratulate yourself after completing a revision. That's hard work. But it's the best kind of exercise you can get. If you can rewrite someone else's lyric successfully, think what you can do with your own!

Now, to the last half of the VVTS.

THE TIME FRAME

Choosing your plot's Time Frame and Setting is rather like making a date: you simultaneously decide both the time and the place. Similarly, to make the rendezvous come off as planned, you'd better remember the arrangements you made. An illustration of what can happen if you forget your plans is "You've Got a Good Love Comin' "

(Morrison/Stephenson/Silbar). An attentive listener heard Lee Greenwood announce his arrival at the singee's place in the first verse with "Guess who's here!" Then the second verse proclaims he's still on his way: ". . . when I get there. . . ." Ooops.

When writers take their eyes off the plot clock, the singer doesn't know where he is. And neither does the listener. Here are some guidelines to help keep your story straight.

Define Your "Now Moment"

The key to handling time frames is to decide your "now moment." Is the singer reacting to events that are happening right now—Saturday night? Or is the singer looking back on last night right now—Sunday morning? Or is the singer looking ahead to next Saturday night, right now—Thursday afternoon?

Here's an example of what can happen when a writer neglects to select the plot's "now moment." After you read each section of this excerpt, we'll pause to analyze the Time Frame, Viewpoint and Voice.

> **LOCAL CALL**
> (An excerpt)

Verse
> *You called today and it made me feel good*
> *Your voice seemed to smile*
> *As we talked of our childhood*
> *We still have so much in common*
> *And it's good to find*
> *Our lives haven't changed,*
> *We're still intertwined.*

With a series of past tense verbs—called/made/seemed/talked—the writer has told us that earlier today she got a call from a childhood friend. That makes the "now moment" *later the same day* with the singer looking back on an action that's over—and makes this a thinking lyric. Okay. So based on what we've heard so far, we expect that we'll continue to hear the singer muse about the phone call and her feelings for her friend. Here comes the chorus:

Chorus

> *Though miles have come between you and me*
> *You've always stayed in my memory.*
> *So somehow it's not long distance at all,*
> *It's just a LOCAL CALL.*

What are those two "it's" (it *is*) doing there? Those present-tense verbs contradict what we've just heard. Did we misunderstand the first verse? Is the action (the phone call) still going on? Well, let's see what the second verse brings.

Verse

What's happening in your life?
How are things with you?
I've got love in my eyes;
No, it's not "I do."
Changed my job last week,
I had to travel too far.
Did you get it together
To buy that new car?

No doubt about it now: The singer is talking on the phone to the singee. The lyricist has unintentionally written a split past-tense/present-tense Time Frame—and by extension a mixed thinking/talking Voice—which of course doesn't work.

The lyric demonstrates the interconnectedness of Viewpoint, Voice, and Time Frame. To prevent such incoherence, decide before you begin to write whether your action is taking place now (present tense), is over (past tense), or anticipated (future tense). It's as simple as that.

Note: That second verse contains another kind of verbal glitch worth calling your attention to: "I do." It's unlikely that any listener would get the writer's intended meaning about not marrying. Remember, the ear can't hear quotation marks.

As Time Moves, Show It

I recall a student song written for a children's album that was designed to show the ambivalent emotions of a three-year-old boy upon the arrival of his new baby sister from the hospital. The Time Frame was set by the second line: "Mommy brought her home *today*." As the song moved from verse to verse the brother expressed his mixed reactions of pleasure and jealousy. In the final verse he puts his sister on his tricycle and pushes her around the living room.

Listeners were befuddled. How could a newborn even sit up, much less steer a bike? The writer had neglected to show that over the four verses, three years had passed.

Unless we're told that a time frame changes, we assume a song is one moment's feeling—which it usually is. Time cannot make big forward leaps in a lyric without your showing that movement to the listener.

"Cat's in the Cradle" (S&H Chapin) does the job the way it needs to be done; the first line of each verse announces the passage of the years: *My son arrived just the other day . . . my son turned ten just the other day . . .* and so on. That's the way to do it.

Now let's examine the three Time Frames with their subdivisions.

The Three-Pronged Present

Looking at the diagram we see that the Present Tense breaks down into *The Nonspecific Present, The Habitual Present,* and *The Particular Present.* We've already noted that the plots of most pop songs take place in some undefined present tense in which the singer is saying, in effect, *this is how I feel.* The viewpoint is predominately first-person, the voice is thinking: "(I Did It) My Way," or "Comin' In and Out of Your Life (Isn't Easy)." I've labeled this time frame the nonspecific present.

PRESENT TENSE		
Nonspecific Present (An Undefined Moment)	Habitual Present (An Ongoing Action or Emotion)	Particular Present (A One-Time Action)
Someone to Watch Over Me	16th Avenue	Touch Me in the Morning
Goin' Out of My Head	In the Ghetto	With Pen in Hand
Annie's Song	Nowhere Man	Saving All My Love for You
I Am Woman	Losing My Mind	How Am I Supposed to Live
Song Sung Blue	Piano Man	Without You?
Time in a Bottle	She Believes in Me	W*O*L*D
Endless Love	Private Dancer	Old School
Book Examples	*Book Examples*	*Book Examples*
Sly Like a Fox	Dying on the Vine	Midnight Mood
Kamikaze		Manhandled
		Present Moves in a Vehicle
		99 Miles from LA
		Tie a Yellow Ribbon
		By the Time I Get to Phoenix
		Book Example
		Red-Eye Flight

Then there's the habitual present in which the singer's emotion or action is on-going rather than expressive of one moment's feeling. Such songs sometimes allude to time frames, morning/noon/night as in "Losing My Mind" and may flash back to how things used to be. They may even mention a place—such as the bus in "I Say a Little Prayer." But the bus in that song is not a setting as such because "I Say a Little Prayer" is a thinking lyric.

Some habitual present lyrics feature both a setting and a time frame. Billy Joel's "Piano Man" for example: "It's nine o'clock on a Saturday" sets up a scene that describes the atmosphere of that piano bar on any given Saturday, rather than on one particular Saturday.

The particular present represents a one-time action and includes letters ("With Pen in Hand" and "Take a Letter, Maria") and phone calls ("W*O*L*D" and "Operator"). Lyrics set in the particular now may also have an implied backdrop: In "Saving All My Love for You," the setting is clearly the singer's place. ". . . when you walk thru that [my] door. . . ."

A subcategory of the particular present is a lyric whose story takes place in a moving vehicle—such as a car, bus, train, or plane. That plot device makes for unusual songs in which the singer moves either closer to or farther away from an emotional situation. To illustrate, here's the first verse of an AABA student lyric.

When I saw him holding her
I packed all that I own.
Now I'm headin down the runway
From the world I've known
I see the lights grow smaller—
They disappear from sight
As I leave behind the hurt and the lies
On this RED-EYE FLIGHT tonight.

© 1986 By Nina Meryl Ossoff. Used with permission.

Know Which Present Tense You've Picked

Many lyrics pin down the particular present with such phrases as "Later tonight I'll be in your arms. . . ." "In the morning when you're gone. . . ." By writing such a line you place your action in a specific moment; your plot must stay there—unless you purposefully change it—and show the change.

If you take your eyes off the clock, time may run amok as in this student first-draft excerpt:

Verse   *This morning*
When you said goodbye,
I tried so hard
Not to let you see me cry.
It hurt so
But there was nothing I could do
To hold a man who just ran out of love.
Now I know that

Chorus   *LAST NIGHT WAS THE LAST NIGHT*
And you'll never again hold me hard and tight
Oh, I know that
LAST NIGHT WAS THE LAST NIGHT
Our very last night together.

Verse   *Each morning*
When I awake
I wonder what I'll do
To make it through the day.
Around me
Empty drawers and empty dreams
Behind the door a pair of jeans remain.

© 1983, By Arline Udis. Used with permission.

Did you notice what happened? The writer inadvertently slipped from the particular present into the habitual present. In her first verse she set up a clear time frame: "Sometime later that day" showing us that he'd left her in the morning. Clear. So where did "*each* morning" come from? This implies that he's been gone for a while.

A plot cannot have two present tenses.

Before Going On
Exercise #13

VIEWPOINT,
VOICE, TIME
FRAME, AND
SETTING

65

The second verse of "Last Night" needs to align with the particular present time frame of the first verse. There's nothing to it. Just keep in mind that the singee left you this morning. Make your statement reflect that *later the same day* consistency:

_____

_____

_____

_____

_____

_____

_____

PAST TENSE	
First-Person Reflections	Third-Person Cameos/Stories

At Seventeen
Taxi
Same Old Lang Syne
Alice's Restaurant
Garden Party
 	
Book Examples
Kiss Me, Carmen
The Man Who Walked
  on the Water
Girls Night
	Frankie and Johnny
	Coward of the County
	The Wreck of the Edmund
	  Fitzgerald
	Bad, Bad Leroy Brown

	The Historical Present
	Eleanor Rigby She's Leaving Home Golden Ring *Book Example* Dirty Little Secret

The past tense frames two main divisions of lyrics: first-person songs in which the singer reflects on some biographical event ("Taxi"), or third-person songs in which the singer acts as an omniscient camera eye narrating a human interest story ("Bad, Bad Leroy Brown").

In the Third-Person Stories column you see a subcategory, *The Historical Present*. This is a story-telling device that gives a narrative more immediacy by telling its events in present-tense verbs. The Beatles used the historical present, as it's called, in two of their most effective camera-eye songs, "Eleanor Rigby" and "She's Leaving Home."

As in the present-tense guideline, be consistent. Whether you've picked the simple past tense or the historical present, stay with it all the way.

Some Subtleties of the Past Tense

In lyrics, as in life, *the past* can be last night, last year, a decade ago, or an eon ago.

To write a coherent lyric, it's important to decide whether your singer is telling of an event shortly after it happened, or long after. The amount of elapsed time will affect the emotional distance between the singer and the event being examined. You could liken your treatment of the past to looking at former events through a microscope, binoculars, or a telescope. Decide how long ago was the "when" of your plot.

"Last Night When We Were Young," for example, presents a singer overwhelmed by the dissolution of his lovelife "in one little daybreak." In contrast, two of Barry Manilow's hit singles, "Mandy" and "Even Now," find the singer viewing a love long gone—as through a telescope—and analyzing with some detachment the muted longing he still feels.

The guideline is, as always: decide the details of your plot, picture the scene, check your clock and calendar, and then *become* the character.

Past-Tense Verbs

You may remember from grade school a grammar lesson about the past-perfect (or pluperfect) tense. This is a verb tense used to express an action or to help make a statement about something completed in the past before some other past action or event. It's formed with *had*. For example, "He suddenly remembered that he *had forgotten* to call her." Correct. Not, "He suddenly remembered he *forgot* to call her." The two past actions occurred at different times; they require two different past-tense verbs. Many lyrics are rendered confusing when the writer mistakenly uses the simple past tense where the past perfect is needed. Remember when alluding to an event that took place prior to another past action, use a verb with *had*.

Before Moving On
Exercise #14
To reinforce the grammar lesson, here's an example of a simple statement that expresses two events that did not happen at the same time. Correct the faulty past tense verb to a past perfect verb, using *had*.

When I dieted for a week, I checked my weight.

_____

FUTURE TENSE

Tomorrow
Somewhere
Blue Room
Come Saturday Morning
Come Rain or Come Shine
Soliloquy (from Carousel)
When I Marry Mr. Snow
If You Go Away
On That Great Come and Get It Day
In the Year 2525
The Miller's Son

The Future Tense is the least complex, and also the least often chosen of the three time frames. If popular songs are any barometer, it appears that we concentrate on the present or ponder the past more than we speculate about the future. The lack of a book example from either the work of my students or from my own catalog would seem to confirm the relative rarity of future-tense songs.

Watch The Clock

As you've seen, good time management is critical to writing a successful lyric. You need Cinderella eyes: What time is it? Is the action going on now, or is it already over? Develop a sense of your lyric's "now moment" even if your character is alone and thinking *I miss her.* Is he staring into his breakfast coffee? Or standing at a bus stop? Does the clock move? If so, announce the change, and then make your verbs match the new time frame.

Here's the last of the VVTS.

THE SETTING

Like the first three parts of the VVTS, the Setting has its own special qualities. Your lyric's Setting can be an insignificant aspect of your plot, or a major one. And similarly to the Time Frame, the Setting can shift—or move.

THE SETTING				
None (Thinking)	Particular Place	Unidentified "Here"	Scenes Change	A Moving Vehicle
Feelings The Way We Were If You Could Read My Mind What a Fool Believes	One for My Baby Last Dance The Gambler Old School Slow Hand Please, Mr., Please	Saving All My Love for You Touch Me in the Morning Leaving on a Jet Plane Baby, It's Cold Outside	Lucille Same Old Lang Syne Class Reunion	99 Miles From LA By the Time I Get to Phoenix Taxi Tie a Yellow Ribbon
Book Example Fool If I Don't	*Book Examples* Dirty Little Secret All Over But the Leaving	*Book Examples* Manhandled Follow Your Heart Good Morning, Goodbye	*Book Examples* Sue and John Girls Night Kiss Me, Carmen	*Book Example* Red-Eye Flight

Pick A Place

It's important that you know where your characters are holding their conversations. A salad bar? A movie line? A dance floor? Pick a place, not solely because the background sounds of tinkling ice cubes and a juke box playing Patsy Cline add atmosphere to your lyric, but more critically, because it will keep you focused.

As a case in point, when writing "Fool If I Don't," I imagined that a woman ran into a former lover and they went to have a drink in a cocktail lounge of a hotel. Although I made no reference to the setting in the lyric, my picturing the scene enabled me to write a clear and consistent scenario.

When a writer works from a clear mental picture, listeners get treated to a coherent story. "How Am I Supposed to Live Without You?" (Bolton/James) for example, resounds with a strong sense of setting (his place) and time (right now): the singer, hearing that her former lover has found someone new, goes to get the facts from him. When Laura Branigan sings "I didn't come here for crying," and "from the look upon your face," we know she's standing inside his door looking him right in the eye.

Watch Your "Heres" And "Theres"

When your character is alone and thinking, you might consider it pointless to visualize where the singer is doing the thinking. Not true. Seeing the scene before your eyes as well as deciding what time it is, will help you avoid the murky plots so common on the top-40. For example, a hit 1986 duet—an attitudinal lyric reflecting one moment's feeling—had the female singing in the first verse, "[I'm] lying here," which she contradicts in the third verse with "here I stand"; then in the fourth stanza her lover invalidates both her statements by saying she'd already "walked out." So are they lying in bed thinking? Or are they facing each other talking? Or are they not even together? And if she's not there, how come it's a duet? Hit or not, the VVTS is a shambles.

The guideline: Identify every *here* and *there* in your own mind so that your lyric won't be full of plot holes, leaving your audience with only an emotion or a groove to listen to.

The Focus Questions

To help make your song make sense, get in the habit of writing a short script outline at the top of your first draft. The sentence should cover these basic questions:

> Is the singer alone or with someone?
> Where is the singer?
> What time is it?
> Is the singer talking or thinking?

For example, your sentence could be: A young man is sitting in a bar at happy hour; a pretty girl walks in and he talks to her. As you write, check back to your outline sentence. If you decide to move your characters from the bar to the bed, be sure to make the transition as clear as it is in the country classic, "Lucille": "From the lights of the barroom/To a rented hotel room/We walked without talking at all." (Bynum/Bowling).

Meanwhile Back At The Ranch. . . .

The whole trick is to make the ear hear where your characters are moving. Take a tip from the script writers of the old radio series "The Lone Ranger" who had to show listeners where the characters were galloping to and from. Hence, the transitional cliché, *Meanwhile, back at the ranch . . . Tonto, his faithful companion, had untied the sheriff. . . .*

A few connecting lines will do the trick: *as we got into my car . . . the next morning at the motel . . . I quietly dress as he sleeps . . . but on Saturday, he didn't call . . . meanwhile, back at the gym. . . .*

Start strong. In your first few lines show whether your singer is alone or with someone, thinking or talking the lyric, and where and when it's all taking place. If anything changes—Viewpoint, Voice, Time Frame, or Setting—make it clear to the ear.

When you get a fix on the VVTS, you'll write easy-to-follow lyrics that will keep your audience listening.

STEP 3   QUIZ

1) Name the four elements that constitute the spine of your lyric's plot.

   ———————— ; ———————— ; ———————— ; ———— .

2) a) What is meant by a *persona* song? ————————————————————

   b) Name a famous one ————————————————————

3) When writing from the camera-eye viewpoint, what two qualities should your plot possess?

   ——————————————————————————————————

4) When designing a lyric in which the singer is asking the singee to do or not do something, what voice is called for?

   ——————————————————————————————————

5) What is the special time frame shared by "By the Time I Get to Phoenix" and "Tie a Yellow Ribbon"?

   ——————————————————————————————————

6) Identify the time frame of this opening line: "You come home from the office/ And flip to Channel 2."

   ——————————————————————————————————

7) If your lyric changes settings, what must you provide for your listener?

   ——————————————————————————————————

(You'll find the answers on page 269.)

A RECAP OF STAGE ONE

You've now got a detailed picture of how to build a sound structure. Don't be surprised if it takes several readings of this section till you've absorbed all the theory and it's become part of your unconscious process. It will, eventually. But don't let yourself feel rushed. There's no timetable on growth. After all, perfecting your craft is a lifetime process.

How To Make Your Words Work

Every minor detail
Is a major decision. . . .
STEPHEN SONDHEIM

Applying the Top-Ten Principles to Avoid the Pitfalls

The same fundamental principles that apply to writing a Pulitzer Prize newspaper story apply to writing a Grammy Award winning song. The objective here is to learn the unwritten rules that underpin all good writing.

> Simplicity
> Clarity
> Compression
> Emphasis
> Consistency
> Coherence
> Specificity
> Repetition
> Unity
> Genuine Feeling

When a lyric doesn't work, that is, when a listener finds the plot confusing or disappointing, some basic writing principle has been violated. Because criteria exist by which to judge good writing, guidelines exist by which to avoid bad writing.

Here then are the top-ten principles of good writing and how to apply them to songwriting.

1. SIMPLICITY

Keep to one idea, and eliminate subplots. The plot of a well-crafted lyric can be summarized in one short sentence. One student designed a lyric with a situational plot about a high school girl who had a crush on a fellow student. But the writer mistook complexity for development. Though not a story song, the verses tracked the teenage relationship from the first day of second grade to second week of eighth grade, which served only to clutter the lyric with irrelevancies. The writer could simply have shown that at the moment the boy was ignoring her and let the chorus's emotional

72

plea to "Show Me You Care" do the rest.

Shun fanciness. Keep your language simple. One student lyric had the singer say that he "*quaffed* down some *brew . . .* and *bantered on* past two." Write the way we talk: *He drank beer and talked till two.*

Before Moving On
Exercise #15

Without regard to rhyme, restate the following two lines to make them conversational:

> *"I've been jettisoned from your heart*
> *And it's tearing my soul apart"*

_____

_____

2. CLARITY

The goal is to make your words move from line to line, holding the listener's interest without ever jarring or confusing. Pronouns—omitted, misplaced, mismatched, or unidentified—can cause major confusion.

Identify Your Characters

Include key personal pronouns—*I, You, He, They*—to make clear who is doing the talking or thinking. Clarify opening lines such as: "Always wishing for something out of reach." Tell the listener who is doing the wishing. *"You're* always wishing" or *"I'm* always wishing."

As a general rule, establish the identity of a person or group *before* you use *he, she* or *they.* For example, a listener would have to be psychic to follow this opening:

> *The years that we were married*
> *Were the best ones of my life*
> *He made my days and seasons rhyme.*
> *I was sitting at my desk at the office*
> *When* she *telephoned out of the blue*
> *I hadn't heard from* her *in a long, long time.*

Midway through that lyric the class learned that *she* was the husband's ex-wife. A listener needs to understand the plot from the beginning, line by line. We can follow the revision:

> *I was at my desk when his first wife*
> *Telephoned out of the blue*
> *I hadn't heard from her in a long, long time.*

Detect "Itosis"

The grammatical rule is to give every pronoun—each *it, this, that, he, she, they,* and so on—a clear antecedent that agrees in number, gender, and person. The listener connects the closest noun to the pronoun. Lyricists often fail to link a pronoun, especially *it,* with an identifiable noun antecedent. This common lyric malady I call *itosis.* First, here's an example of good pronoun use:

You took my trust and abused it.

It clearly refers to *trust,* the nearest noun. Here's another instance of doing it right:
You'd think we'd learn as the old world turns

How to keep it safe and sound.

It clearly stands for *world.* Occasionally a short phrase serves as the antecedent:
My bedtime stories always have a happy end

You make it happen.

Now here comes itosis:
All it takes is the right face at the right time
And it's certain to last.

What's certain to last? The right time? The right face? The writer presumably meant that upon meeting the right person a *relationship* could start that would last. To avoid itosis, supply a noun. Because the first line already contains a colloquial use of *it* in the expression *all it takes,* the revision eliminates the second *it:*
All it takes is the right face at the right time
And a love will start that's certain to last.

By establishing a clear antecedent, *love,* and changing *it* to *that* the meaning becomes unmistakable. Here's a *they* that doesn't work:
I have a dream
That lives inside of me
I want to bring the world together
In perfect harmony.
And if they would only listen . . .

We know the writer's intention is to link *they* with the noun *world.* But *they* (plural) disagrees with world (singular). There are two ways to fix the glitch: change *world* to *people of the world* (plural); or change *they* to *it* (singular).
A meaningless *this* or *that* can cause another kind of vagueness; for instance:
What will I say when I see her?
What if she's wearing that dress?

It's pointless to point a finger at *that* dress if the listener doesn't know what significance the dress holds for the singer. It could be that red taffeta dress he hated, or the black silk she wore on their first date. He might have meant something like "What if she's wearing that low-cut blue dress that turns me on?" It's not the listener's job to fill in some meaning, but the writer's job to clarify it.
I've heard many lyrics that contained the non sequitur ". . . but *this time. . . .*" a

phrase unrelated to any former statement in the lyric. If you want to say *this time,* then precede it with a setup line: "I've always rushed into love before . . . but *this* time. . . ." or "on my last flight I missed the plane . . . but *this time*. . . ."

Catch the Culprit

Three more culprits cause ambiguity: *word fusion, unfamiliar allusions,* and *multiple meanings.* A student's line caused puzzled expressions: Did we hear "grey day beaches," or "Grade A beaches"? The context didn't tell us. To detect word fusions, read your words aloud to yourself as you write.

Watch your allusions. When your lyric makes reference to a well-known person, place, or thing, it's important that all your listeners recognize the allusion. One student lyric contained the phrase "with her 501 blues"—a word combination filled with semantic possibilities. Some listeners puzzled whether the reference signified a commuter bus or train ride, or the post-workday letdown, or a ritual after-work drink. The writer was referring to *501 brand jeans,* a product unfamiliar to many in the audience.

Eliminate any word or phrase that will force a listener to choose between two (or more) meanings. Do not confuse ambiguity (undesirable vagueness) with layered meaning (successful puns). As a case in point, the first draft of "Midnight Mood" (page 29) contained a small ambiguity: the third verse began "Cancel your reservations/Sample some forbidden fruit." By *reservations* the writer meant *mental restraints.* But some listeners wondered what restaurant (or hotel, or plane) reservations the singee was being asked to cancel. The two denotations of the word *reservations* distracted the audience from the song's story. The writer wisely removed the ambiguity by revising the line: "Take a short vacation/Sample some forbidden fruit." No confusion now.

Before Moving On
Exercise #16
Here's a case of itosis that's causing plot vagueness.

> *Your clothes are in my closet*
> *You've even got the key*
> *Don't put* it *off any longer*
> *You're the one for me.*

Instead of stating the antecedent of *it,* the writer implied it, and presumed that a listener could connect the dots. *It* refers neither to *key* nor to *closet,* nor to getting married. What the writer wants to express is the idea that the (female) singee has the key to his apartment and some of her clothes at his place; he wishes that she'd make a commitment to the relationship and move in. Knowing the writer's intended meaning, rewrite the four lines to make the scenario clear to an audience.

_____

_____

_____

_____

3. COMPRESSION

Aim to say a lot in a few words. Be mindful that the closer the effect is to the cause, the stronger the impact: Instead of "Once I thought that down deep in your heart you loved me," contract to "Once you loved me."

Identify and delete meaningless modifiers such as *(old) adage, (quick) glance* and those two notorious redundancies *(free) gift* and *reason (why)*.

Banish *-ly-* adverbs like *slowly* and *sadly* and limp adverbial phrases. Make verbs do the work: Instead of "she *walked slowly* into the party," replace two weak words with one strong one, "she *ambled* into the party"; similarly, compress " 'I'm leaving,' he *said in a low voice*" to " 'I'm leaving,' he *mumbled.*"

Limit the use of qualifiers like *very, really, just,* and *a lot*. The phrase "you matter to me *a lot*" is unconvincing because it's been blown up with hot air. Someone matters, or someone doesn't matter. By qualifying the statement, you undercut the sincerity of the speaker: "You matter to me" says it all. Perhaps the worst de-emphasizer is *really*—as in "I'm *really* sincere." That statement is about as trustworthy as the familiar evasion, *"the check is in the mail."*

Before Moving On
Exercise #17
To make this opening verse punchier, delete any word unnecessary to the meaning; and you may reduce two words to one: For example, the line, "Between the two of us we could light up this here night" would be improved by reducing *this here night* to *the night.*

> *Are you standing there takin' inventory?*
> *It sure feels that way to me,*
> *'Cause your eyes keep cruisin' up and down*
> *Ev'ry single inch of me.*
> *I only came into this bar tonight*
> *Just to cool off from the heat,*
> *But now it seems hotter in this place*
> *Than it was out there on the street. . . .*

_____
_____
_____
_____
_____
_____
_____
_____

If you took out fewer than ten words, go back and trim some more fat. Then, from the following two lines of the lyric's second verse, compress two phrases. In the first line condense *that pair of* to one concise pronoun; in the second line replace *pressed so tight* with one verb:

Wish I was that pair of leather jeans
Pressed so tight against your hips

4. EMPHASIS

Proper emphasis is central to forceful writing. Cutting worthless words and reducing the syllable count, which you just practiced, contributes to emphasis. Your lyrics will gain additional punch if you follow the following guidelines.

Prefer active verbs and one-syllable words. Here, for example, are two sentences that make essentially the same statement—only the second makes it more emphatically than the first: *The subway was overflowing with commuters returning home from work.* A compound verb *(was overflowing)* and three multi-syllable words *(overflowing, commuters, returning)* weigh down the sentence for a total of eighteen syllables. Here's the second sentence: *Rush hour crowds jammed the subway.* Now a one-word verb *jammed* makes *crowds* perform the action, and two words *rush hour* replace the prepositional phrase *with commuters returning home from work.* Seven syllables say it all.

Position your words in a strong place. Put words with semantic weight—verbs and nouns—at the end of a line. That's where they gain emphasis and are therefore remembered. The next best position is at the beginning. For example, instead of "she had that red dress on," reposition *dress:* "she had on that red dress." Not, "this photograph of you is all I have," but "all I have of you is this photograph."

Keep words in their natural order. Avoid reversing words to accommodate meter or rhyme: Not "on your smile I still depend," but "I still depend on your smile."

Avoid exaggeration. New writers often believe that exaggeration creates drama. As a result lyrics thud with overstatements: "*All* your nights are full of passion/*All* your days are full of fun." That's synthetic. "Love doesn't know any reason/Love doesn't need any rhyme": parallelism without meaning.

Avoid pluralizing: For instance, here's an ineffective way to show missing someone: "I found a lot of your old tee shirts. . . ." More touching would be: "I found your Yankees tee shirt. . . ." Prefer the singular to the plural.

Avoid overblown clichés: "You went away and took my soul with you . . . my heart begins to die . . . the pain is tearing me apart. . . ." If you treat a weighty subject in an offhand rather than a heavy-handed manner, you'll be more likely to evoke an emotional response in your listener. Once again: write the way we talk.

Remember the VVTS: When designing your lyric, try to choose the first- and second-person viewpoint over third-person, the talking voice over the thinking voice, and the present tense over the past and future tenses.

Match words to music. When setting words to music or music to words, match content words to stressed notes—those whose pitch rises or those held for several beats. In other words, don't emphasize articles (*a, an, the*), auxiliary verbs (*will, may, can*) or prepositions (*of, on, in*), which will weaken your thought. For example, in the line "I miss you in spring," the content words are the verb *miss,* the pronoun *you,* and the noun *spring.* The natural emphasis would therefore be "I MISS YOU in

SPRING." Yet we commonly hear in pop songs such misplaced emphasis as "I miss you IN spring." Fit emphasis to emphasis.

Before Moving On
Exercise #18

Rewrite this passive voice line, turning *be comforted* into an active verb: (Give *touch* the action).

> *I can be comforted by the touch of your hand.*

_____

Rephrase this line to place the emphasis on a noun.

> *Between the cradle and the grave the time is short.*

_____

Reduce this excessive generality to a specific incident that reminded the singer of the singee today.

> *I think of you every minute of every day.*

_____

5. CONSISTENCY

Determine that your character is consistently drawn. The unconvincing lover of "Let Me Pretend" (page 57) illustrated the need for consistency of diction and tone: Sustain your singer's language style—hip or romantic—and attitude—teasing or entreating—throughout your lyric.

The consistency principle also governs the effective use of figurative language. Keep your lyric's fundamental image such as *rain* consistently either literal (real rain, as in "September in the Rain") or figurative (hard times, as in "I Made It Through the Rain." Within one lyric don't shuttle between literal and figurative meanings of the theme word. (Step 5 deals fully with figurative language.)

Consistency is the essential message in "Get a fix on the VVTS." To recap Step 3's key caveats on viewpoint and voice: In a second-person song addressed to an abstraction ("Luck, Be a Lady") or to an absent place ("Galveston") or thing ("Skylark"), keep that singee the lyric's only *you*. In a third-person narrative, be sure that you maintain your *he, she,* or *they* references throughout. And to write a convincing talking lyric, make your singer's dialogue sound consistently conversational.

Before Moving On
Exercise #19

a) The language style of the following two lines lacks consistency:

> *The symphony of our love*
> *Has got a real hot beat.*

Take each line and pair it with a new mate that matches it in both diction and tone without regard to rhyme or rhythm. Complete this thought:

> *The symphony of our love*

_____

Now, provide an introduction to the line below.

A real hot beat.

b) In the following second-person lyric addressed to the moon, a reference to a second singee *(us)* confuses the listener.

Pale summer moon sailing by,
I'm so glad you brought us *here*
To hold each other near
In the glow of your light.

Retain the first line and revise the second to clarify *us*. Obviously *us* does not mean the moon and the singer (you and me, *us*) but alludes to a person not yet introduced to the listener. A hint: Sometimes the best solution for murky pronouns is to use the missing noun.

_____

_____

_____

_____

6. COHERENCE

Coherence is primarily a matter of logic. Keep all the elements of a lyric centered on the topic and put ideas in an easy-to-follow sequence.

Remember that the brain works by association: It processes new information by associating it with data previously stored. Your listeners can deal only with what they already know. Each line therefore should support and elaborate on the preceding one, and lead to the next one with clear connectives: *if . . . then . . . but . . . therefore.*

Make an action *precede* a consequence. And a premise *precede* a conclusion. And a cause *precede* an effect. Here's an example of a poor sequence of thoughts:

I know it's easy, easy to run from
Something like heartache when it comes.

We understand the first line only after we've heard the second line. Give your listener meaning line by line. Let's make *heartache* precede the pronoun *it* instead of follow it, like this:

A heartache, when it comes,
Is easy to run from.

The revision gains emphasis as well as clarity by eliminating the common verbal tic *like,* which, by qualifying heartache, diminishes it.

Here's an opening verse that lacks coherence because it omits the action that caused the *reaction.*

I can't believe it! It's been a real long time
Though I won't deny you're often on my mind
I hope life is good and she's makin' you happy
But I also hope you sometimes think of me.

That's third-degree *itosis*. By neglecting to precede "I can't believe it!" with a cause for the exclamation, the writer forces us to interpret the words instead of experience them. What can't she believe? That she unexpectedly ran into the singee? Did the singer just learn that the singee got married? Here's an orderly statement of the facts—without regard to meter and rhyme:

> *Only a couple of minutes ago*
> *The band played our old song*
> *I'd just been wond'ring how you were*
> *So I can't believe you've walked in*

Now we know what's going on: the singer is in a public place thinking about the singee as he walks in. Here's another opening line with an unset setting:

> *Back to where I started from*
> *Where it all began*
> *Goin' round and round again*
> *Forgettin' the best I can.*

"Back to where I started from" is a consequence of some event. Because we have no idea what the singer is back to, or trying to forget, the entire four lines lack meaning. It was not until nearly the end of the lyric that the writer revealed that the singer's love affair ended and he's back to playing one night stands. *Meaning is not retroactive.*

If, in the opening line, the writer had set up the cause for the effect, we could have enjoyed the song from the beginning. Here's how it might have started:

> *I thought that when I'd finally found you*
> *I was through with the single scene*
> *But now that you've walked out of my life*
> *I'm hitting the clubs again*

Watch where you put modifiers. If misplaced, they can distort meaning and thereby create incoherence. Be especially careful, for example, where you position the adjective *only:* If you say "I *only dance* at weddings" that implies I don't talk, eat, or drink at weddings. If, on the other hand, you say "I dance *only* at weddings," that implies I don't dance at proms, church suppers, clubs, or restaurants. A student lyric titled "It Ain't Only Rainin' on You," unintentionally conveyed the sense that it was also snowing, hailing, sleeting on the singee. Her intended meaning was, "It ain't rainin' only on you; it's rainin' on me, too."

Keep a meaningful sequence. To be coherent, maintain a logical chronology from line to line—*morning, noon, night.* Put ideas in ascending emotional order, "old wood to burn, old wine to drink, old friends to cherish."

And of course if the lyric changes viewpoint, voice, time frame, or setting, lead the listener in a clear transitional phrase.

Before Moving On
Practice Critique #4
As you read these two verses consider the sequence of the thoughts. Are they logically organized?

My heart is feeling weary.
The tears run down my face.
This bed was once a haven,
Now it's just a barren space.

The house is dark and empty;
When you left you left no light.
I press my pillow close to me
Through another lonely night.

Which principle is being violated here? What should the rewrite accomplish?

Your critique: _____

_____

_____

_____

_____

(To compare your critique with mine, turn to page 270.)

7. SPECIFICITY

Remember that your listener wants to see, hear, touch, smell, feel. Abstract words—kindness, sorrow, memories—are impersonal and shadowy. Because they cannot produce a picture for the mind's eye, they leave no after-image in the listener's memory.

Whenever possible, turn shadow into substance with words that will involve the senses by evoking color, texture, flavor or aroma. Try to be specific rather than general. For instance, you could vivify the imageless "memories of you," with "that velvet valentine"; the colorless "jewelry you wore" with "gold bangle bracelets"; the non-specific "that weekend party" with "that marshmallow roast."

Specificity comes in degrees: You can upgrade the line "Let's play some music" to "let's play some records," and particularize it even further with "let's play some Brubeck." Similarly, "pour my wine" can be made more memorable if made more specific: "pour my Bordeaux."

Here's an example of what I mean by using photographable images—what I call Kodak words—that objectify the emotion the singer is feeling:

You keep showing up in all the wrong places
Your aftershave clings in the dresser drawers
And those old running shoes
With the knotted up laces
Are still under the bed
On the side that was yours.

© 1986, By Francesca Blumenthal. Used with permission.

That's a fine example of how to bring authenticity, atmosphere, and universal truths to your lyric through the specific truths of detail. What the mind's eye can see more clearly, the heart can feel more deeply.

Lastly, use specificity to *show* an emotion, rather than tell it. In "The People That You Never Get to Love," Rupert Holmes drew a picture of shyness: "...and [you] take a sudden interest in your shoes."

Before Moving On
Exercise #20
a) Replace each shadowy generality with a specific example:

I've got faith in you. _____

Want to go out tonight? _____

They've got a lot in common. _____

b) Janis Ian showed she slept alone through an image: "And in the winter, extra blankets for the cold." Create a picture for each of the following emotions:

Show loneliness: _____
_____

Show nervousness: _____
_____

Show elation: _____
_____

8. REPETITION

Satisfy the listener's need to recognize the familiar. Repeat important words and/or lines for emphasis—especially the title. In the verse/chorus form the repeated chorus brings instant satisfaction to the ear; in the AAA, it's the refrain ("For the times they are a'changin' ") and in the AABA ("The Way We Were"), it's the title.

The Greeks identified dozens of separate repetitive figures of speech. The names for some of these figures, such as alliteration, are commonly known. The terms for many other significant devices, however, are both unfamiliar and unwieldy. In giving the following list of useful repetitive tools I have sometimes, for simplicity's sake, "translated" the Greek term.

Alliteration features the repetition of accented consonant sounds in successive or neighboring words. This classic device creates phonic patterns by lightly linking words (ideas) you want to emphasize. Here's an example from "Manhandled" (on page 176):

> *I want to be*
> *Manhandled tonight*
> *Tied up in the arms of*
> *Someone holding me tight.*

Here's another from "He Belongs to the Land" (Sue Stater):
> *He's worked these fields for forty years*
> *And it's the Good Book he's followed*

Assonance uses a repeated vowel sound to lend cohesion and emphasis. In her lyric "New York Boys" Arline Udis yokes ideas through a succession of long *a* sounds:

> *They play with the flame*
> *But they keep it cool.*
> *They name the game*
> *And they write the rules.*

In "Dying on the Vine," Maureen Sugden helps unify two lines by accented *en* sounds:

> *She has spent each morning shopping,*
> *And the men here are divine.*

Keep your ear peeled for places to give your lyric more impact by picking words whose inner sounds can connect your ideas.

Parallelism presents similar or contrasting ideas in a similar grammatical construction and lends both cohesion and polish to a lyric. This excerpt from the first verse of "Changing, Changing" (page 49) uses parallelism as its framework·

> *Tasting wine from many vineyards*
> *Testing truth from many shores*
> *Looking into funhouse mirrors*
> *Looking out of prison doors.*

Look for lyric lines you could tighten by putting a series of thoughts in the same grammatical form.

Word Motif (Repetend) is any repeated word, phrase, or line that reappears, often irregularly, to add emphasis and unity to a lyric. In "Sue and John," you heard several word motifs at work unifying the three stanzas: "are busy moving . . . needs improving . . . perfect wife" (page 24). You'll find two more examples of motifs in the lyrics on pages 162 and 170.

Word Derivatives (Polyptoton: po-LYP-toe-ton) reinforce meaning by repeating the same word or root in different grammatical functions or forms. Franklin D. Roosevelt's memorable phrase "the only thing to fear is fear itself" gives us first the verb and then the noun. You heard this device used in "Tell Your Story Walkin' " (page 39) "you've overstayed your stay"—again a verb and a noun. "Midnight Mood" (page 28) employed this repetitive figure of speech twice:

> *I've got an indecent* proposition
> *That I'd like to* propose *to you.*

is more memorable than

> *I've got an indecent* proposition
> *That I'd like to* offer *you.*

and

> *What I'm* needing *I* need *right away.*

is more emphatic than

> *What I'm* needing *I* want *right away.*

Start-of-line Echoes (Anaphora: a-NAPH-or-a) A device that repeats a word (or like-sounding words) or a short phrase at the start of successive lines or verses and thereby reinforces meaning as it echoes the words. Here's the opening verse from "Dirty Little Secret," a lyric printed in its entirety on pages 228-30.

> What a pretty little *picture*
> What a pretty little *scene*
> What a pretty little *dwelling*
> *On a lawn that's lush and green.*

Starting successive verses in the same manner acts to unify your lyric. "Girl's Night" (page 162) announces its changing settings and time frames with this device:

> *Verse #1* In a *teenager's bedroom in Pittsburgh*
> *Verse #2* In a *studio apartment in Manhattan*
> *Verse #3* In a *split level house up in Larchmont*

End of Line Echoes (Epistrophe: e-PIS-tro-fee) features a repeated word or phrase at the end of successive lines. For example:

> *I had* the chance
> *But I blew* the chance

Here's another example extended for dramatic effect:

> *Every night I spend*
> *Waiting* for your call
> *Hoping* for your call
> *Living* for your call
> *Desp'rate* for your call

Small Craft Warning. The two foregoing repetitive devices will strengthen your lyric. But there's a kind of repetition that will weaken it—a haphazard repetition of a word that's already been used in a different sense. In a student lyric the word *feeling(s)* was scattered carelessly over two verses and a bridge:

> . . . *shining bright on* feelings. . . .
> . . . *you're* feeling *sure of yourself.* . . .
> . . . *our* feelings *are strong.* . . .

Weed out such faulty echos. Make your repetitions purposeful, for effect.

A *Borrowing* is a word or phrase taken from another place—a literary allusion. In lyrics we often hear recycled slogans, song titles, and fragments of poetry. "What Are You Doing the Rest of Your Life" weaves in William Blake's famous image, "forests of the night"—a direct borrowing. In "Who Will Answer" I changed Longfellow's "Under the spreading chestnut tree" to " 'Neath the spreading mushroom tree' "—an altered borrowing that makes an oblique reference to the atomic bomb. The title "Goodbye, Yellow Brick Road" derived of course from *The Wizard of Oz*. The 1987 hit "Diamonds" incorporated the 1949 show-stopping title from *Gentlemen Prefer Blondes*, "Diamonds Are a Girl's Best Friend."

Small Craft Warning. "Dying On the Vine" (page 197) contains an allusion to T.S. Eliot's memorable phrase from *The Love Song of J. Alfred Prufrock*, "I have measured out my life with coffee spoons." In the lyric's first draft, however, the line read "She has measured out her life with coffee cups." Substituting *cups* for *spoons* serves only to confuse the listener: did the writer unintentionally misquote her borrowing, or was she possibly trying to pass it off as an original phrase? A guideline: Either borrow exactly or alter the phrase in some definite way to create a fresh twist; anything in between sounds inept.

The Return—the reappearance of a significant word, or line, or entire verse— was discussed in Step 1 as a development technique. The return, by its nature, is a repetitive device that helps unify your lyric with the ring of the familiar.

Before Moving On
Exercise #21

a) Strengthen the following lines by linking ideas through alliteration. Replace the verb *match* with a verb that alliterates with *feel,* then read the verse aloud to appreciate the improvement.

> *The travel poster on my wall*
> *Has lost its old appeal*
> *And songs I liked a while ago*
> *Don't (match) _____ the way I feel.*

b) The third in the following series of ideas is in a different grammatical form from the first two. Rewrite the third line to give it a parallel structure to the others.

> *We need more gas in the car*
> *More milk in the fridge*
> *And the breadbox could use more bread.*

---

c) Using the same word instead of a different one will add impact to this thought.

> *This night with you*
> *Is like no other (evening) _____ of my life.*

d) Using a series of word derivatives here instead of new words will make these lines more memorable. Replace *went* and *loving* with derivatives of *fall.*

> *At least I wasn't afraid to* fall.
> *Though the man I (went) _____ for may have been wrong,*
> *The (loving) _____ was right.*

Again, read your revision aloud to appreciate the punch of repeated sounds.

9. UNITY

In this outline of writing principles, you've seen how consistency and coherence contribute to clarity, how compression and repetition contribute to emphasis, and how they all ultimately contribute to the unity of your lyric. Unity can be said to be the goal of every work of art.

Unity also requires a balanced relation of parts to one another and to the whole. So treat elements with a length that's appropriate to their importance and maintain a logical relationship between the verse and the climb, the climb and the chorus, and the chorus and the bridge.

Here's a trick to help channel your ideas in a logical order: Say to yourself, "And then what? . . . and then what? . . . and then what?" Your objective is to weave the elements of time, action, and place into a harmonious whole that produces a single general effect. The simple guideline to achieve unity: apply all the foregoing principles of good writing.

Before Moving On
Exercise #22
Rewrite the line in this series of images that destroys the verse's unity.

> *The stocking hangs by the mantle*
> *The star shines atop the tree*
> *And a pumpkin smiles at the window*
> *Announcing the holiday season.*

---

10. GENUINE FEELING

Each of the foregoing nine writing principles lends itself to a practical how-to exercise. The principle of genuine feeling, however, is one you must exercise independently. It can't be taught. A lyricist either writes with genuine feeling or does not. And without it, all the alliteration, imagery, and parallel constructions won't help. There is no substitute for sincerity.

I can offer only the age-old injunction: Write about characters, situations, and emotions you understand. To illustrate, I recall a student lyric in which the singer wistfully enumerates a series of romantic scenes he shared with the singee—an amusement park ride, a summer picnic, a Christmas dinner—as though the couple could never enjoy such moments in the future. At the song's end we learn that the relationship is still going on. The lyric is fabrication. It rings false because it's not true to life: We miss what can never come again, not what is still possible. In genuine "reminiscing" standards such as "These Foolish Things," "Thanks for the Memory," and "Traces," the relationship, appropriately, is over.

It's not uncommon for new writers to go about the songwriting process by trying to write hits. Looking for the formula for a quick payoff, many grind out best-seller themes: for example, the cheating song. A cheating song is all right as long as you've got something genuine to say—an honest point of view to express. I recall a student lyric in which a long-married man is suddenly swept up in a tumultuous office affair with a young secretary. The writing lacked believability. I asked the married student if he identified with his character: "Heavens, no!" was his quick response.

Oscar Hammerstein put it succinctly: "Most bad writing is the result of ignoring one's own experiences and contriving spurious emotions for spurious characters."

To move and convince others, *you* must first be moved and convinced. Be true to be believed.

STEP 4 QUIZ

1) From the top-ten principles, name "the four C's"
   C _____; C _____; C _____; C _____

2) How do you avoid "itosis"? _____
   _____

3) Where is the best placement for important words?
   _____

4) The following line is made more memorable by the interlacing of two repetitive
   devices:
   "The sunny glow of summer's golden scene is gone."
   a) Name the two devices and b) identify which words they link.
   a) _____ and _____;
   b) _____

5) The principle of unity demands the weaving together of what three plot elements? _____

(You'll find the answers on page 270.)

Figuring Out Figurative Language

We think and talk in two kinds of language—literal and figurative. Sometimes we say just what we mean—"It's raining"—literal. Sometimes we exaggerate a fact for emphasis—"It's raining cats and dogs"—figurative. Sometimes we give a word a non-literal meaning to dramatize how we feel—"It's raining in my heart"—figurative again.

Figurative means "not in its original, usual, or exact sense or reference." To say it's raining cats and dogs is not a fact but rather an overstatement to emphasize the size of the raindrops. To say "it's raining in my heart" is to compare the feeling of unhappiness to the bleakness of a rainy day—a figure of speech called a metaphor. Metaphor is principally a way of achieving a deeper understanding of one kind of experience in terms of another kind of experience.

We use metaphors when we have strong feelings to express; for example, Bette Davis' memorable quip in *All About Eve* as she braces herself for a turbulent party: "Fasten your seat belts. It's going to be a bumpy night." Comparing an impending fracas to a stormy flight vivifies the emotion.

Muddling Our Metaphors

In conversation we sometimes muddle our metaphors. It's not uncommon, for example, to hear someone blunder, "That was water under the dam," when what was meant was either "that was water *under the bridge*" or water *"over the dam."* I recall another scrambled metaphor from the manager of a rock and roll band as he discussed launching his group: "We want to get the show *off the road*"—a mishmosh of "get the show *on the road*" and "get the show *off the ground.*" Such verbal booboos, which everyone commits on occasion, often go by unnoticed. But if such a glitch gets set in print or vinylized on record, it tends to discredit its author.

Understanding how figurative language works will help you work it successfully into your lyrics.

THE METAPHOR UMBRELLA

A metaphor is both a particular figure of speech and an umbrella term for a number of other figures which include apostrophe (a-POS-tro-fee), personification, simile (SIM-a-lee) and pun, as well as the expanded forms of symbol, fable, and allegory.

Creating fresh metaphors requires an eye for resemblances: Music critic Stephen Holden in a *New York Times* review of a Shirley Bassey concert said, "She made George Harrison's gentle lyric for 'Something' sound like the reflections of a barracuda zeroing in on a goldfish." That's a vivid comparison in which Holden used a simile, the most common subtype of metaphor.

Picture the metaphor umbrella like this:

It is these types of metaphor—rather than the extended forms of allegory and fable—that songwriters employ the most. So we'll center our discussion on the seven figures under the umbrella.

Lyricists use figurative language in two basic ways: casually as a decoration in a lyric line or two, or significantly as the central device of the song. The more weight the metaphor bears, the more critical it is that it be used properly.

In ascending order of importance we'll examine what it takes to make your metaphors work. In each discussion I'll suggest—for your future study—some song titles that employ that figure either as a decoration in a single line or two, or as the lyric's central device.

Personification

When we give human qualities to inanimate objects or abstractions, we are personifying them. When we say: the stars *look* down, volcanos *spit* fire, or inflation is our biggest *enemy,* we are making animate things out of the inanimate.

Lyric Line Examples: From "Marcie" (Joni Mitchell): "and the sand/all along the ocean beach/*stares* up empty at the sky." In Sondheim's *Sweeney Todd* the chorus exhorts the barber "lift your razor high, Sweeney/Hear it *singing* 'Yes!'"

Central Device Examples: Songs designed with Personification come in two styles. The more common of the two has the singer make animate an abstraction as in "Hungry Heart" and "The Summer Knows." In the more dramatic approach the singer *becomes* the place, or thing, or abstraction as in "I Write the Songs" (I am Music), "(I'm the train they call the) City of New Orleans."

Guideline: The key caveat is don't overdo the properties of the thing personified. For example, in a student lyric, *heartbreak* paid a return visit. A line like "I've been just fine without you" works because it expresses the singer's attitude toward the feeling. But what you don't want to do is attribute to *heartbreak* something as outlandish as having personal property: "I'll go get your coat and hat/Let me help you with your bags." That's carrying personification past the point of believability. When probability fails, the illusion breaks.

Apostrophe

In this figure, an absent or dead person, or more commonly an absent place or thing, is addressed as if it were alive and present and will presumably answer. Apostrophe is closely related to personification; "Good Morning, Heartache," for example, is a lyric in which the subject is both personified and addressed.

Lyric Line Examples: "The Old Songs" (Kaye/Pomeranz) contains an aside: "Sweet old songs, I'm counting on you to melt the lady's heart." "You're Gonna Hear From Me" opens with "Move over, sun, and give me some sky." (D&A Previn)

Central Device Examples: Songs featuring apostrophe come in four main categories: *Places:* "Swanee," "Galveston," "California, Here I Come"; *Nature:* "Willow, Weep for Me," "Blue Moon," "Evening Star," "Green Finch and Linnet Bird"; *Abstractions:* "Luck, Be a Lady Tonight," "Mr. Sandman," "Time, Don't Run Out on Me"; *Absent People:* "Blow, Gabriel, Blow," "Papa, Can You Hear Me?" "Vincent."

Guideline: First, set up the apostrophe so that the audience knows immediately who or what is being addressed, unlike this student first draft: "Slidin' off from shore/Raisin' my sail/And with you at my back I'm off to explore." Who's you? The next line tells us *you* is the wind. That's too late. Identify in your first line the one being apostrophized: "Moon River . . . I'm crossing *you* in style. . . ."

Be consistent. When you address an absent thing or person ("Swanee," or "Papa, Can You Hear Me?"), that object or person becomes your singee—the one sung to—throughout the lyric. In a country hit of Anne Murray's, "Time, Don't Run Out on Me" (Goffin/King), a major inconsistency went unnoticed. The lyric was conceived as a plea to *time* to help the singer get back her ex-lover. The writers lost their focus in the second line: After the title line we hear "gotta make *you* love me the way *you* used to do." The line, of course, should have been "gotta make *him* love me the way *he* used to do."

The Pun

A pun is essentially an "auditory metaphor" (Auden) that can be used humorously or for serious purposes. Puns come in several forms.

In one form of punning, a word is repeated with a shift in meaning. The first use of *line* in "Wichita Lineman" (Webb) referred to the main telephone line; the final use suggested that the singer's emotional feelings were unchanged *(still on the line)*. The payoff in the last chorus of "Class Reunion" (Henry/Morris)—a story of the meeting of two high school classmates—has the word *class* take on the added meaning of quality: "what a *class* reunion!"

In another form of pun, two meanings of a word are suggested simultaneously. The country song "Macon Love," makes evident to the ear that the title phrase refers both to the Georgia city and sexual activity. In *Sweeney Todd* Stephen Sondheim built "A Little Priest" upon a string of black humor puns that suggest the potential culinary properties of members of certain professions if they were made into meat pies: priest/*too* good, actor/overdone, politician/oily, fiddle player/stringy, piccolo player/

piping hot, and so on. The trick in this form is to set up the pun in such a way as to play on two (or more) of the possible applications—which are instantly apparent.

In yet another form, the second time the word (or part of the word) is used it sounds the same, but has both a different meaning and different spelling as in Sondheim's "weighty affairs will just have to wait" ("Comedy Tonight").

Lyric Line Examples: In addressing the abstraction, luck, in "Luck, Be a Lady," Frank Loesser simultaneously used apostrophe, personification, and pun: "At times you have a very unladylike way of *running out.*" In "Putting It Together" (Sondheim) an artist declares "first of all you need a good foundation"—both craft and financial support.

Central Design Examples: The country song "Harmony" (Berefford/Hinson) works on two levels of meaning: the singer's parents sing *in a chord* and live *in accord.* Layered meaning is always apparent to the ear. The title of the prize winning country hit "On the Other Hand" (Schlitz/Overstreet) simultaneously conveys two senses: the colloquialism and the singer's left hand on which he wears a wedding ring.

Guideline: Set up your intended punning word or phrase so that it conveys *two meanings*—either simultaneously or sequentially. In the following student attempt, the key word switches meaning in midair: "You're the Spam/You're the bread and butter/You're the jam/In my mental clutter." It's quirky, but it doesn't qualify as a true pun. Instead of conveying two meanings, *jam* causes the listener to instantly revise his first thought of "preserves," and shift to "a block" in order to arrive at the sense of the last line.

Another ineffective student pun evolved from the dialogue of two strangers in a movie line. Eager to begin a relationship, the fellow quips, "Let's get on with the show." The writer hoped to express that the singer both wished the movie would start and that he and the girl would get together after the film. But *get on with the show* suggests either beginning something that's been delayed, or resuming something that's been interrupted. Since neither of those two meanings fits the lyric's scenario, the line falls flat.

Double Entendre

Double Entendre, a form of pun, is a word or expression capable of two interpretations, one of which has a risqué connotation. With *double entendre* we say one thing and actually mean another. Since pop music is mainly a radio medium, suggestive puns are limited pretty much to sophisticated theater songs and supper club special material.

Central Design Example: In "I Never Do Anything Twice" (Sondheim) a madam recounts her S&M encounters with a baron and an abbott in which she won't permit her partners to repeat any painful pleasure—even though "it's *hard.*" She recalled with pleasure ". . . the baron who *came* at my command."

Guideline: As with the pun, the *double entendre* makes two levels of meaning simultaneously apparent—with the emphasis on the risqué one. In "Come and Get It While It's Hot" a student intended to offer a sexual invitation. But with lines like "I'm cooking the spaghetti/I'm simmering the sauce" she unintentionally wrote single *entendre.* She thought she was cooking up a sensual delight, but there's no way spaghetti sauce means more than spaghetti sauce.

The trick is to choose words that work on two levels of meaning—one of which is risqué. Had the writer added some menu items like "buns," "dessert," and "taste treat," for example, she could have served up some suggestive puns.

Simile And Metaphor

Simile and metaphor are closely related—figurative cousins, we might say. Since the hazards they pose to the songwriter are governed by the same guidelines, I will treat the two together.

A simile compares dissimilar things, using *like, as,* or *than.* When we employ a simile, we say, in effect, this almost equals that. A metaphor equates dissimilar things without *like, as,* or *than.* In the case of metaphor, this *is* that.

Lyric Line Simile Examples: "The tide's creepin' up the beach *like* a thief (Hammerstein); "I'm as corny *as* Kansas in August" (Hammerstein); "(He's) meaner *than* a junkyard dog" (Croce).

Central Design Simile Examples: In "It Might As Well Be Spring" Oscar Hammerstein "proved" his title by filling the verses of this classic AABA with a string of similes to illustrate the singer's restless-jumpy-starry-eyed-giddy feelings. Similarly, in "I Remember (Sky)," Stephen Sondheim chose a series of memorable similes ("…trees/Bare *as* coatracks/Spread *like* broken umbrellas") to vivify the recollection of a character in *Evening Primrose* who had lived for years inside a department store.

Lyric Line Metaphor Examples: "Love *is* a game of poker" (Mercer); "Love *is* pure gold and time a thief" (Nash); "Some say love it *is* a razor" (McBroom).

Central Design Metaphor Examples: "(You *Ain't* Nothin' But a) Hound Dog" (Leiber/Stoller); "I *Am* a Rock" (Paul Simon); "Running on Ice" (Billy Joel); "(Life *is* a) Cabaret" (Kander/Ebb); "Merrily We Roll Along" (Sondheim).

Guidelines: Looking at similes and metaphors as verbal equations will help you visualize how they work. And when they don't. Any word or phrase used in a figurative sense on the right side of the equal sign should apply to the word or phrase used in a literal sense on the left side of the equal sign:

$$\text{bare trees} = \text{coatracks}$$
$$\text{gambling on love} = \text{a poker game}$$
$$\text{a strong man} = \text{a rock}$$
$$\text{T H I S} = \text{T H A T}$$

Picturing verbal comparisons as equations is only the first step to writing successful similes and metaphors. To help you avoid the many minefields of figurative language, ten guidelines are coming up in a minute. But first, let's look at the final figure under the metaphor umbrella, the symbol.

The Symbol

When an image is combined with a concept, it becomes a symbol—the richest form of figurative language. For example, when Frank Sinatra sings "I Like to Lead When I Dance" (Cahn/Van Heusen) he's not merely telling the singee that he'll decide the moves on the dance floor but that he'll call the shots in the relationship. The title's image signifies one thing but represents (symbolizes) something much bigger.

Symbolism is rarely found in isolated lyric lines; it is used more commonly as the song's organizing principle.

Some Central Design Examples: In the Paul McCartney and Stevie Wonder duet "Ebony and Ivory," black and white piano keys represent the two races and their potential for living side by side in harmony.

When the singer of Thom Schuyler's country classic "My Old Yellow Car" longs for his "rusty old shell of an automobile"—as he's chauffered in his bar-equipped Mercedes—we know he really longs for what his old car symbolizes: the friend-filled "richer" times of his youth.

When we hear the line in "September Song" (Anderson/Weill) that *the days dwindle down to a precious few,* we realize that the months of the lyric's calendar represent the seasons of the singer's life.

Guideline: As these examples illustrate, you produce a symbol by making one image consistently convey a second, broader meaning.

TEN GUIDELINES TO THE SUCCESSFUL USE OF FIGURATIVE LANGUAGE

Guideline #1—Complete your metaphor

If you start an analogy, then finish it. For example, in an opening verse a student started to compare being in love with taking a journey. Then he stopped.

> *I've been down the road to love*
> *A time or two before*
> *But each time ended up with a broken heart.*

That's an incomplete metaphor. In other words, if you're going to say that being in love is like traveling down a road, then follow that claim by showing love's roadlike qualities. Because a metaphor is a verbal equation, the sides should compute.

$$\text{IF BEING IN LOVE} \quad = \quad \text{GOING DOWN A ROAD}$$
$$\text{then}$$
$$\text{ON THE ROAD OF LOVE} \quad = \quad \text{ROADLIKE QUALITIES}$$

But what we got was:

$$\text{ON THE ROAD OF LOVE} \quad \neq \quad \text{NON-ROADLIKE QUALITIES:}$$
$$\text{a broken heart}$$

That lacks emotional closure. A broken heart is not something roadlike. After the critique, the writer made this revision.

> *I've been down the road to love*
> *A time or two before*
> *But green lights turned to red along the way.*

That's the way. We now feel satisfied because we heard a complete metaphor: The equation balances.

$$\text{ON THE ROAD OF LOVE} \quad = \quad \text{ROADLIKE QUALITIES:}$$
$$\text{green lights}$$
$$\text{red lights}$$
$$\text{along the way}$$

Guideline #2—Make realistic comparisons

Be sure your claims on the right side of the equation fit your word on the left. If, for example, you compare a person to a rock (as Bob Seger did in his 1986 hit "Like a Rock") each listed quality should be rocklike. Some were. Some weren't.

I'M LIKE A ROCK	=	ROCKLIKE QUALITIES:
		Strong
		hold firm
		solid

So far so good. But then we hear

LIKE A ROCK	≠	NON-ROCKLIKE QUALITIES:
		Arrow straight
		Charging from a gate
		Carrying a weight
		Having skin

None of those qualities applies. The more weight you put on your metaphor the more likely it is to collapse. Midway through the song, this simile sank—like a rock.

When Irving Berlin said that "A Pretty Girl Is Like a Melody" every claim to likeness worked:

A GIRL IS LIKE A MELODY	=	SONGLIKE QUALITIES:
		haunts you
		spins around your brain
		in your memory
		leaves you
		comes back

It's complete. It equates. It's a standard.

Guideline #3—Avoid mixing metaphors

I remember a lyric with the line: "You've got me covered, but I won't take your bait." That's an example of the infamous mixed metaphor. The writer started out by using a hunting (gun) metaphor and ended up with a fishing (bait) metaphor. Let's look at it as an equation:

You've got me covered	≠	but I won't take your bait.
(LOVE IS LIKE HUNTING)	≠	(LOVE IS LIKE FISHING)

Comparing love to two things instead of one mixes the metaphor. Each half of that misstatement can easily be made into a complete metaphor.

Before Moving On
Exercise #23

Take the mixed metaphor above and make two balanced metaphoric statements from it. First, complete the gun metaphor with a reference that has gunlike qualities:

You've got me covered = but _____ .

Now introduce the fish metaphor with a phrase that can apply both to the sport of fishing and romance:

_____ = but I won't take your bait.

To avoid mixing metaphors stick to your subject. Check over your first drafts with a mental equals sign to verify the accuracy of your verbal equations.

Guideline #4—Use sparingly

Metaphors are like seasonings: use sparingly—not too much of one kind and not too many different kinds. Here's an overseasoned verse:

> *The past is a drug imprisoning my soul*
> *Regret is a shovel digging a hole*
> *Fear is a master standing over me*
> *Oh, where is the power to set me free?*

That's overwriting—what's known as a purple patch.

Guideline #5—Keep a series of related terms consistently either literal or figurative

The mind expects to hear more of the same of what it's been hearing. We are therefore thrown by a series of seemingly related ideas that turn out to be part literal and part metaphoric. For example this series of bodily parts: "she frosts her hair, paints her fingernails pink, and often puts her foot in her mouth." I think you get the idea: make your series either consistently literal or figurative.

Guideline #6—Make your metaphor true to life

Here's a well-developed metaphor from Maureen Sugden:

> *We used to be so sure that when the time came*
> *We'd walk away without a backward glance,*
> Cash in our chips *and say, "Thanks for a* fine game*"*
> *Satisfied that love had had a* sporting chance.

LOVE IS A GAME OF CHANCE	=	GAMBLING QUALITIES:
		cash in our chips
		fine game
		sporting chance

The analogy is complete, and the specific allusions to chips, game, and chance are appropriate to the chosen comparison. But even more important, the concept that love is a gamble fits our view of the world. The metaphor rings true. In some songs it does not. Here's a cartoon scene:

Verse
> *There's a storm to the north*
> *And it's movin' south*
> *Honey, there ain't no way*
> *You can shut it out*
> *But don't be afraid*
> *You're gonna like it a lot*
> *And you won't need a coat cuz I'm blowing hot*

Chorus
> *MY LOVE IS COMIN', COMIN' YOUR WAY*
> *My love is comin', comin' to stay*
> *Better hold on tight for all your life*
> *MY LOVE IS COMIN' YOUR WAY.*

Verse
I know many have come
And then gone with the wind
They've left you cold
And you think "never again"
But I promise I won't be passing on through
I'll funnel my energy only on you

(Chorus)

Bridge
You won't wanna run for cover
When you see my lightning and feel my thunder

(Chorus)

© 1986, Student lyric. Used with permission.

It isn't until the chorus hits that the listener understands that the words "north" and "south" are being used in an anatomical (figurative) sense. Then we gather that the singer is telling the singee that she's about to face some passionate love making—in a tone that could be characterized as menacingly assuring. Since all the storm allusions should work on a physical level, what in the world is a person's lightning?

And tossing in the colloquialism, "gone with the wind," which is unrelated to "hot" love, serves only to call attention to itself and undermine the believability of the emotion.

One reason the lyric rings false is that the writer has overplotted the lyric: the singer is making three unrelated (and thereby unconvincing) claims instead of one genuine one: 1) I'm a hot lover; 2) I'll be more than a one night stand ("I won't be passing on through"); 3) I'll be faithful ("I'll funnel my energy only on you"). The latter two, incidentally, are about love in general rather than sex in particular, which is the song's manifest subject.

Although this lyric has a range of flaws, the central one is its false metaphor: Who views passion as a fearsome storm to be "shut out?" Ground your metaphor in reality.

Guideline #7—Give a figurative image a figurative setup

When you design an entire lyric around an image used in a figurative sense—rain, for example, as troubled times—alert the listener immediately with a figurative setup. Here's the wrong way to introduce a metaphoric chorus:

Verse
Set my course for sunny Spain,
Crashed the reefs off rocky Maine,
Mid wind and wave and blinding rain,
Won't put foot on land again.

Chorus
OVERBOARD, lost at sea.
Girl, you made a wreck of me.
I'm doomed to drift my whole life through,
I dove OVERBOARD over you.

Verse	*Water here, more water there,* *Frigid water everywhere* *I looked for love and found despair,* *Love can be so damn unfair.*
	(Chorus)
Verse	*Don't understand why* *I've been abandoned on a sea of salty tears* *That won't run dry until you rescue me.* *And now you won't even talk to me*
	(Chorus)

© 1986, Student lyric. Used with permission.

As a song streams by we continuously sort out what we're currently hearing, what we've already heard, and what we've been led to expect next. The opening of "Overboard," with its real-place names of Spain and Maine, leads us to expect a literal story. So we were jolted by the obvious figurative use of the title word in the chorus' opening line.

An effective metaphoric image results from setting it up figuratively and maintaining it figuratively. To underscore this important principle, consider some famous rain-equals-trouble songs—"Stormy Weather," "Raindrops Keep Fallin' on My Head," "Don't Rain on My Parade." The opening line of each song announces its figurative stance by using its key words—*weather, clouds, rain, sun*—in a nonliteral way. And all subsequent theme words support the plot's metaphor.

Had the writer sprinkled the opening verse with a few expressions like *a stormy time on the sea of love; love boat was shipwrecked; the tide's gone out for us; no shore in sight,* and so on, and then titled the lyric "Man Overboard," he could have steered his song to safe harbor.

Before Moving On
Practice Critique #5
Here's a lyric that suffers from two serious problems—one involves figurative language, the other the VVTS. a) First identify the metaphoric pitfall, cite the guideline it flouts, and suggest a solution. b) Then identify the glitch in the VVTS that renders the lyric incoherent.

	MENU OF MEN
Verse	*I met Lisa at the diner.* *Over lunch she took my heart.* *She's the only one I think of.* *It tears me up when we're apart.* *But Lisa's also seein' Billy* *And she's been spendin' time with Neil.* *I wish I had the courage* *To tell her how I feel.*

Chorus *But now Lisa's lookin' over her MENU OF MEN*
And I'm the waiter at the table waitin' on her again
And she can't decide who to order—is it gonna be me?
She won't be tippin' at the diner tonight—
But she'll be leavin' me in misery.

Verse *Well a couple of weeks have passed*
And things are still the same.
Last night it was her and me
But today she spent with what's his name.
Tonight she's at the diner
And I've got to call her bluff.
I've got to make her choose between us
Because a part of her just ain't enough

Chorus *But now Lisa's lookin' over her MENU OF MEN*
And I'm the waiter at the table waitin' on her again.
And she can't decide who to order—is it gonna be me?
She won't be tippin' at the diner tonight—
But she'll be leavin' me in misery.

Bridge *So the very next day I told her "them or me"*
Backed into a corner she said "tonight you'll see."

(repeat Chorus)

© 1986, Student lyric. Used with permission.

Your critique: a) _____

_____

_____

_____

_____

b) _____

_____

_____

_____

_____

(To compare your critique with mine, turn to page 270.)

Guideline #8—Maintain one central image

Rain as a metaphor for heartbreak or troubled times has long been a popular song staple: "Look for the Silver Lining," "Stormy Weather," "Here's that Rainy Day,"

"Rainy Day Woman," "I Made It Through the Rain" and on and on.

Follow the lead of these classics and keep your metaphor consistent. If, for example, you've picked rain, then make sure to stick to rain. As a case in point, here's the first verse and chorus of a student lyric:

> *You're not the only one without an umbrella*
> *Followed by a dark cloud*
> *Pouring water in your eyes,*
> *I'm out here in a leaky boat*
> *Just doin' my best to stay afloat*
> *And find myself a place that is dry.*
>
> *IT AIN'T ONLY RAININ' ON YOU*
> *Sometimes I feel like I'm drownin' too.*
> *So take my hand, let's swim together.*
> *Maybe love can change the weather,*
> *'Cause IT AIN'T ONLY RAININ' ON YOU.*

If the singee is on a street without an umbrella, how is she going to start swimming with the singer who is on the water in a leaky boat? And how will a change in weather improve the leak? What's the metaphor here? Rain? Water?

This lyric also illustrates what happens when you don't get a fix on the VVTS. Had the writer picked an imaginary setting (street?/lake?) and also decided voice (thinking?/talking?), she could have prevented her lyric from falling into the drink.

Guideline #9—Don't milk your metaphor

I'll illustrate this point with the second verse of "It Ain't Only Rainin' On You":

> *God don't play favorites*
> *We each get our share*
> *Of walkin' through the puddles*
> *Gettin' mud into our shoes.*
> *Yeah, I know where you're coming from*
> *'Cause I'm one of the muddy ones*
> *Searching for my own little patch of blue.*

Puddles and muddy shoes (which strain to work figuratively) on top of umbrella, rain, dark cloud, pouring water, leaky boat, afloat, swimming, drowning—are tooooo much! The writer has made the means become the end. That's what's known as milking a metaphor. When you squeeze every drop of similarity from your comparison, your lyric runs dry of credibility. The flaws in many figurative lyrics are curable. But I'm afraid that "It Ain't Only Rainin' On You" has a terminal case of water on the "hook."

A fine example of a lyric built on a simile is "(Like a) Bridge Over Troubled Water." Paul Simon knew that all he had to do to make his point was complete the simile: "I will lay me down." To develop the lyric, he turned to literal statements about the rough times when friends can't be found. Remember, a metaphor should make a point, not be the point.

Guideline #10—Make your theme word consistently literal or consistently figurative

There's a widespread delusion among new writers that shuttling between the literal and figurative aspects of a given word results in layered meaning. Not so.

The meaning of a student's title "The Only Music" was diffused by three semantic shifts: in its first two figurative uses *music* represented the joy of life that left with a former romance; the third use was literal where *music* referred to the songs played by a cocktail lounge pianist; the last reference flipped back to figurative—this time expressing the singer's elation at finding a new love. A semantic blur. The aim is to make your image signify one meaning.

When we see the title, "Make Your Own Kind of Music," the song's fundamental meaning springs to mind as a metaphor for being true to yourself; the singer exhorts the singee to heed Thoreau's injunction to follow a different drummer. Barry Mann and Cynthia Weil, by being single-minded and consistent, turned "Make Your Own Kind of Music" into an anthem for self-actualization.

In pop songs the word *music* can stand for two other figurative contexts—as a loving feeling and as a sexual feeling. Although in life the state of loving and the sexual act are not necessarily mutually exclusive, in lyrics, 'tis better so. For example, in "How Do You Keep the Music Playing?" the question asked is, "How do you sustain love over a lifetime?" That's one idea. In my own "You Turn on My Music," an uptempo dance song, the singer extolls the physical pleasure that comes with a tuned-in sexual partner. That's another idea. And they're both different from that of "Make Your Own Kind of Music." All three songs work because their lyricists didn't switch implications of the theme word in the vain hope of writing layered meaning.

To write a successful metaphorical song, pick one meaning from among the several a word may connote, then stick to it. As the principle of consistency helps you to maintain your lyric's Viewpoint and Voice, so does it govern the use of figurative and literal theme words.

Before Moving On
Exercise #24

In the title "It's Hard to Leave While the Music's Playing," the word *music* could be treated either literally as records, a band, the radio, and so on; or figuratively, conveying a romantic or a sexual feeling. In this exercise, treat the title figuratively, making it connote either the beginning of romance or the throes of passion. Write an introductory verse (or two, if necessary) showing your listener that the singer is hearing music from within rather than from without. Design the verse so that its last line leads inevitably into the first line of the chorus, the song's title. Caveat: Be sure that all music-related words that you employ—*tune, key, song, harmony,* and so on—make literal sense when applied to a relationship.

Verse _____
_____
_____
_____

Chorus *IT'S HARD TO LEAVE WHILE THE MUSIC'S PLAYING*
_____
_____
_____

SOME LAST THOUGHTS ON FIGURATIVE WRITING

It's clear that creating fresh metaphors requires an eye for resemblances. But that gift, rather like having 20-20 vision, is not given to everyone. Joni Mitchell looked at an oilslicked puddle and saw "taffeta patterns"—a stunning metaphor. Many of us look at an oilslicked puddle and see an oilslicked puddle.

Although Aristotle argues that "the greatest thing by far is to have a command of metaphor; it is the mark of genius," he adds the qualifier: "This alone cannot be imparted by another."

Working with many lyricists over an extended period of time has led me to conclude that the facility to create unique metaphors is an innate knack rather than a learnable skill.

If you see life more through a magnifying glass than through a prism, don't view that as a liability. You are no less a writer for not using similes. I remember a student who, after being enthralled at a performance by Amanda ("The Rose") McBroom, became despondent over his unmetaphorical lyrics; "When am I ever going to write images like hers?" he moaned. My reply was *never*.

Nor should he want to try. That's the wrong goal, and worse, a self-defeating one. Your objective as a lyricist should not be to become another Amanda McBroom, but to become the only you—with your own unique vision. And if that vision should lack figurative allusions, so be it.

Just remember the success of the imageless *"Feelings, wo, wo, wo. . . ."*

STEP 5   QUIZ

1) Match each example of figurative language with its proper label:

   1) The clock must be lying   a) simile   _____
   2) Make the song sad and slow, clarinet   b) metaphor   _____
   3) Our love is an unfinished chapter   c) personification   _____
   4) "The Last Word in Lonesome is Me"   d) apostrophe   _____
   5) Her touch was like eiderdown   e) pun   _____

2) Change this simile to a metaphor: "Your smile's like a light at the end of the tunnel."

   _____

3) Punning can take several forms: in one, a word is repeated with a shift in meaning ("What a *class* reunion!"); in another, the second time the word (or part of a word) is used it sounds the same, but has both a different meaning and different spelling (as in "weighty affairs will just have to wait"). Identify a third form and give an example:

   _____

   _____

   _____

4) What's the guideline for writing effective *double entendre?*

_____

_____

5) Pinpoint the problem here: "You've got a run in your panty hose/And you're coming apart at the seams."

_____

_____

(You'll find the answers on page 271.)

You Got Rhythm

As we enter a room, our gait—strolling, striding, marching, charging—announces our emotional state. Similarly, the meter of a lyric reflects the mood of its writer. Because meter is a matter of emotion, it's instinctive. Rarely, if ever, will a lyricist construct a rhythmic scaffold and drape words over it, or will a composer build a melody from a metric pattern.

If rhythm is an unconscious choice—as it seems to be—what, you might ask, can a songwriter be taught about it? Practically speaking, not a lot. But since good instinct favors the informed mind, the more informed the better. Knowing some basic theory will help you enliven your writing with variety and avoid that dreaded pitfall—a singsong rhythm. To discuss the subject, we need to define a few terms.

A Rhythmic Miniglossary

Rhythm refers to any steady movement distinguished by regular accents of strong and weak beats—the TICK tock/TICK tock/TICK tock of a clock; the lub DUB/lub DUB/lub DUB of a heartbeat. There's a rhythm in the way we brush our teeth, scramble an egg, peddle a bike. Conversational speech is rhythmic, too. Our words pour out in a stream of stressed and unstressed syllables: WANna rent a VIDeo SATurday NIGHT? Unstructured and unmeasured, yet rhythmic.

Meter, from the Greek word *metron,* is measured rhythm. Music, of course, is metered. Because a lyric is written to be sung to music, its words must be conceived in measured rhythm, a song beat.

The Greeks identified all the common rhythms of speech, giving a name to each two- and three-stress group. As time is measured by units of the second, the minute, and the hour, verse is measured by the units of the foot, the line, and the stanza. A *foot* is a unit of syllables in a set pattern.

Prosody (PRAHS-a-dee), according to the dictionary, means the study of metrical structure. The Greek word *prosodia* meant both a song sung to instrumental music and the tone or accent of a syllable. Contemporary songwriters use the term prosody to describe the way words fit with the music—whether they mean perfectly (good prosody) or poorly (bad prosody).

Scansion is a visual system of reading verse and lyrics with the help of special marks. Analyzing the meter that's being used fosters an understanding of metric technique.

Prosodic Symbols, or metrical marks, are the signs used to aid in scanning verse. Those most helpful to lyricists are: ˘ unstressed syllable; ′ stressed syllable; / virgule—the diagonal line that marks off metric feet.

Here are the most commonly used meters in lyrics, along with their equivalents in music:

FOOT NAME	ACCENT	SCANNED EXAMPLES	MUSICAL NOTATION (in triple meter)
Iamb	taTUM	tŏ-DÁY, thĕ SNÓW	
Trochee	TUMta	ÁL-wăys, TRÝ ănd	
Spondee	TUMTUM	QÚICK-SÁND, TÍN CÚP	
Pyrrhic	ta ta	ŏn thĕ, ĭn ă	
Dactyl	TUMtata	HÉAV-ĕn-lў, RAÍN ŏn thĕ	
Anapest	tataTUM	ĭn-tĕr-JÉCT, ŏn ă TRÁIN	
Anti-bacchius	TUMTUMta	HEÁRT HÚNTĕr, FRÉE WHÉELĭng	

Counting Feet

A lyric line is measured by the number of feet, or stressed syllables, it contains. The sophisticated and sometimes ironic expressions of theater writers from Cole Porter to Stephen Sondheim are often contoured in two- and three-foot lines. Pop songs extend generally to five- and six-foot lines. And the loping statements of folk and country writers commonly shape themselves into lines of seven or eight feet.

FOOT LENGTH	TERM	SCANNED EXAMPLE
Two feet	Dimeter	SEND ĭn thĕ / CLOWNS /
Three feet	Trimeter	YÓU dŏn't / BRÍNG mĕ / FLOẂ-eřs /
Four feet	Tetrameter	Ĭ'd LÍKE / tŏ TEÁCH / thĕ WOŔLD / tŏ SÍNG /
Five feet	Pentameter	RÁIN- / DRÓPS kĕep / FÁLL-ĭng / ÓN m̆y / HÉAD /
Six feet	Hexameter	IT'S sŏ / NÍCE tŏ / HÁVE ă / MÁN ă- / ROÚND thĕ / HOÚSE /
Seven feet	Heptameter	STÚCK ĭn- / SÍDE ŏf / MÓ-bĭle / WÍTH thĕ / MÉM-phĭs / BLÚES ă- / GAÍN /

By combining the foot name with the number of such feet, we label the meter of the poem or lyric line. For example, three feet of dactyls (TUMtata TUMtata TUMtata) produces dactylic trimeter; five feet of iambs (taTUM taTUM taTUM taTUM taTUM) creates iambic pentameter, one of the most common in songwriting. Meters that start with a stressed accent (TUMta, TUMtata) are called falling rhythms; those that begin with the unstressed accent (taTUM, tataTUM), rising rhythms.

The Limerick

If any meter could be said to be lighthearted it would be the rising rhythm of the anapest, especially as it's used in the limerick—a five-line pattern in which lines one, two, and five are anapestic trimeter and the third and fourth are anapestic dimeter. Here's the limerick pattern:

> TataTUM tataTUM tataTUM
> TataTUM tataTUM tataTUM
> TataTUM tataTUM
> TataTUM tataTUM
> TataTUM tataTUM tataTUM

A limerick meter—if adapted to a lyric—should of course be fused to an appropriately humorous content.

Since songs are extensions of speech, lyrics are designed to be conversational. Their meters, therefore, are looser than such strict poetic forms as the sonnet or villanelle. A lyric, if written in unvarying iambic pentameter, for example, would lead to a less than inspired melody. Uniformity sounds mechanical. It cries out for variation.

Before Moving On
Practice Critique #6

After reading the following introductory verse, give your immediate reaction. Were you moved? Analyze how the meter contributed to your response.

> *In a doorway in lower Manhattan*
> *She sleeps on a bed of concrete.*
> *Tomorrow she plans*
> *To hunt bottles and cans*
> *That she'll cash in for something to eat.*

Your critique: _____

_____

_____

_____

_____

(To compare your critique with mine, turn to page 271.)

Theme And Variations

All art is built upon an interplay of repetition and variation. The best tunes reflect that interplay in repeated melodic motifs and varied rhythm and harmony. The best lyrics pleasure the ear with verbal echoes and unexpected shifts of meter.

Ideally, as writers we are flexible, adaptable, versatile—we easily alter our accents and line lengths as the style of the song demands. Perhaps no songwriter better personifies this ideal than Irving Berlin, whose hundreds of hits resound with an almost unbelievable variety of rhythms.

Like all desirable qualities, versatility comes more easily to some than others. Composers, for example, tend to demonstrate a far greater rhythmic diversity than lyricists. And lyricists who can write music—or at least hear "head tunes"—display more rhythmic variance than lyricists who can't.

The objective here, then, is to help you become more rhythmically versatile. First let's dispel the common misconception that counting syllables is the way to create uniform rhythmic patterns. Not true. Lyric writing is not a matter of counting syllables: It's a matter of feeling stressed beats.

Since composers clearly have the cutting edge in rhythmic versatility, the obvious objective for a lyric writer is to learn to think more like a composer. With that goal in mind, let's look at rhythm from a composer's point of view.

Writing "Musical" Lyrics

Songs are made up of both sound and silence. Each unit of sound and silence has a specific value with its own symbol: a note and a rest respectively. Here's a composer's basic tool kit of notes and rests:

whole note	o	whole rest	▬
half note	𝅝	half rest	▬
quarter note	♩	quarter rest	𝄽
eighth note	♪	eighth rest	𝄾
sixteenth note	𝅘𝅥𝅯	sixteenth rest	𝄿

Below is a table of notes and rests. Each note or rest has a value one half that of the note or rest above and double that of the note or rest below:

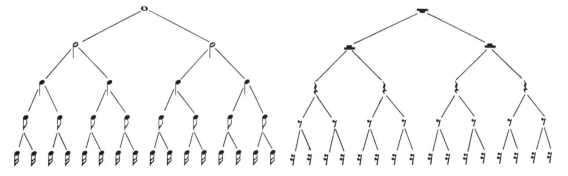

Now we'll assign a word to every note.

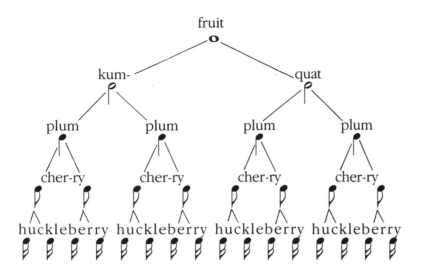

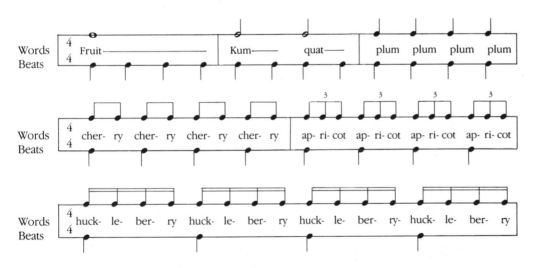

The majority of pop songs are written in 4/4 time—four beats to a bar of music with a quarter note getting one beat. Using 4/4 time (common time), we'll distribute the fruit words in the music bars in order to visualize some of the rhythmic substitutions available to you.

In addition to slicing up the whole note into half notes, quarters, eighths, and sixteenths, we'll divide it another way, into eighth-note triplets that look like this ♪♪♪ and assign to the triplets the word *apricot*.

The "fruit bars" illustrate that you can say huckleberry, a sixteenth-note word, or apricot, an eighth-note-triplet word, on the same quarter note beat as you can say cherry, an eighth-note word. Thus, you can write a four-beat line containing a rhythmic mixture of such "fruit words." They scan like this:

/ Húck-lĕ-bĕr-ry̆ / aṕ-rĭ-cŏt / cher-ry̆ / píe /

Here are those rhythms translated into a more lyriclike thought:

/ Év́ry̆ tĭme yŏu / smíle ăt mĕ, / hów Ĭ / sígh. /

That line could serve as a welcome variation in a series of unvaried lines such as:

/ Év́ry̆ / tíme yŏu / go Ĭ / díe. /

Read the last two lyric lines again. How many syllables are in the first line? How many syllables are in the second line? You can see that despite the variation in syllable count, from ten to seven, the lyric lines share the same number of the stressed beats—four. That's what matters. Therefore the basic melody written to the even seven-syllable line could also be sung to the varied ten-syllable line by adding three unstressed notes. Here's how:

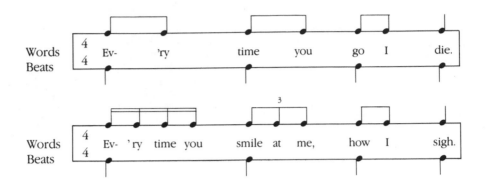

The point is: don't count syllables, because syllables don't count. Instead, feel the stressed beats.

Before Moving On
Exercise #25
To practice varying the unstressed beats within your meter, alter the rhythm of the line *Summer leaves are turning into gold* (TUMta/TUMta/TUMta/TUMta/TUM) to TUMta/TUM/TUMta/TUMtata/TUM—which replaces two of the cherry (TUMta) syllables with one apricot (TUMtata) and one plum (TUM). Rhyme the new five-beat line with "gold."

SUMmer	LEAVES are	TURNing	INto	GOLD,
(TUMta	TUMta	TUMta	TUMta	TUM)

(TUMta	TUM	TUMta	TUMtata	TUM)

An Example of Rhythmic Contrast in Action

The general guideline, then, is to vary your meter a bit both from line to line and from section to section; that is, in a verse/chorus song, make your chorus contrast with your verses, and in an AABA, make your bridge contrast with your A sections.

Here's a student sample of rhythmic variety both within the verse itself and from verse to chorus. The lyric was designed to become an uptempo dance song—which it became. I've tried to represent on paper the vivid rhythm the writer clearly heard in her head. Each line represents one bar of music in 4/4 time—four beats to the bar.

To get a rhythm going, count a slow ONE, two, three four, ONE, two, three, four, as you slap your leg.

HEART HUNTER
(An Excerpt)

Verse
/ (beat) / (beat) / Yóu're / oń thĕ /
/ Prowl / tŏníght / (beat) / (beat) /
/ Dressed / tŏ kíll / (beat) / (beat) /
/ (beat) / (beat) / (beat) / (beat) /
/ (Beat) / Yóu're ňot / lóokĭn' / fór /
/ Love / tŏníght / (beat) / (beat) /
/ Just / ă thrill / (beat) / (beat) /
/ (beat) / (beat) / (beat) Yŏu / got /

Climb
/ All thĕ / ríght / móves / ańd yŏu /
/ Kńow / hów tŏ / máke thĕm / (beat) /
/ (beat) / Fáll / doún ŏn / their /
/ Kńees / (beat) / (beat) ănd / év'ry /
/ (beat) / Tíme / próves / thát yŏu /
/ Kńow / how tŏ / fáke thĕm / (beat) /
/ (beat) / Ńow yŏu're / gunnĭn' / fór /
/ Me / (beat) / (beat) / (beat) /

Chorus
/ Stóp, / (beat) / ríght whĕre / yóu /
/ Aŕe / (beat) / (beat) / (beat) /
/ (beat) / HEART / HUNTĔR / (beat) /
/ (beat) / HEART / HUNTĔR / (beat) /
/ Stóp, / (beat) / dón't gŏ / tóo /
/ Fár / (beat) / (beat) / (beat) /
/ (beat) / HEART / HUNTĔR / (beat) /
/ (beat) / Dón't / cápture / my /
/ Heart / (beat) / (beat) / (beat) /

© 1986, Lyric by Jan Kramer/Music by Shami Arslanian & Steve Weisbart.
Used with permission.

"Heart Hunter" throbs with a syncopated rhythm; that is, it often places the emphasis on a weak beat (the second and fourth of the measure) or between the beats. The writer, though not a composer herself, is inherently musical. Her words express such strong rhythmic patterns that they communicate to collaborators her desired effect.

More Means Of Rhythmic Variation

As "Heart Hunter" demonstrates, one way to achieve contrast is to vary the placement of your stresses. Although falling rhythms (those starting with a stressed beat) dominate the lyric, we are never bored because the stresses keep hitting in different parts of the measure.

Another way to vary stresses is to change from falling rhythms (TUMta, TUMtata) to rising rhythms (taTUM, tataTUM). Or, put in a composer's parlance, change from starting a measure on the downbeat, to starting on the upbeat. For example "Over the Rainbow," an AABA, begins the A section on the downbeat (SOME - WHERE), (TUM - TUM); then the bridge begins on the upbeat "someDAY I'll WISH upON a STAR" (taTUM, taTUM, taTUM, taTUM).

Changing the end punctuation also acts to lend variety to a lyric. It's a songwriting convention that the end of a thought should coincide with the end of a line. That junction creates a natural pause that's often marked with some kind of punctuation— a dash, comma, or period. This is known as an end-stopped line. Most of "Heart Hunter's" lines are end-stopped.

But because we enjoy variety, the ear welcomes an occasional *run-on line,* one in which the thought continues past the structural end into the next line. The climb of "Heart Hunter" has such a line: When we hear "You got all the right moves/And you know how to make them," we at first think that *them* is the end of the thought and refers to *moves.* Then we discover that the thought continues into the next line and that *them* actually refers to the girls who succumb to the singee's charms: " . . . You know how to make them fall down on their knees."

Here's another example of a run-on line from the first verse of "Sue and John" (page 24):

> But she'll sew a flowered curtain
> Have a baby, and John's certain
> Sue will be the perfect wife.

Although *certain* punctuates the end of the line, it doesn't complete the thought. It's therefore required of the singer to keep the vocal inflection up until the arrival of *wife* at the end of the next line. Because run-on lines make the listener work to follow the sense, they can become wearying. To place several in succession is to risk audience fallout. The guideline—use sparingly.

The most popular way to ward off a singsong rhythm is to vary the number of unstressed syllables within a foot. The fruit bars demonstrated how that works. And you've already had some practice with cherries, apricots, and huckleberries.

Putting variety into your lyrics is as easy as p_ fruit bars.

Weighing Your Words

Turn back now to the rhythmic diagram on page 104 and read aloud the examples of scanned feet. You'll notice that it took longer to say *TIN CUP* (a spondee), than it did to say *in a* (a pyrrhic). A spondee (TUM TUM) requires more time to articulate than a word or phrase that goes tata, TUMta, or taTUM, and is therefore useful when you want to emphasize a thought. For example, compare the weight of the final word in each of these treatments of the same idea:

> Your kind of lovin' brings MIS'ry
> Your kind of lovin' brings HEART BREAK.

HEART BREAK expresses misery more than *mis'ry* does because it takes longer to say. Snail-paced spondees can also create midline emphasis. For example, here's a thought (in line one) whose emotion is emphasized (in line two) by substituting a spondee (LAST NOTE) for a trochee (LETter).

With its slower pace, LAST NOTE elbows the listener for attention. And the finality of *last* heightens the wistfulness of the line.

Small Craft Warning: Be careful not to let a spondee highlight an idea you don't mean to stress. Imagine, for instance, if Yip Harburg, instead of writing "We're off to see the wizard, the WONderful wizard of Oz," had written "We're off to see the wizard, the *WISE OLD* wizard of Oz"? That would certainly have slowed down the joyous skip along the yellow brick road.

When you want to speed up a line, try adding anapests (tataTUMs). To illustrate, I'll rephrase that sentence, using anapests: If you WANT/every WORD/to go TRIP/ping aLONG/then you ADD/a few MORE/tataTUMs. See how it works?

Before Moving On
Exercise #26
Speed up this line by replacing SHINE BRIGHT (TUM TUM) with a more appropriate TUMta word, (which may require changing the word *in*).

> *How do stars SHINE BRIGHT in the sky?*
> *How do stars _____ the sky?*

Laminate Words And Music

Regardless of which one came first, the words or the music, they should fuse emotion to emotion, phrase to phrase, and accent to accent. Perfect prosody all the way.

The best craftsmen demand of themselves that every word sing exactly as it's spoken. For example, if the music goes taTUM, the word should go taTUM—not TUMta: *We're THROUGH* and *to YOU* fit taTUM. But *resCUE* is a misfit; it's been warped out of its natural TUMta (trochee) shape of REScue.

Similarly, if the music goes tataTUM, just any old three-syllable word won't do. For example, *in the NIGHT* would make a perfect fit. But *toMORrow* (taTUMta) or *DARKness FALLS* (TUMtaTUM) would be a mismatch.

Today, we hear a common complaint about pop songs: "I can't understand the words." This epidemic inability of audiences to discern a song's lyrics and to thus understand its meaning, results, more often than not, from a particular aspect of poor prosody: slow words have been fused onto speedy notes; that is, syllables that require quarter notes (♩♩) are rushed into the space of eighth notes (♫). For example take the phrase "BACK-SEAT LADy." If the words BACK SEAT (a slow spondee) are sung on quick eighth notes instead of slower quarter notes, the phrase "BACK-SEAT LADy" is likely to hit the ear as "BAXy LADy."

Not only can poor prosody twist a word out of its natural pronunciation and make meaning unintelligible, it can result in something even worse: insincerity. As a case in point, I recall a #1 ballad whose closing words were misemphasized by the pitch of the music: *I LOVE you* came out *I love YOU*. With that emphasis, the implica-tion is *I don't love HER, I love YOU*. But that meaning didn't match the lyric plot. I find it difficult to imagine anyone ever speaking those three words—and meaning them—except with the inflection, *I LOVE you*.

Study The Best

The best way to learn any art is to immerse yourself in the work of its masters. Stephen Sondheim has a lot to teach all aspiring songwriters—even if they're aiming for the pop chart.

Every aspect of Sondheim's work is worth studying—his forms, literary devices, wordplay, verbal motifs—but perhaps particularly, his mastery of the natural rhythms of speech. I especially recommend that you study the original cast album of *Sunday in the Park with George*. The diversity of metric patterns, the dovetailing and counterpointing of rhythmic figures is peerless. Analyzing how Stephen Sondheim attains his effects will enrich your understanding of what true craftsmanship is about.

Sondheim is also without equal in the realm of rhyme, the next step in making your words work.

STEP 6   QUIZ

1) The following lyric line illustrates the meter that is most like conversational speech: "If only you and I could meet again" (taTUM taTUM taTUM taTUM taTUM). What is it called?

_____

2) "Everyone considered him the coward of the county" is the opening line of a famous story song. a) Copy it over below to illustrate its meter: syllabify the two- and three-syllable words, mark the stressed and unstressed syllables with the prosodic symbols, and place a virgule between each stressed beat.

_____

How many feet in the line? _____

Is that a rising or falling meter? _____

3) Identify the three ways to avoid a singsong rhythm.

   a) _____

   b) _____

   c) _____

4) The following lyric line is written to fit one measure of 4/4 time: "Wish I had a dime for ev'ry time you made me cry." Write the appropriate note values on the top line.

Notes

Words $\frac{4}{4}$ Wish I had a dime for ev'ry time you made me cry.

Beats

5) What foot would you use to emphasize an important thought or to slow down a speedy line? _____

(You'll find the answers on page 271.)

A Rundown Of Rhyme

Since rhyme is essentially a kind of stress, it plays a rhythmic role. Words that chime in a discernible pattern—especially at the end of lines, accent structure. Linking words of similar sound helps to emphasize meaning.

Rhyme—A Definition

Two or more words are said to rhyme when each contains the same final accented vowel and consonant sounds and a different consonant preceding that vowel, such as *shoe/true, barrel/*ap*parel.*

The word that sounds first is termed the rhyme agent, and the second of the pair, the rhyme mate.

*Street/re*treat is a perfect rhyme because the same final accented vowel sound of each is preceded by different consonants; but *day/*to*day,* or *leave/*be*lieve,* or *loud/*al*lowed* are *Identities* (or Identical Rhymes). They sound flat because instead of having a different preceding consonant they have the same one. Identities which try to pass themselves off as rhymes—whether in poetry or in lyrics—have traditionally been considered a flaw.

The spelling of a word is not a factor in rhyme, as you can see and hear in the pairing *bronze/swans.* Rhyme is solely a matter of sound. Thus homonyms—words that are spelled differently but sounded alike, such as *size/sighs* and *one/won*—are also considered identities, or nonrhymes.

The Major Accent Rhymes

The three most common types of rhyme are made up of one, two, and three syllables and are termed "major accent rhymes."

Masculine, or single rhyme, occurs with the matching of two or more one-syllable words *wide/slide, mate/fate* or with the last syllable of a longer word *free/*de*bris, late/*re*late.*

Feminine, or double rhyme, occurs when the last two syllables of words agree: *ended/*pre*tended/*con*de*scended*/when did; sad to/had to; kissing/missing.*

Triple Rhyme or trisyllabic rhyme results when the last three syllables of words match in sound: *chasable/*em*braceable/*ir*replaceable/trace a bul/*(let); *would you try/could you try.*

When a double or triple rhyme results from more than one word, it's termed a *Mosaic* or *Composite Rhyme: nocturne/clock turn* (Sondheim); *wreck to me/*appendectomy (Hart); Sir *Lancelot/romance a lot* (Mercer); *feminine/lemon in* (Harnick.)

The Minor Accent Rhymes

In terms of quality, there's nothing minor league about some minor accent rhymes. To the contrary, conceiving them takes both ingenuity and craftsmanship.

Broken Rhyme is a much admired artifice that breaks off the last word in a line to make its inner sound chime with the rhyme mate. Stephen Sondheim achieved surprises with *blander/Ander/* (sen) and (cha)*teau/o-/* (verstaffed). Lee Adams scored in "Put On a Happy Face" with (mask of) *tragedy/glad ya de/*(cided); it sings so smoothly that it slips by virtually unnoticed.

Trailing Rhyme is a device in which a one-syllable rhyme agent is paired with either the first syllable of a two-syllable word or the first of two words, making a perfect rhyme—plus a trailing syllable. In "Mountain Greenery," Larry Hart matched Richard Rodgers' trailing notes with *cook/look*ing, *you/blue* laws, and the unique mosaic trailing rhyme *play/*(uke)*le*le.

Apocopated Rhyme is trailing rhyme in reverse. A one-syllable rhyme mate chimes with the first syllable of a two-syllable word or the first of two words creating a cut-off (apocopated) effect: *an*swer/*chance, clung* to/*sung, wide*r/*pride.* (You heard the device in the verse of "Thank God for Music": *forty/more* (page 43).

Contiguous Rhyme results from the touching of two matched sounds within a line. Alan Jay Lerner butted -ate- sounds in "the *late, great* me." Other examples include "What's the *diff if* I live or die," (Cole Porter) and "Some people of *one hun*-dred and five. . . ." (Stephen Sondheim).

Linked Rhyme is an end-rhyme artifice common to early Welsh verse. It requires linking the last syllable in one line to the first sound of the next:

> *Are you gonna get my* vote?
> *You're not gonna* know
> T*ill tomorrow.*

The rhyme is formed by fusing the -t- in *till* to the -o- in *know* to make a perfect ping with *vote.*

Light or *Weakened Rhyme* contains one accented syllable paired with an unaccented one. The device, a favorite with Emily Dickinson (*bee/*reve*ry*), is common in songs. In "She's Leaving Home" we hear "thoughtless*ly/me."* In Joni Mitchell's "Cactus Tree," we find "memo*ry/tree,* eterni*ty/free."* In the songs just cited these three-syllable words are sung as they are normally spoken: THOUGHTlessly, MEMory, eTERnity. That's good prosody. All too often we hear poor prosody: the natural pronunciation of a three-syllable word warped by an unnatural stressing of the final syllable—THOUGHTlessLY, MEMoRY, eTERniTY.

Internal Rhyme, also called interior or inner rhyme, is that extra ping that chimes in midline: "You're the closing *scene* of a Balan*chine* ballet." Internal rhyme rang out in musical comedy and film scores by Cole Porter, Rodgers and Hart, and the Gershwins. Now that movie songs mirror pop music's casual attitude toward (perfect) rhyme, this decorative dividend is rarely heard today except on Broadway.

Mirror Image Rhyme is my term for a rare device the Greeks call *Amphisbaenic*

Rhyme. A subtle echo effect is created by making the rhyme mate reverse the sound of the rhyme agent: for example, *peal/leap, rail/lair, mid/dim.* In "The Day Off" (Sondheim) we hear this mirror image pairing: ". . . with the *pale*tte . . . *lap* at last."

Experiment

When writing "dry" lyrics (without music), experiment. Break out of the overused male and female major accent rhymes. Substitute some minor accent variations for the habitual patterns of *say/may* and *trying/flying*: try *ring/ling*er or *night*bird/*flight*. You'll not only create fresher lyrics, it's likely that a varied rhyme pattern will evoke a more interesting melody from your collaborator.

Getting Clever

Top-notch lyricists enjoy playing with words. Here are a few tricks of the trade as practiced by our finest craftsmen.

Lettering—eighteen out of twenty-six letters of our alphabet are rhyme sounds. Johnny Mercer in his "G.I. Jive" made a feature of abbreviation with PVT, L.I.E.U.T., and M.P. who did K.P. on the Q.T.

Stretching—A favorite technique of Ira Gershwin's made short words fit a longer musical phrase: *Parties* expanded to *partiays* to match up with *shopping at Cartiers. Velvet* became *vel-a-vit/tell of it,* and *Garfield* stretched to *Gar-a-field/far afield.*

Mispronouncing—Larry Hart reminded us that "English people don't say *clerk,* they say *clark,*" and added that anybody who says it like that is a *jark!* Cole Porter coupled Milton Berle/Castor "erl," and in "Nobody's Chasing Me" he altered the title in one verse to match up with "Ich liebe *dich*"—"Nobody's chasing *mich.*" Note: When you employ the device, be sure to adjust the word's spelling to make your intended pronunciation clear on the page.

Inventing—Sometimes the right rhyme doesn't exist. So the ingenious create *nonce words* to meet momentary needs. When the Cowardly Lion in *The Wizard of Oz* needed an expletive to echo "rhinoceros," Yip Harburg fused impossible and preposterous and made "imposerous!"

Clipping shortens a two- or three-syllable word to create a fresh rhyme mate: *Spa*/Tampa "*Fla*" (Lerner); *got*/Frank "*Sinat*" (Morgan); *dish*/dispo*sish* (Gershwin). Because clever rhymes call attention to themselves, they are usually reserved for comedy songs.

Top-Of-The-Line Rhymes

The poet Wallace Stevens once acknowledged feeling chagrined for having committed the hackneyed mating *breeze/trees:* "I've never forgiven myself. It is a correct rhyme, of course—but unpardonably *expected.*"

Surprise, the main pleasure of rhyme, depends on some unlikelihood inherent in the mating. The kind of rhyme that therefore earns the highest praise from experts is the linking of different parts of speech or of words that are semantically unlike. Rhymes made by the same part of speech, often make a lackluster sound, like this string of verbs: *glow/show/flow/blow/know.*

What pricks the ear is the contrast inherent in such pairings as a noun and verb: *skies/revise;* a verb and adjective: *sneer/clear;* adjective and noun: *smartest/artist;*

noun and pronoun: *zoo/who,* and so on. Even teaming up the same parts of speech will deliver delight when the mating makes an incongruous team: *trapeze/trees, shallot/palette, tunics/eunuchs* (Sondheim). Quite simply, we are more entertained with rhymes that contrast vividly, yet sound unforced.

Before Moving On
Exercise #27
a) Give each of the following words an apocopated rhyme:
nightly/_____; had to/_____; Eastern/_____.
b) Write a fourth line that creates a trailing rhyme with *through.*

> *Every day it's the same old scene*
> *Same old nine-to-five routine*
> *I do the job, and when I'm through*

Near Rhyme: Substitutes For Perfect Rhyme

Perfect rhymes in pop songs are a contemporary rarity. Rhyme's most common substitute is assonance.

Assonance links words by means of echoed vowels—*time/life/revive;* the end consonants differ but the accented vowels agree. Also called Slant, or Oblique Rhyme, assonance allows for a greater naturalness—the hallmark of today's pop style. Commonly heard on the charts are such examples as: m*ee*t/s*ee*n/, tr*a*de/w*a*ste, l*oo*se/intr*u*de, n*i*ght/str*i*ke, sl*a*m/h*a*nd, g*e*t/poss*e*ss.

Unstressed Rhyme is a pairing where the final syllable of both words is unaccented as in given/heaven, hollow/willow, matter/after.

Consonance (also called Half Rhyme, and Off Rhyme) is the agreement of final consonant sounds, but with a differing preceding vowel sound, as in soo*n*/ow*n*; the final -n- sounds agree, but -oo- and -ow- differ. Over the last two decades consonance has joined assonance as a popular rhyme substitute in such examples as ca*n*/me*n*, be*t*/a*te*, sol*d*/wil*d*, ba*th*/fai*th*.

Because there are over a dozen vowel sounds, consonance gives the lyricist many possible sound links with any given word. What if, for example, you want a fresher mate for *love*—rather than the clichéd pairings: *of/above/dove/glove/shove.* Consonance offers such alternatives as: sa*v*e/ha*v*e/slee*v*e/ne*v*(er)/arri*v*e/sie*v*e/co*v*e(r)/star*v*(ing)/groo*v*e/conser*v*e/. Rather than a stale rhyme, or one that doesn't truly reflect your idea, experiment with consonance.

Para Rhyme is a subtype of consonance where the initial and final consonant sounds of the rhyming pairs are identical, but the vowel sounds differ: *moan/mourn, loft/left, sign/scene.*

Feminine Para Rhyme is two syllable para rhyme where the two final consonant groupings of the rhyme agent and the rhyme mate agree: *broode*d*/bearde*d*, summer/simmer, winter/want her.* Substituting feminine para rhyme for feminine perfect rhyme eliminates the problem of that predictable pinging of "stalemates" like *sadly/badly, kiss you/miss you.*

Augmented Rhyme is a term I've given to the linking of like sounds where the rhyme mate is enriched by an additional consonant—the most common of which are d, g, s, t, and v. For example: blue/gratitu*de,* rain/staine*d,* plunder/wondere*d,* harbor/

starboar*d*, pain/strange, rent/cents, mess/chest, play/cra*ve*.

Since the rhyme agent sets up the expectation to hear a perfect mating of sounds, augmented rhyme delivers what we expect—and more. For that reason, I find it the most satisfying substitute for perfect rhyme. Its use greatly extends the possibilities of fresh sounds in end rhymes.

Diminished Rhyme is augmented rhyme in reverse—with the enriched sound coming first. Because an incomplete rhyme mate disappoints the ear, diminished rhyme is less satisfying. If we hear *stairs*, for example, we expect to hear *glares/dares/pears*, not *care*. In addition to being a let-down, diminished rhyme can cause confusion. For example, on hearing the rhyme agent *around*, we expect to hear a mate such as *found, ground*, etc. If the mate doesn't match, as in the word *down*, we must strain to distinguish exactly what word was sung. *Downed? Drowned?* While the listener labors to decipher words already sounded, the song is moving relentlessly on. Diminished rhyme yields diminishing returns. Use at your own risk.

Before Moving On
Exercise #28
Write a fourth line in which you use para rhyme to mate with *team*.

> *I was sure that we would make it,*
> *That we'd always be a team,*
> *Baby, what a fool I was*

Design A Rhyme Scheme That Surprises

A lyric, like a poem, has an overall end-rhyme pattern called a *rhyme scheme*. We identify the pattern by assigning the same lowercase letter of the alphabet to lines that rhyme with each other. Here's the first verse of "Midnight Mood":

Turn off the television	(a)
Put down that paper, too	(b)
I've got an indecent proposition	(a)
That I'd like to propose to you	(b)
I'm gonna unhook the receiver	(c)
As soon as I send out for Chinese food	(d)
Although the sun's still high in a daylight sky	(e)
I'm in a MIDNIGHT MOOD.	(d)

A common goal of fine craftsmen is to surprise the listener with the rhyme. The rhymes in the verse sound both unexpected and inevitable. It often happens, however, that on hearing a song for the first time we can predict a rhyme a line or two before it arrives. That's known as "telegraphing" a rhyme, and it's been traditionally considered hack writing. To make words sound inevitable and simultaneously sound fresh requires some effort.

Three elements conspire to produce predictable rhymes: the choice of feminine rhymes (especially of the *singing/bringing* variety), the abab rhyme scheme, and lines of even length. Telegraphing wasn't permitted to be a problem in "Midnight Mood" because the writer sidestepped those potential pitfalls. She shunned the more obvious two-syllable rhymes; then she altered the abab pattern of the first half of the verse to cded (or abcb) thereby reducing the number of end rhymes from two to one; and lastly, she extended the length of her seventh line—creating an interior rhyme (*high/sky*)—that cleverly keeps us waiting for the final ping of *mood*. Well done.

An unaltered pattern of ababcdcd virtually invites predictable rhymes. The easiest way to avoid telegraphing is to choose the abcd pattern, which rhymes only every other line. Fewer end chimes will keep your listener focused on the meaning of your words rather than wondering what rhyme is coming next.

Rhyme For A Reason

The guiding principle: keep rhyme to a minimum. When used excessively, rhyme can sound silly, especially those -ing- feminine rhymes: singing/bringing, trying/crying, kissing/missing. If humor is your intention, multiple feminine rhymes can build to a laugh as in Stephen Sondheim's purposeful excess of feminine para and perfect rhymes in "The Day Off": "What's the muddle/In the middle?/That's the puddle/Where the poodle did the piddle." If humor is not your intention, feminine rhymes can trivialize your thought. Constant end-of-line chiming wrenches our attention away from the important thing—the song's meaning.

Be mindful that the shorter the length of the lyric line, the more conscious the listener becomes of rhymes as they quickly hit the ear. Ira Gershwin, being aware of this hazard, solved the problem posed by the three successive feminine notes of "I Got Rhythm": he refrained from rhyme. Instead he used a series of unrhymed feminine words—*rhythm/music/my man; daisies/pastures/my man; starlight/sweet dreams/my man.*

Because rhymed words are the ones we remember most, make it a practice to rhyme only those words that highlight the lyric's plot, reinforce its emotion, and unify its atmosphere. In short, rhyme for a reason.

Before Moving On
Exercise #29
Three elements combine to make the following four lines singsong: an unvarying meter, an abab rhyme scheme, and the feminine rhymes *met you/forget you:*

I still have dreams about the night I met you,	(a)
I still can feel your arms around me tight,	(b)
Tho ev'ry day I swear that I'll forget you	(a)
I wake to find your mem'ry just as bright.	(b)

The goal is to eliminate the telegraphed rhyme *forget you,* and to make the listener wait for the rhyme mate to *tight.* Following the pattern shown in "Midnight Mood" (page 117), rewrite the third and fourth lines to create an abcb rhyme scheme and lengthen the third line by means of an inner rhyme. You might want to shorten the last line to a four-beat line for variation.

I still have dreams about the night I met you,	(a)
I still can feel your arms around me tight,	(b)
_____ (c) _____	(c)
_____ *-ight.*	(b)

Rhyme Theory And Song Forms

One of the functions of rhyme is to lend emphasis and unity to your lyric by outlining its structure.

Because varied sounds please the ear, the basic guideline is to treat your listener to a broad spectrum of end-rhyme sound colors. Deciding when to repeat them and when to vary them depends to a degree on where the song's title appears—in effect, on what song form you're using.

We'll start with the verse/chorus. To emphasize the importance of your chorus, make it a practice to restrict your chorus end-rhymes to the chorus. I'll illustrate: The chorus of "Just Once" features three rhymes—*wrong/long, right/night, to it/through it*. Those sounds—*ong/ight/ooit*—are not repeated as end rhymes elsewhere in the lyric. In the song's verses and bridge we hear a succession of new sounds: *before/door, change/strangers, anywhere/prayer, blowin'/goin', stand/hand, better/together*. By tapping the complete range of vowels—A, E, I, O, U—Cynthia Weil constructed a lyric that pleasures the ear as it makes its point. That's what the best lyricists do intuitively.

This principle of reinforcing structure through rhyme applies similarly to the title line of an AABA. A good example is "Saving All My Love for You," in which lyricist Gerry Goffin saved all his -oo- rhymes for *you (do/blue/through)* to emphasize his title. Each of the four A sections features fresh sounds: *share/there, alone/own, more/door, night/right*. The bridge brings the additional contrast of the first -e- sound: *me/free/fantasy*. Intuitively or consciously, that's the way to do it.

The foregoing principle applies of course to the AAA form: reserve the end rhyme of your title line or refrain section to those lyric spots. A good example of doing it well is John Hartford's classic, "Gentle On My Mind."

Before Moving On
Practice Critique #7

The first verse and chorus of this student lyric show a grasp of form and an understanding of universality, but the lyric could easily be improved. Based upon the rhyme theories discussed so far, pinpoint the lyric's major flaw and make a recommendation for fixing it. If a couple more minor things bother you (and I hope they do), note them too.

Verse

*The tender smile you used to smile's
Been fading day by day.
And the closeness that we used to feel
Has almost gone away.
But one thing I am sure of—
I still believe in our love.
And with a will, there's a way.*

Chorus

*LET'S START OVER, BABY
What 'ya say?
LET'S START OVER, BABY
Starting today.
Let's really try to give and take
And make love stay.
LET'S START OVER.
What 'ya say?*

Your critique: _____

_____

_____

_____

_____

(To compare your critique with mine, turn to page 271.)

Keep Your Character In Character

Rhyme in general and internal rhyme in particular reflect an educated mind; not only the lyricist's, but by extension, that of the singer of the song. It is critical for the integrity of the song that the kinds of rhyme and the amount of rhyme be appropriate to the song's "character"—in each sense of that word.

In the majority of pop songs the singer is simply speaking for him- or herself in universal contexts such as "My Way" or "One Less Bell to Answer." In some cases, the singer is a character in a musical, like the side-show barker of *Carousel* or the phonetics professor of *My Fair Lady*. In a persona song, it might be the pregnant teenager of "Papa Don't Preach." Madonna's character would have sounded absurd, for example, sputtering the trisyllabic rhymes that sounded so natural coming out of Professor Higgins' mouth. Make sure your rhymes suit your character.

Make Your Words Sing

Not only should the words of your lyric convey the meaning you intend, ping in all the right places, and suit your character, they should *sing*.

The key ingredient is vowels. The basic principle is to use lots of open-ended long vowel sounds, -a-, -e-, -i-, -o-, -oo-. Such words as *rain, ear, lime, tote,* and *gloom* are more resonant, for example, than the short vowels in *ran, err, limb, tot,* and *glum*.

Consonants, the framework of a word, make noises rather than music, although a few sing fairly well; the most singable consonants are the liquids -l- and -r-, and the nasals -m-, -n-, and -ng-. Cole Porter said that he used the word "thing" so much ("What Is This *Thing* Called Love," "Just One of Those *Things*," "Any*thing* Goes") because it sang so well.

When writing slow ballads that feature sustained notes, be mindful of the all-important word at the end of a phrase: can it be held? Again, think vowels. It's no mystery why ballads often contain such end rhymes as I/lie/try/sigh/cry/die; you/true/through/knew/blue; pay/play/day/say/way; be/me/free/see/agree. A singer can hold on to these open vowels because they are not closed off by any plosive consonants—p, b, t, d, k. Since such words as talk/dump/ask/trade/snob/last are impossible for a singer to hold, they're a poor choice for a sustained note.

Certain word combinations are also difficult to sing: for example, in order to clearly articulate *dark corner,* the mouth must perform some acrobatics or the words may come out sounding like *dacorner*. As a general rule avoid placing words back-to-back when the identical consonant sound ends one word and starts another.

The simplest way to insure writing singable words is to sing them—really sing them out loud. If you're not writing to a melody, make up a dummy tune. That's how many pros go about it. When every word feels good in your mouth, flows easily to the next one, and sings exactly the way it's said, you've done the job.

STEP 7   QUIZ

1) Link each of the following word pairings with its correct label. Think—this one is tricky.

    a) soar/sore   1) light rhyme   _____

    b) intrepid/lid   2) identity   _____

    c) simper/whimper   3) feminine rhyme   _____

    d) unfinished/diminished   4) triple rhyme   _____

    e) ballast/calloused   5) masculine rhyme   _____

    f) tramps/lamps   6) feminine para rhyme _____

2) Why is diminished rhyme a poorer choice than augmented rhyme?

    _____

3) To which pairing would rhyme experts give a higher grade

    a) simper/whimper or bread/red? _____

    b) Why? _____

4) What kind of rhyme often produces an unwanted trivial effect?

    _____

5) Which of the following two lines would a recording artist prefer to sing? Why?

    a) Don't stop doing such sweet, sweet things.

    b) I love the things you do to me.

    _____

    _____

    _____

    _____

    _____

(You'll find the answers on page 272.)

A RECAP OF STAGE TWO

This concludes the basic theory of the course. In time, you will internalize these writing principles and unconsciously arrange all your words in a clear, coherent order. By experimenting you'll find fresh metaphors, unpredictable rhythms and surprising rhymes. But there's no rush. You learn as you practice. And until the time that all the theory becomes second nature, you'll have these steps to return to as a reference.

How To Put It Together

Putting it together,
That's what counts. . . .
STEPHEN SONDHEIM

Writing with the Whole Brain

To produce coherent lyrics, two brains are better than one. And I don't mean yours and your collaborator's. I mean both of yours.

We've known for over a hundred years that our brain is divided into separate hemispheres connected by the corpus callosum, a three-and-one-half inch muscle by which one side communicates with the other. We have, in effect, two brains. But only since the 1960s have discoveries documented that the two sides process information differently.

There is abundant evidence that the left brain conducts activities that are primarily verbal, logical, and analytical. The right hemisphere functions in a more nonverbal holistic manner. Just as we are generally right- or left-handed, so are we generally right- or left-brain dominant. Brain dominance means that our behavior, our activities—in effect our personalities—are shaped by our favoring one hemisphere more than the other.

The ways in which our two brains interact have interesting implications for the songwriting process. The drawing on page 124 reflects characteristics——more descriptive than absolute—that experts attribute to our right and left brains. My placement of these characteristics is not meant to imply their exact locations in the brain, but only to indicate the particular hemisphere in which they reside.

A look at the distinctive abilities of each brain makes evident how researchers can identify brain dominance merely from occupation. For example, lawyers, mathematicians, and chemists are usually left dominants because these professions require logical, sequential skills; athletes, artists, and musicians are right dominants, since these occupations demand physical coordination and visual/spatial skills.

A person who possesses strongly developed talents in each hemisphere is called a mixed dominant: an Olympic swimmer (right), for example, who enjoys analyzing the stock market (left), or an accountant (left) whose hobby is gardening (right). Perhaps the quintessential mixed dominant was Leonardo da Vinci, a painter, sculptor, architect, engineer, and scientist!

Throughout a day we shuttle between using our right and left hemispheres. When we walk, mow the lawn, throw a ball, the right side controls the motor activity.

123

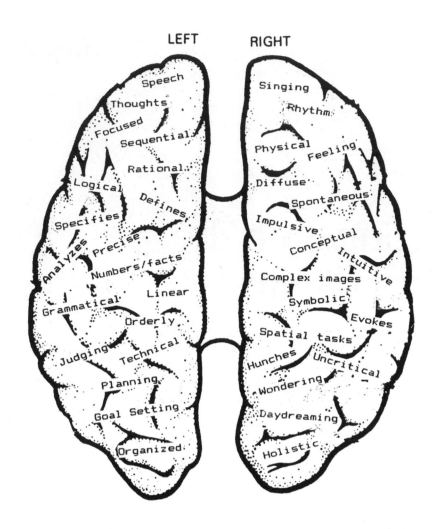

When we balance a checkbook, write a letter, plan a trip, it's the left that tallies the facts. Ideally, we possess strong skills in each hemisphere and shift easily from one to the other according to the skill required. Tasks such as cooking and driving a car, for example, require the interaction of both hemispheres.

GETTING THE BEST FROM BOTH SIDES

To write an easy-to-follow lyric with an intriguing opening, a logical middle, and a conclusive end requires the cooperation of both brains. The more that a songwriter is able to move at will from right to left and vice versa and thereby integrate the assets of each side, the more effective the lyric.

Let's see how to get the best out of both modes of thinking.

Brainstorming on the Right: Clustering

Because our imaginative right side produces the broad picture, the intuitive answer, and the colorful image, it makes good sense to begin the lyric writing process by tapping the talents of the right brain.

To mine this rich terrain I suggest that students *cluster*—a warmup technique developed by Gabriele Lusser Rico, professor of Creative Arts at San José State University and author of *Writing the Natural Way*.

Clustering may be defined as brainstorming on paper—letting uncensored ideas radiate from a central "nucleus" word or phrase. Its purpose is to allow you to free associate, drawing upon random thoughts and stored experiences. The exercise puts you in touch with unconscious thoughts and feelings and usually generates a song title.

I introduce clustering to a class by assigning a common word in song titles as the jumping off place for a lyric; for example, to write a lyric with the word *blue* or *music* or *love* in its title. The process of clustering triggers a pattern of ideas that is unique to each writer. Look for instance at the diversity of emotions sparked in two students by the word *night*.

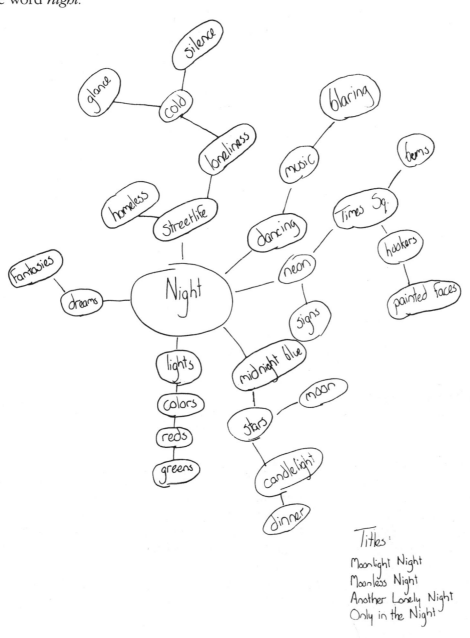

Titles:
Moonlight Night
Moonless Night
Another Lonely Night
Only in the Night

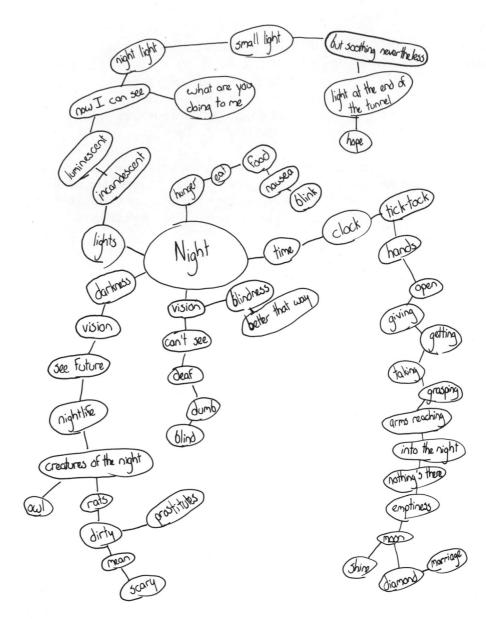

Before Moving On
Exercise #30

Here's a way to access your right brain. On a following page, the nucleus word *heart* has been written in and circled. Get a pen or pencil. You're going to cluster. The purpose is to allow your ideas to flow uninhibitedly. So encourage yourself to be imaginative, illogical, outrageous. At this stage the trick is to not permit your critical left brain to censor the stream of ideas from your right. Let associations spill out as quickly as possible. Connect each fresh associated word or phrase by a line from the preceding one and follow your progression of thought in one direction as far as it will go. Then return to the word *heart* and start again to write down the next mental connection that it suggests, repeating the process until you fill the paper or run out of associations. Don't edit as you go. Sequencing comes later. In a matter of minutes it's likely you'll discover that an idea has appeared to lead you into a lyric.

Shift Left to Make the Key Decisions

Let's imagine that a title emerged. Although you've got a title, resist the temptation to plunge right into writing the lyric. It's focus time. You now need to mull over the potential plots that the title suggests. Your thoughts need to be clarified. This requires a shift to the left brain, which likes to put ideas in logical sequence.

Before you begin to write, try to get a clear picture of the lyric scene: Who is singing your title to whom and why? The sharper your focus on your plot details before you write, the more coherent your first draft will be. Here are the key decisions to give you a fix on the VVTS:

Choose the gender

Will your singer be male or female? Choosing your singer's gender will give your lyric greater definition. Decide before you write. The lyric may of course work for either gender.

Select the viewpoint

Will you set your lyric in first person with the emphasis on "I"? In second person with the emphasis on "you"? In third person with the emphasis on "he," "she," or "they"?

Decide the voice

Will the singer be *thinking* (an interior monologue) or *talking* (dialogue)? In thinking lyrics the singer may be: 1) Alone and thinking; 2) With someone and thinking; 3) Addressing an absent person, place or thing; or 4) Addressing the collective "you." A talking lyric is a conversation with someone present. Decide the voice and stay with it.

Define the time frame

Is your action going on now (present tense), over (past tense), or yet to come (future)? Decide. Keep your eye on the clock. If it moves, state it.

Set the scene

Where is the singer doing the thinking or talking? Even if your lyric doesn't state where, you should know where. If the scene changes, show it.

Identify the tone

What is your singer's emotional attitude toward the events—wistful, playful, grateful, rueful? Pick one tone and stay with it all the way.

Pick the diction

Is your character educated? Street smart? Poetic? To keep the diction consistent, you must understand your character. Pick one style and keep consistent.

Determine the structure

Which one of the three major song forms best suits the effect you seek? Know what you want your audience to feel.

Put Your Decisions in Writing

A focused first draft requires making those key decisions. Left dominants do this intuitively. Dominant rights often need an enforced shift to the left to channel a lyric concept into a coherent script.

For some right-brain dominants the act of running down those key questions is enough to engage their left-brain and keep them focused. But the right "extremists" require more than a mental exercise to enforce their linear thinking. So I designed a Focus Sheet.

The writing down of objectives—whether a grocery list, the day's agenda, or lifetime goals—helps us to get the job done. List making—a left-brain activity—both clarifies and organizes our thoughts. So after you've mentally answered the key questions, confirm them on paper; putting your plot decisions in writing will help you keep the scene before your eyes. On the next page, you'll find the Focus Sheet, a preview of what you'll be using for the ten writing assignments in Stage Four.

THE FOCUS SHEET

Who is singing? _____ male; _____ female; _____ either; _____ duet

What is the Viewpoint of lyric?
_____ First person (emphasis on "I").
_____ Second person (emphasis on "you"). If yes, is singer addressing _____ a particular you; _____ the collective you; _____ an absent person, place, or thing.
_____ Third person (emphasis on "he/she/they"). If yes, _____ is it an omniscient camera-eye view lyric? _____ or a singer-singee connection lyric?

What is the Voice? _____ thinking _____ talking.
Does the Voice change? _____ no; _____ yes.
If yes, in what line did you make it evident? _____

What is the Time Frame?
_____ The Nonspecific Present (one moment's feeling)
_____ The Habitual Present (an ongoing condition)
_____ The Particular Present (a one-time action)
_____ The Past (first-person reflection)
_____ The Past (third-person narrative)
_____ Historical Present (a past event told in present tense)
_____ The Future
_____ Does time move during the lyric? _____ no; _____ yes.
If yes, how did you make it clear to the listener? _____

Does the lyric have a Setting? _____ no; _____ yes.
If yes, where: _____
Does the setting change? _____ no; _____ yes.

If yes, in what line did you show the change? _____

Did you imply a setting by using the word "here"? _____ no; _____ yes.
If yes, where do you picture "here"? _____
How does the lyric convey that setting? _____

What is the (one) Tone of the lyric?
_____ self-assertive (I Will Survive)   _____ reflective (Private Dancer)
_____ tongue-in-cheek (Short People)   _____ ironic (Send in the Clowns)
_____ wistful (The Way We Were)   _____ romantic (Endless Love)
_____ playful (Dress You Up)   _____ (specify other) _____

What is the relationship between singer and singee? _____
In what line did you show that relationship? _____

What is the lyric's basic form? _____ AAA; _____ AABA; _____ V/C?

Synopsize the lyric in one short sentence: _____

What is the universal situation or emotion with which you expect millions to identify? _____

What is the song's title? _____
(It should sum up your idea and be identifiable after one hearing.)

Telling the Lefts from the Rights

After only one or two classes of a new semester, students make evident to me their dominant thinking modes, both in their lyrics and in their attitude toward the writing process itself.

The left brains and mixed dominants generally write clear, coherent first drafts; they don't need a focusing sheet (though they dutifully fill it out and hand it in) because their highly developed left hemispheres instinctively line up the lyric elements in sequential order. Often these students earn a living in such left-brain occupations as book editing and advertising copywriting.

Conversely, composers and singers often turn in first drafts diffused by ambiguous pronouns, murky metaphors, and vague time frames. It is ironic—though not surprising—that these students consistently resist making the key decisions, shun the focus sheet, and experience difficulty in rewriting with success.

For right-brain (feeling) dominants, the sound of a song often supersedes the sense of it. (That's understandable in view of the fact that feeling supplants thought.) When, for example, I point out to a right dominant that a particular word or line is contradictory, or even meaningless, I often get the response, *but it SINGS GREAT!* I of course reply, *but it doesn't make sense.*

A song can both *sing great* AND *make sense;* the two qualities are not mutually exclusive—as our first-rate standards verify.

"Righty" or "Lefty"?

Perhaps you've been wondering if you're a right- or left-mode thinker. Your response to the focus sheet should give you a fairly reliable clue. If you resist using it, you're likely to be a right dominant who's uncomfortable with imposed linear thinking; if you easily (even eagerly) fill it out, you are probably a left dominant who finds the sequencing of ideas pleasurable.

Quite obviously, the more annoyance or anxiety you experience at coming to terms with the details of your lyric before starting to write, the more you need to do just that. Until clarifying the VVTS becomes an automatic process, make filling out the focus sheet a routine procedure—however much it annoys you. Regard feeling uncomfortable as a sign of growth—which it is.

If your editorial left-brain gifts are less developed than your intuitive right-mode talents, you can strengthen your powers of analysis by practice—just as pumping iron makes muscles.

TRACKING THE CREATIVE PROCESS

To illustrate the interaction of the right and left modes of thinking over the five-step lyric writing process—brainstorm clustering, focusing, first draft, critique, and rewrite—I will retrace the evolution of a class assignment.

On the next page is the result of a student's clustering from the word *heart*—the first step in an assignment to write a lyric with the word *heart* in its title. As you can see, her clustering produced the title "Follow Your Heart."

Because the assignment included filling out the focus sheet, we'll assume that before she began to write, the student made the key decisions: whether her character is talking or thinking, what time it is, and where the action is taking place.

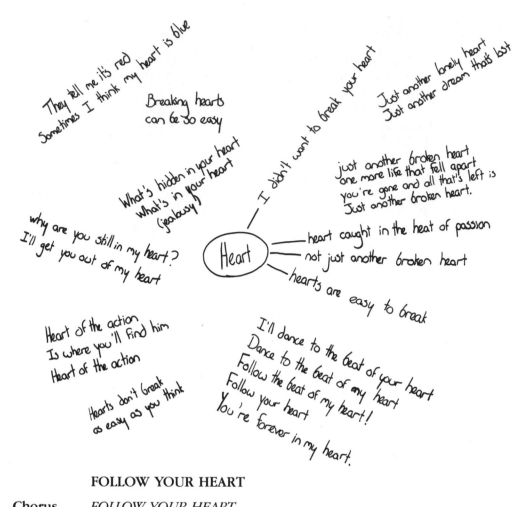

They tell me it's red
Sometimes I think my heart is blue

Breaking hearts
can be so easy

What's hidden in your heart
What's in your heart
(jealousy)

why are you still in my heart?
I'll get you out of my heart

I didn't want to break your heart

Just another lonely heart
Just another dream that's lost

just another broken heart
one more life that fell apart
you're gone and all that's left is
Just another broken heart.

Heart

heart caught in the heat of passion
not just another broken heart
hearts are easy to break

Heart of the action
Is where you'll find him
Heart of the action

Hearts don't break
as easy as you think

I'll dance to the beat of your heart
Dance to the beat of my heart
Follow the beat of my heart!
Follow your heart
You're forever in my heart.

FOLLOW YOUR HEART

Chorus   *FOLLOW YOUR HEART*
Wherever it leads you,
To someone you love,
Someone who needs you.
Reach out for a dream
Give it all that you got
FOLLOW YOUR HEART, just
FOLLOW YOUR HEART.

Verse   *Saying goodbye was not so easy.*
Friends like you are hard to find.
You know that last song you sang me?
Can't get it out of my mind; you sang:

Chorus   *FOLLOW YOUR HEART*
Wherever it leads you,
To someone you love,
Someone who needs you.
Reach out for a dream,
Give it all that you got.
FOLLOW YOUR HEART, just
FOLLOW YOUR HEART.

Verse	*You turned away to hide the tears* *I said New York is not that far* *As we sat on my old couch* *And you played your new guitar, you sang:*
Chorus	*FOLLOW YOUR HEART* *Wherever it leads you,* *To someone you love,* *Someone who needs you.* *Reach out for a dream,* *Give it all that you got.* *FOLLOW YOUR HEART, just* *FOLLOW YOUR HEART.*
Bridge	*I have no doubt you will make it.* *The whole world will sing your songs.* *But if you stumble, you just call me,* *Don't you ever feel alone.*
Chorus	*FOLLOW YOUR HEART* *Wherever it leads you,* *To someone you love,* *Someone who needs you.* *Reach out for a dream,* *Give it all that you got.* *FOLLOW YOUR HEART, just* *FOLLOW YOUR HEART.*

Analysis

The first draft reflects the student's potential as a lyricist. Right off, the title sounds as if it has always existed: you can imagine saying it to a friend, or having a friend say it to you. The writer struck a common chord with a variation on one of songwriting's timeless themes, friendship.

The lyricist has a strong grasp of form: the verse, chorus, and bridge each performs its proper function. The chorus, outlined top and bottom with the title, resounds with a synopsis of the theme. The bridge adds a new dimension to the plot and paves the way for a smooth return of the chorus.

A nice variety of rhyme and near rhyme pleases the ear: mosaic feminine rhymes in the chorus (leads you/needs you) play off masculine ones in the verses and bridge (find/mind, far/guitar, song/alone). Rhythmically, the three-foot lines in the bridge contrast with the four-foot lines in the verses and chorus. Good work.

That's a lot of Brownie points to rack up—especially for a sixteen-year-old whose native language is Russian! Now let's examine what doesn't work as well as it should.

You may have already figured out that the central problem stems from the writer's failure to make some key decisions. For example, is the singer thinking or talking? Hard to tell. Is the action over, or going on now? Hard to tell. Are the singer and singee lovers or friends? Hard to tell. The scene is foggy to the listener because the scene is foggy to the writer.

The writer confessed she hadn't filled out the focus sheet. It's not uncommon for beginning lyricists to resist this procedure. (For many, it conflicts with their notion that lyrics spring from inspiration.)

Maria realized that she had two options: A thinking lyric looking back on a past action, or a talking lyric taking place in the particular present. She opted for the latter, the more compelling of the two choices.

In my critique I noted that to begin this particular song with the chorus was a poor idea: the chorus seems to be addressing the world at large (set in the second-person collective you viewpoint). By placing it *before* the first verse, the audience is (mis)led into thinking that it is being addressed. The verse's opening lines then contradict that assumption and force a listener to reassess what was just heard: Guess I'm wrong—the singer's not talking to me but to a particular person.

The scenario of "Follow Your Heart" requires that a verse set up the singer-singee relationship; this done, there'll be no mistaking that the chorus, when it hits, counsels the singee, not the audience.

Did you catch the double message expressed in the chorus? Instead of one theme, two separate ones compete for attention: *find someone to love* AND *reach out to a dream.* The first principle of lyric writing is simplicity: stick to one idea. The song should be either (consistently) about finding someone to love OR following a dream, not both. Since the content of the verses and the bridge relate solely to the singer's career, *that* appears to be the idea that the writer most wants to express. Thus the lines *to someone you love/Someone who needs you* should be replaced with a thought that supports what the song's truly about: go for your dream.

There's a second duality in the chorus: it changes from being the words of the singee's song to words of advice from the singer. This shift lessens the chorus' impact. These are the lyric's major flaws.

Two minor ones also need repair. The line "you turned away to hide the tears" states a consequence without its cause; the line distracts the audience by making us wonder who the singee is, and why he or she is crying. Is the singee a female friend who'll miss the singer? Is it a male lover who feels guilty at leaving the singer behind for his big city dreams? A simple setup line preceding the action of crying would clear up both the singee's relationship to the singer and the cause of the tears.

The second small point is an unsuccessful attempt at antithesis: *old couch/new guitar.* The writer was trying to put into practice an element of good writing—to make a vivid contrast with antonyms. Unfortunately the two nouns she chose to link—the singer's couch and the singee's guitar—lack a relationship, so the antithesis sounds stuck in for effect. A more appropriate pairing would be *you're heading for New York with your old guitar and your new dreams.*

Like all promising writers, Maria Lopotukhin took the criticism as a challenge to hone her skills. I asked that she confirm her chosen viewpoint, voice, time frame, and setting at the bottom of her lyric sheet.

FOLLOW YOUR HEART
(The Rewrite)

Verse

Saying goodbye is never easy.
Friends like you are hard to find.
Still I'm glad you're heading for New York
And that you're ready to leave your doubts behind.

You've got your guitar and your suitcase,
Your eyes are shining with a distant glow,
You'll be on that plane before you know it,
But I can see, that for you, the clock is moving slow.

Climb

There isn't much for me to say
Except I hope that every day you'll

Chorus

FOLLOW YOUR HEART
Wherever it leads you
FOLLOW YOUR HEART
'Cause everyone needs
To give a dream all they've got to give.
So FOLLOW, FOLLOW YOUR HEART.

Verse

There's music deep inside you—
Songs the world will someday play.
If you believe in yourself as I believe in you,
Success is surely on the way, just

Chorus

FOLLOW YOUR HEART
Wherever it leads you
FOLLOW YOUR HEART
'Cause everyone needs
To give a dream all they've got to give.
So FOLLOW, FOLLOW YOUR HEART.

Bridge

The road to the top can be hard and slow.
And when you stumble, hold on.
And if ever you feel that nobody cares,
Just call me; you are never alone.
I'll remind you to

Chorus

FOLLOW YOUR HEART
Wherever it leads you.
FOLLOW YOUR HEART
'Cause everyone needs
To give a dream all they've got to give.
So FOLLOW, FOLLOW YOUR HEART.

Viewpoint: Second person singular
Voice: Talking
Time Frame: The Particular Present
Setting: Nonspecific Here (at the singer's place)

That's a successful rewrite. This time, because Maria clarified the VVTS before she began the rewrite, she controlled her plot. Putting the action into the particular present, choosing the talking voice, and making the chorus consistently the words of encouragement to the singee combine to produce a forceful lyric moment of two parting friends.

This revision makes evident that only when a lyric is clear to the writer can it be clear to the listener.

BRAIN SHIFTING TECHNIQUES

The five-stage process of "Follow Your Heart" illustrates the distinct skills of each hemisphere: brainstorming for ideas, organizing the elements, creating the product, evaluating the first draft, and polishing it to perfection. Of course there's much more to integrating your two modes of thinking than the exercise of free association (right brain) and filling out the focus sheet (left brain). But these activities characterize the separate abilities of our two brains: the right to let the free play of uncensored ideas produce the broad picture and the left to put elements in logical order and detect first-draft flaws.

Understanding when and how to switch modes may lessen or even prevent some of the frustrations inherent in the songwriting process. There will be times, for example, when you want a more compelling opening line, or a fresh approach to the second verse. Whenever your creative motor gets stalled, you can jump start it by shifting into the opposite hemisphere from the one you're in.

The ability to switch modes, and thereby write with more ease, is a matter of first getting the feel of each mode and then learning how to cross over to the other.

Brainstorming for Tune Titles

For those times when you need to come up with a title for a tune, you'll find your right brain the place to go.

Some lyricists prefer to write words to music: the form, the rhyme pattern, and emotional peaks have all been laid out. When you work from a melody, I recommend three steps: to memorize the tune till it becomes organic; to identify the tune's title spot—its most memorable motif; then to start from a title.

Because searching for a title—in effect, free associating—is a right-brain activity, brainstorming on paper can help you discover that subtle statement the music is making.

As in clustering, you need to suspend your logical left side. The objective is to let your intuitive right brain freely suggest any random thought that would match the musical phrase you've picked as the title spot. I'll illustrate the process by reproducing a page of successful brainstorming from an old notebook of mine.

I'd been assigned by a publisher to write an English lyric for a French record. On hearing the song once, the title spot announced itself. And memorizing the tune was easy. The real work always begins with trying to discover what that melody is saying: the title.

Some instinct told me to busy myself with a mindless physical activity—ironing. My objective was find a title that would fit both the rhythm (TUM TUM ta TUM ta) and the emotion of the song's minor motif (E F E B A—that rose on the B).

As I pressed some napkins, I scribbled down every phrase that popped into my head—regardless of how banal. After ten minutes, I picked up my notebook and looked over what I'd written:

Once in a Lifetime
When Was It Over
Say It's Not Over
This Is Our Moment
Riding a Whirlwind
If This Is Living
Only a Woman
What Kind of Woman
How Can You Leave Me
Time Is a River
This Time Tomorrow

A little more than midway through the list, I saw *What Kind of Woman*. A mental bell went off. When I read those words I knew I could write that title because it suggested a common emotional situation: the female singer would be thinking "I wonder what kind of woman will turn you on; I want to be the one...." In an hour or so I had a first draft. The next day, after some polishing, I presented "What Kind of Woman?" to the publisher. He was as pleased as I was with the mating of words and music, so I got a contract and an advance.

The ideal title sprang to mind as a result of accessing my imaginative right side through a repeated mechanical (mindless) physical action. Rearranging ash trays or scraping carrots may have done the trick just as well. But had I sat at my desk staring at the blue lines on a white pad, I might still be facing a blank page.

Switching from Right to Left

Let's say you're pacing up and down racking your brain for a rhyme-mate. It's been over a half hour and nothing's come. Since the right brain controls motor activity, the act of pacing means you're operating in the right mode. You'd have a better chance of finding the perfect chime if you crossed from the wide angle lens of the right to the closeup lens of the left; stop pacing, sit down, take out a pad and pencil and your rhyming dictionary. You might begin your search by making two columns, one for words in consonance with your rhyme agent and a second to list those letters of the alphabet that could produce augmented rhymes. Such a systematic approach is likely to generate enough potential rhyme mates to give you several to pick from. (Example on page 116.)

Analyzing, alphabetizing, and list making are all left-brain activities. Such tasks put your organizational skills in motion. As just noted, a good way to shift from right to left is to narrow your field of vision, concentrate on an isolated problem, and break it down into parts.

Before Moving On
Exercise #31
To experience the feeling of your left brain, stop reading for a few minutes and write down a personal agenda for tomorrow: errands, phone calls, appointments, and so

on. The activity of planning your day will give you a sense of functioning in your left mode.

_____   _____
_____   _____
_____   _____
_____   _____
_____   _____

When Right Is Right

Now let's suppose you're stuck in a lyric scenario that puts two lovers on a dance floor; you can't seem to bring the scene to a satisfying emotional conclusion. You've been struggling with transitional lines but they just keep paraphrasing a point already made in the first verse. You're about ready to chuck the lyric in the wastebasket.

The frustration stems from trying to make your left brain do a job that it can't do: picture the scene. Stop struggling. Close your notebook and get up from your chair. Stretch. Sharpen a pencil. Check the mail box. Physical activity acts to suspend your narrow-focus, linear, left brain and thus allow your broad-view, imaging right brain to produce a 3-D picture of the couple on the dance floor. Hear the throb of the music. See the flashing lights. Notice what your couple's wearing. Improvise their dialogue. Let the scene unreel. As the picture sharpens and the emotions of your characters develop, the lyric lines will come.

To reach your right brain requires a suspension of your left's questioning, comparing, judging activities. Something as simple as getting a glass of water could cross you over. And of course such right-brain inducers as a predinner cocktail, TV viewing, dancing, jogging, or meditating will definitely do the trick to put your left on hold.

Integrating

But despite a preference for one mode of thinking over the other, we possess the capacity to develop the latent talents of our less-favored brain. The revision of "Follow Your Heart" proved that. It's simply a matter of practicing some mental calisthenics.

Practice getting the feel of both sides, so that when you sense that it's appropriate, you can purposefully shift to the opposite mode: move right when you want to rehearse the dialogue of your characters, visualize the landscape of your plot, or map its emotional payoff; move left to organize the chronology of your story, correct itosis, and detect mixed metaphors.

Whenever you hear yourself think, _I'm spinning my wheels and getting nowhere on this lyric,_ heed that voice. It's a message that you're working on the wrong side. It's time to shift.

In Stage Five's writing assignments you'll find a "Post-First Draft Quiz" that will put your logical left in gear and help you revise and polish. (For a sneak preview, turn to page 158.)

SOME LAST THOUGHTS ON WHOLE BRAIN THINKING

This step has illustrated a few ways to enhance your technical facility by applying some of the new knowledge of brain dominance to the creative process.

If the subject intrigues you—and what can be more intriguing than learning more about how our minds work?—I recommend that you check out three books. First, *Whole Brain Thinking* by Jacquelyn Wonder and Priscilla Donovan, Ballantine (1985). These experts present many more techniques to help you switch hemispheres. They also provide a Brain Preference Test so you'll be able to identify your preferred hemisphere—in case you haven't figured it out by now. *Centering Through Writing* by Margaret Hatcher, Ed. D, University Press of America (1963) offers a number of devices to enhance perceptual and conceptual thinking through free association, pattern making, and multisensory imaging. *Writing the Natural Way* by Gabriel Lusser Rico, J. P. Tarcher Inc. (1983) illustrates the subtleties of clustering and offers additional insights into the creative process. These books will enrich your understanding of brain dominance and thereby improve your writing skills.

And now to finding your voice.

Finding Your Voice

First-rate lyrics can affect us even when recited. Otto Harbach demonstrated that one night years ago on the Ed Sullivan Show when, to a hushed audience, he quietly spoke his lyric "Smoke Gets in Your Eyes."

And judging from reissues of the lyrics of Oscar Hammerstein, Cole Porter, and Noel Coward, and the newly compiled complete writings of Larry Hart, the public enjoys simply *reading* lyrics. Well, some lyrics. Craftsmen such as these achieved the goal of all serious writers—an identifiable style. Each found his voice.

When we say that a writer has a distinctive voice, we mean that he or she has a unique way of expressing experience. That uniqueness can cut through the din of party chatter or the wail of a fire engine to stop us in our tracks to catch the rest of an intriguing line: . . . *going where the weather suits my clothes . . . was I standing up too close or back too far? . . . wearing the face that she keeps in a jar by the door. . . .*

Words of genius? Not really. They are the words of writers who think with independence of mind.

DEVELOPING A DISTINCTIVE VOICE

When we turn on the radio we hear, more often than not, lyrics that lack distinctiveness. Anyone could have written "I never felt like this before/And deep down inside I know I'll love you forever/So it cuts me like a knife. . . ." In fact many *have* written it. Many times. But that's not *writing,* that's duplicating. In place of hearing the charm of a fresh thought, we hear the thud of a rubber stamp.

How do you find your voice? I wish I could offer a magic formula like: Every day for seven days read twenty pages of *Roget's Thesaurus,* meditate ten minutes, click your heels three times, and voilà! at the end of a week your distinctive voice will emerge. Unfortunately, there is no formula.

It's been said—more in truth than jest—that what a writer needs more than a course in creative writing is a course in creative living. To write with a fresh voice, we must see with a fresh eye. Easy to say—much harder to do.

Think No Cliché, Speak No Cliché, Write No Cliché

Certainly a small step in the right direction is not to talk in clichés. We all do it in varying degrees—drop readymade expressions into our conversation—mostly out of laziness. It's just so much easier to use verbal shorthand: *he pulled the rug out from under me . . . she feels like a fish out of water . . . I threw in the towel . . .* than to think of a fresh response. But the more we permit threadbare phrases to impoverish our small talk, the more we'll continue to write with an unidentifiable voice. Because, after all, we write the way we talk (think).

So the first step is to think for yourself. Bite your tongue the next time you sense you're about to say: *She's been burning the candle at both ends . . . the green-eyed monster's getting to him . . . there's just no rhyme or reason. . . .* Only the people who originated those (now clichéd) phrases were independent thinkers: Edna St. Vincent Millay, Shakespeare, Sir Thomas More. By constantly leaning on the thoughts of others, you weaken your ability to think your own.

Be Curious

Curiosity about what makes people tick is characteristic of original writers: *I wonder what would happen if a bored lover answered a personals ad? I wonder how it would feel to be a released ex-con going back home unsure if his girl's still waiting?* Such wondering resulted in two number one songs: "Piña Colada," and "Tie a Yellow Ribbon Round the Old Oak Tree."

Look, and listen, and wonder. . . .

You Are the Genre

It's a given that songwriters tend to write the same kinds of songs they loved in their youth—whether pop, or theater, or country, or rock. On occasion, exposure to an unfamiliar genre may strike a responsive chord in a writer who, after internalizing its style, can authentically reproduce it. But generally, what's bred in the bone comes out in the beat; the point is that it's pointless to try to write in a style that's alien simply because you think it'll sell better than the kind of music you really love. For example, if you dote on Noel Coward and have a flair for sophisticated cabaret songs, it would be crazy to affect a backwoods twang and spin tales of eighteen-wheel truckers. Admittedly, there's a greater market for country songs than for cabaret songs. There is *no* market, however, for synthetic songs. But a song that rings true—whatever the genre—will find an audience.

Write Your Reality

The well-worn injunction still applies: write what you know. The verb *know*, however, does not suggest that you write only about first-hand experiences. *Know* extends to what you intuit that a particular person would feel in a given situation. Harry Chapin never drove a cab ("Taxi") or shot thirty-seven people ("Sniper") but he was a keen observer of human nature. He possessed both insight and empathy. He *knew* how his characters felt. He *became* the character.

Learn to Be Brave

In addition to thinking independently, being curious, and writing from your own reality, finding your voice requires emotional grit. It takes courage to put your thoughts on paper—to let the world see how your mind works. Because, ultimately, writing means to expose yourself. But to risk exposure is exactly what every first-rate writer has been brave enough to do.

Discover Who You Are

To write with a strong voice, you must know what you think. What concerns you? What delights you, turns you off, outrages you? As an exercise to help students sharpen their perception of the world I sometimes give a special home assignment: write down ten concerns—personal and/or social. The next week I ask how they found the experience. The responses range from "fun" to "scary."

The students most in touch with themselves find it easy. Others—more estranged from their own emotional centers—find it hard. Some are unable to think of as many as ten items. And occasionally a writer feels too threatened to even pick up a pencil. But the exercise, however anxiety-provoking to some, helps everyone see the need for self-definition.

Before Moving On
Exercise #32

Try the experiment now. List as many things as you can think of that interest you, intrigue you, bug you, worry you, obsess you. The items could range from railing at junk mail to concern about the country's rising illiteracy rate. Try to put down at least five items before reading on.

1) _____
2) _____
3) _____
4) _____
5) _____
6) _____
7) _____
8) _____
9) _____
10) _____

Clarifying the Goal

Every Basics Class brings together budding lyricists whose musical tastes cover a diversity of styles—pop, R&B, country, cabaret, theater—even sacred music. A common desire unites them: to express themselves in song.

Consequently the purpose of every class assignment is to help the writer find his or her individual style. Never is the objective to design a hit—a pointless pursuit for two reasons: one, a hit record results from a number of factors beyond the writer's control; second, and perhaps even more to the point, to attempt to second guess what a fickle marketplace wants, rather than to write about what truly interests the lyricist, sabotages his effort to find his voice.

Each assignment is designed to stimulate the expression of some personal view of the world that will touch a responsive chord in an audience—make them dance, make them laugh, make them cry. Maybe even make them think.

SOME DISTINCTIVE VOICES

To illustrate what I mean by a distinctive voice, here are lyrics by three writers whose work rings with authenticity because it reflects an aspect of his or her unique view of the world.

Brian Sitts

Irony often underpins Brian Sitts' lyrics; the surface appearance belies the reality beneath. We can identify with his real people struggling with such contemporary dilemmas as estrangement. Here's a *cinéma verité* sample.

IT'S ALL OVER BUT THE LEAVING

Lying in our silent bedroom,
We take separate sides and turn away,
Pulling covers tight around our shoulders,
Counting all the lies it took to get us through today.
Tomorrow at the breakfast table
We won't even meet each other's eyes:
Wordlessly we'll share some toast and coffee,
Wondering when it was we began to realize

IT'S ALL OVER BUT THE LEAVING,
Too late now to even try.
IT'S ALL OVER BUT THE LEAVING
Nothing left to do but wonder why.

Greeting guests at Sunday's party,
We'll be holding hands, yet feeling miles apart,
Hoping that the wine will liven up the evening,
Hoping that the jokes we tell will hide our broken hearts.
And later when the laughing's over,
Sweeping crumbs and ashes from the floor,
We'll remember embers of desire,
Knowing neither one of us is burning anymore.

IT'S ALL OVER BUT THE LEAVING,
Too late now to even try.
IT'S ALL OVER BUT THE LEAVING
Nothing left to do but wonder why.

What'll be the straw that breaks us?
Who will play the villain in the end?
Who will take the car and just start driving?
Who will stay behind to explain to our friends?

IT'S ALL OVER BUT THE LEAVING,
Too late now to even try.
IT'S ALL OVER BUT THE LEAVING,
Nothing left to say except goodbye.

The title, a twist on the colloquialism, "it's all over but the shouting," promises an original voice. The lyric delivers with a fresh treatment of the how-did-we-go-wrong theme.

By means of an interior monologue, we see a relationship play itself out against a backdrop of changing suburban scenes: the bedroom, the breakfast table, the party, the car speeding off in the distance.

Action verbs vivify the progressive alienation: *Pulling covers tight . . . greeting guests . . . sweeping crumbs and ashes . . . and just start driving. . . .*

Because good writing is demonstrable, we can pinpoint the devices that animate the lyric. Listen, for example, to the way echoed sounds link ideas with assonance—*lying/silent/sides/tight/lies,* and alliteration—*hold/hands/hoping/hide/hearts;* and hear how anaphora reinforces structure—*Who will play/Who will take/Who will stay.*

Sitts maintains his listener's attention with classic devices: shifting the rhythms (some rising, some falling), varying the number of stressed beats per line (from three to four), altering meters (from TUMtatata to taTUMta), and choosing unobtrusive rhymes—sometimes perfect, sometimes augmented.

Supporting his personal vision of reality with good craftsmanship, Brian Sitts creates a lyric that rings true. As a consequence, we are touched.

Francesca Blumenthal

Francesca Blumenthal's lyrics spring from a totally different response to reality. She's the wishful dreamer: Why isn't life more fun, more glamorous, more like Fred Astaire movies? This lyric resulted from a special assignment to "cover" the New York mating scene. A lyricist steeped in the traditions of the Cole Porter *list song* delivered a sophisticated treatment.

MUSEUM

I've given up on singles bars.
Can't stand the line and the leer.
The losers—the boozers,
I've had them up to here.
Now Saturday and Sunday
I find I just can't miss—
My modus operandi is this:

I meet a better class of man in a MUSEUM.
His approach seems more refined and debonair.
Last month I met a basso
Perusing a Picasso.
The paint is still not dry on our affair.

You see a suaver style of suitor at the Modern.
Find a finer kind of fellow at the Frick.
If you both can dig Vermeer,
You won't end up drinking beer,
And a champion of Chagall won't call you "Chick."

There's something about the lighting,
Something about the hush
That makes the game inviting
When he's giving you the rush.

One discovers lovely lovers at the Cloisters
And monumental moments at the Met.
I was gazing at a Goya
Near a corporation lawya—
Soon we flew off to LaJolla on his jet.

At the Guggenheim you get a handy preview
As you gaze upon the patrons from above;
When you pick your man, decamp
And trip lightly down the ramp,
That's the start of falling artfully in love.

Then suddenly you're communing,
Gliding from frame to frame,
Before you can say "DeKooning"
He is asking for your name.

So next weekend as you wander through the Whitney
With an impeccably selective roving eye
Don't doubt your motivation—
This is art appreciation.
And da Vinci would have understood just why.

It is certainly no folly
If you dally at a Dali
And you're far from indiscreet
If you meet at a Magritte
Only savvy kinds of dudes
Keep their cool among the nudes
Nothing rises to the top like heavy cre-um
Like the men you get to meet in a MUSEUM.

Francesca's knowledge of theater songs led her to set up the AABA scenario with an introductory verse and to wrap it up with an extended climax. Her verse rhythm (TUMtatata/TUMtatata/TUMTUM) was appropriately treated as a tango.

From a *suaver style of suitor* to *the men you get to meet in a museum,* she lets alliteration lead her lightly to her laughs. Her appropriately frequent and close rhymes *the losers/the boozers, discovers lovely lovers, dally at a Dali*— illustrate intentional overkill for comic effect.

Her inventive sound mates are the kind that earn the highest praise from rhyme theorists: *basso/Picasso, beer/Vermeer, Magritte/indiscreet, dudes/nudes.* We laugh, not merely at the juxtaposition of such incongruous pairings, our laughter also signals the recognition of a contemporary scene—purposely exaggerated.

Some writers try to be clever, but put us off because the cleverness sounds forced. Francesca Blumenthal can't help but be clever—it's her natural voice.

Jim Morgan

Jim's style cannot be neatly categorized as romanticist, realist, or fantasist. His far-ranging interests enable him to not only mix styles but cross genres: his lyrics have earned such diverse credits as cuts by Kool and the Gang, a best original revue-of-the-year award, and a pop opera premiered by the Houston Opera Company. Whatever the challenge, he meets it with an identifiable voice. Here's a lyric that resulted from an assignment to write a song for the Christian market.

THE MAN WHO WALKED ON WATER

There was a little girl
Sittin' beneath a tree—
Freckled and funny,
Nose a bit runny,
That little girl was me.
I was readin' The Good Book,
Havin' a good look
Matthew 14, I read;
I was confounded,
I was astounded,
Ran in the house
And I said: Momma,

There's a Man in the Bible
Who could walk on the water,
He walked on the water,
He walked upon the water,
There's a Man in the Bible
Who walked on the water
On the Sea of Galilee.

Now I'm a mother too
Oh, how the years flew past—
Four o'clock feeding,
Next thing she's reading
Golly, they grow so fast.
I gave her The Good Book,
Said, take a good look,
And out by the tree she read.
I was delighted
'Cause she got excited
Tugged on my sleeve
And she said: Momma,

There's a Man in the Bible
Who could walk on the water
He walked on the water
He walked upon the water
There's a Man in the Bible
Who walked on the water
On the Sea of Galilee.

So I told my baby
What my mama used to say
His wonders and His miracles
Happen every day
The love He has for everyone
Is very clear to see;
His love lives on and on and on
Inside of you and me—
You and me—
Now we sing together

There's a Man in the Bible
Who could walk on the water
He walked on the water,
He walked upon the water;
There's a Man in the Bible
Who walked on the water
On the Sea of Galilee.

There's a Man in the Bible
And he walked on the water,
He walked on the water,
He walked upon the water;
There's a Man in the Bible
Who walked on the water
I know he walks with me.

That compelling tataTUM tataTUMta rhythm seems to say, "Everybody, clap your hands and sing along": *There's a man in the Bible who could walk on the water. . . .* You can almost hear the tune.

The charm of the returning scene under the tree, the simplicity of language, the winsome mother and child image combine to make even a nonbeliever join in the chorus.

Note: The female demo of "The Man Who Could Walk On the Water" was compelling enough to make Josh White, Jr. want to join in the chorus. So he requested a few word changes in the lyric to accommodate a male singer and recorded the song.

SUMMING UP

Imagination plays a key role in the work of all original lyricists. Such writers can obviously access the right brain's rich inventory of stored images and visualize a scene right down to the small details of toast and coffee on a breakfast table or freckles on a face.

A striking feature of the work of these lyricists is the absence of clichés. Instead of the prefab phrase and the obvious rhyme, we hear the fresh expression of the writer's view of the human comedy: . . . *sweeping crumbs and ashes from the floor* . . . *I was gazing at a Goya near a corporation lawya* . . . *Momma, There's a Man in the Bible.* . . .

It would appear that finding your voice is both as easy and as hard as being yourself. You will soon get a chance to exercise your voice on a series of ten lyric writing assignments. But before we begin I want first to touch upon the relationship between the songwriter and society.

The Moral Dimension

In 1821, in "A Defense of Poetry," Percy Bysshe Shelley called poets the unacknowledged legislators of the world. At that time the work of a best-selling poet circulated in the thousands. How, I wonder, would Shelley characterize the influence of a hit lyricist whose words are heard around the globe by tens of millions?

In this increasingly acoustic world, the attitudes and urgings of popular songs are walked to, danced to, chanted—and internalized: "I get high with a little help from my friends," "We don't need no education . . . teacher, leave us kids alone," "What's love got to do, got to do with it?" Lyrics provide America's youth with musical slogans for living. Might it be that as the words go into the mouth, the values go into the unconscious?

There is a moral dimension to writing of any kind; it comes with the territory. But because songs wield an incalculable power to influence—for good or bad—a special responsibility falls on the shoulders of lyric writers.

Before we send a song out into the world, we might ask ourselves, "What values do my words promote?"

Life-Affirming Lyrics

The power of lyrics to affect, to persuade, and even to incite to action has long been recognized.

At their life-affirming best, songs can encourage self-determination ("Ac-cen-tchu-ate the Positive"), celebrate a reconciliation ("Reunited"), imbue us with faith ("You'll Never Walk Alone"), unite us against injustice ("We Shall Overcome") and encourage brotherhood ("We Are the World").

The positive influence of pop lyrics was reported in the *Music Education Journal* (February 1986). Dr. Robert Phillips of the Center for Chronic Conditions, Garden City, New York, found certain songs with upbeat messages are therapeutic. Using recordings of "You're Only Human (Second Wind)," "Over and Over," and "You Can Get It If You Really Want It," Dr. Phillips treats patients suffering from depression.

But just as songs wield power to uplift the spirit, so can they also debase it.

Songs and Society

We are living at a time when the social fabric of our country would seem to be unraveling. Nightly in our living rooms the six-o'clock news documents the latest episodes of drug abuse, street crime, preteen pregnancy, and adolescent suicide.

What, you may ask, have lyrics *got to do, got to do with it?* Pop songs not only speak for their time—not only mirror society, they contribute to shaping it; the media and society constantly shape and reshape each other. By endorsing and thereby promoting practices which society deems illegal or immoral, pop lyrics cannot help but accelerate the acceptance of such behavior as the norm.

Raising Your Consciousness

According to a report published by the Human Development, Family Studies, and Psychology Departments of Cornell University (1986) "The U.S. has by far the highest rate of teen-age pregnancy of any industrial nation—twice the rate of England, its nearest competitor." Bearing that statistic in mind, let me illustrate what I mean by the moral dimension of lyric writing; here's a first draft of a student lyric purposely targeted for the teen market.

READY

I'm so tired of just kissin'
Kissin' goodnight at the door.
The way I feel about you
Has me wanting more.
'Cause kid stuff's not enough
To satisy me
And I can't deny
All the things I feel
Want to make them real
'Cause I'm

READY
READY for the big time
READY
Gonna make you all mine.
READY
The waiting time is through
And baby, I'm READY for you.

So when you come over
To take me out tonight
I don't want to go home
'Till I see the morning light
'Cause tonight's the night
For my lovin' education
And I'm not leavin' class
'Till I know I've passed
Gonna learn real fast
'Cause I'm

READY
READY for the big time
READY
Gonna make you all mine.
READY
The waiting time is through
And baby, I'm READY for you.

I'm gonna give my love to you, and then
I won't ever be that girl again
Bye, bye to my innocence.

(Repeat Chorus)

In terms of craftsmanship, "Ready" is a good first draft with a well-constructed verse/chorus/bridge format, memorable title, and a simple, clear emotional situation. After I congratulated the writer on a well-written assignment, I told her that the lyric troubled me. I asked how she'd feel if she learned that her song had contributed to the pregnancy of even one teenager.

Heavy question.

The writer replied that she had never given any thought to the effect her words might have on anyone; she'd just been trying to write what she believed the marketplace wanted.

The following week she brought in a revision that eliminated such pointedly teenage references as *kid stuff, class, education, girl, and innocence.* The rewrite was just as recordable but a lot less potentially damaging because this time the message wasn't aimed so blatantly at the endangered species—teenage virgins.

Documentation

Sociologists have long studied the relationship between songs and society. A few are now testing the potential of lyrics to wield a global influence on population control. The January 1, 1987 telecast of ABC's "20/20" program documented the story of a Mexican hit song "When We're Together" recorded by the teenage duo Johnny and Tatiana. The song had been specially commissioned by the Population Commission Services of Johns Hopkins University as an experiment to help curb teenage pregnancies throughout Latin America.

Although its uptempo dance beat and melodic hook are standard top-40 fare, the lyric content is unique. Unlike the provocative singer of "Ready," the teenage singer of "When We're Together" says *no* to a sexual invitation.

The platinum hit spun that suggestion to teenagers in seventeen countries in Central and South America. Then in August, 1987, the song and its follow-up "Detente" ("Wait") were released in the U.S. targeted for the nation's Spanish-speaking community. Thanks to a lyric, millions of young girls both north and south of the border have been helped to discover that it's all right to say no—that maybe it's even hip.

Sexual Violence in Lyrics

In his testimony before a Senate Committee (9/19/85) Dr. Thomas Radecki, psychiatrist and chairman of the National Coalition on Television Violence, gave the results of an NCTV study on rock lyrics: "We have found a 115 percent increase in the use of violent lyrics since 1963 in the top-40. Songs of rape and sadism—almost nonexistent in 1963—have become fairly common in the 1980s. Monitoring 1300 rock music videos, almost half contained violence between men and women. A major theme was a portrayal of hatred and intense violence between the sexes as being commonplace and acceptable."

Music videos are now competing with TV as the prime glorifier of antisocial behavior. Lyrics that link images of knives and guns to sexual acts—a pervasive rock metaphor—that feature sadism and degrade women, must be considered as contributing to the ever-spiraling rate of violent sexual crime.

Suicide and Murder in Lyrics

It has been documented in studies conducted by Columbia University's Division of Child Psychiatry that after TV programs in which a suicide takes place, or after TV news stories reporting suicides, the national rate of suicides increases significantly—especially among teenagers.

Research has also found a direct correlation between a bizarre fictional TV crime (such as igniting a bed with kerosene) and a spate of copycat crimes.

Pop lyrics too have portrayed both murder and suicide as acceptable solutions to personal problems—from "Frankie and Johnny," "Delilah," and "Coward of the County" to "Gloomy Sunday," "Sandra," and "Moody River." And just as studies have linked a fictional TV crime to a rash of similar real life crimes, so have "Gloomy Sunday" and "Suicide Solution" been cited as related to self-inflicted deaths.

It would seem time for lyricists to seriously consider the potential effect of their words upon their listeners, to be mindful that any audience may contain highly unstable teenagers as well as emotionally depressed adults. And thus a song perceived as suggesting suicide or murder as a viable solution to a personal problem might become a contributing factor to an act of violence.

An Implied Message

Even a subtle subtext of a lyric could prove just as potentially harmful as a blatant message. As a case in point, the lyrics of a "Sesame Street" song "I Want a Monster to Be My Friend" came under scrutiny when the program received a letter from a concerned parent who feared the song might encourage child molestation. The lyric writer's intention was to teach children that they need not fear the monster images conjured up by their fantasies. But sometimes a lyric can transmit a message that the writer hadn't intended. When the implications of the words "I'll let him do whatever he wanster—especially if he's bigger than me" were reviewed, the show's producers decided to drop the lines from the song.

Commercial Success

It is not uncommon for new lyric writers to believe that the sole route to the top of the charts is sex—and the blunter the better—as in "Sugar Walls" and "Lick It Up."

But as the top-40 hit "We Don't Have to Take Our Clothes Off (to have a good time)" demonstrated, it ain't necessarily so.

Similarly, a *non*-cheatin' song can rack up record sales equal to the flip side of the story. In both "The Old School" (Schlitz/Smith) and "On the Other Hand" (Schlitz/Overstreet) a singer turned his back on an extramarital affair in favor of fidelity and thereby put self-restraint on top of the charts. The Country Music Association honored "On the Other Hand" with the 1986 Song of the Year Award.

The Power of Suggestion

The awareness that a song's message affects the collective unconscious appears to have reached the federal government. In the spring of 1987 the U.S. Department of the Interior sent out a call to the country's songwriters to create a theme song for the national campaign, "Take Pride in America." The government guideline requested "A song that will inspire and motivate people to take better care of our beautiful and bountiful natural heritage. This will not be an easy job, but it is achievable."

Could that mean that the government believes that the words to one song might actually help reform a few million litterbugs into neatniks! It appears so: the government guideline concludes *A song, more than any one individual effort, will create public awareness.*

A RECAP OF STAGE THREE

First-rate lyrics bear the imprint not only of the interplay of the right and the left brain, but of the writer's integrity and social conscience.

Since the lyricist of "Ready" had her consciousness raised, she's had her first songs recorded. Not one of the lyrics urges the listener to drop out, take dope, or commit adultery. And they just might be hits anyway.

Now, on to how to keep your ideas coming.

How To Keep The Ideas Coming

Having just the vision's no solution,
Everything depends on execution. . . .
STEPHEN SONDHEIM

Ten Lyric Writing Assignments

Well, this is it—the big time you've been training for in Steps 1-10. You've written a verse, a refrain, a bridge, a climb, and a chorus. You've practiced clarity, compression, consistency, and coherence. You've gotten a fix on the VVTS. You've learned about figurative language and the functions of your right and left brain. You've pruned, rhymed, alliterated, critiqued, and revised. Now you're ready to put your newly-acquired skills to work. So here come ten lyric writing assignments.

HOW TO APPROACH THE ASSIGNMENTS

Each assignment, in addition to developing your technique in a particular aspect of craft, is meant to suggest a concept category that will get you into the self-assignment habit.

Some assignments will reinforce your understanding of song forms, some will strengthen your grasp of viewpoint, voice, time frames, and figurative language. Others will, I hope, prompt you to express your opinion on a subject of personal concern.

Please resist any temptation to randomly select assignments. Do them sequentially. Do them fully. Do them all. Some will appeal to you more than others. Some might not appeal to you at all. But the very ones that may put you off are probably those from which you'll derive the most benefit. After all, if you find an assignment a snap to do, you've learned nothing new. If on the other hand you feel uncomfortable, even anxious, that's terrific! It means you're being made to stretch your talent and that you are growing.

So do every assignment—and in order. Developing craft is a step-by-step process. There are no shortcuts.

Build From Form

We start of course with form—the bedrock of it all. You may still think that the verse/chorus format is the sole road to a hit record. But by acquiring proficiency in the AAA and AABA structures—two cornerstones of songcrafting—you triple your skills. Mas-

156

tering form will help you to pick the most appropriate song structure, not only for the remaining workbook assignments but for the future assignments of your career.

Through a Glass Backwards

In structuring the assignment guidelines, I've chosen to reverse reality and present the final draft of the example first. After you've seen a well-written model and I've pointed out its good features, we'll sometimes glance back to the first draft to see how criticism helped the writer polish to the final product.

Getting Under Way

After absorbing the assignment guidelines and doing your background homework, give your imagination free play. Allow time to let ideas germinate. As soon as you feel ready to put some random thoughts down on paper, turn to the brainstorming page. When your right brain's given you a broad picture of the idea you want to express, switch left, and fill out the focus sheet to clarify the viewpoint, voice, tone, time frame, and setting of your plot.

Before you start the lyric, write a one-sentence synopsis of your intended lyric at the top of your first-draft page. Looking up at it now and then will keep you writing the song you mean to write.

Let It Flow

I've found that first drafts completed in one setting (and in one sitting) are often more unified than those written at different times and places. For example, starting a verse Monday night at home and completing the lyric Tuesday morning at the office can sometimes result in a shift in tone or language style. Whenever it's feasible, let your first draft pour out in one uninterrupted block of time.

During that process don't allow your left-brain critic to stop the word flow in order to perfect the rhyme or adjust the meter. Polishing comes later. Let your whole brain take the lyric uninterruptedly where it wants to go. Your left hemisphere's turn will come later at editing time.

When you've got a rough draft down, put it away—ideally for a day or two. The greater the emotional distance between the first outpouring and the second look, the better. Elapsed time helps your editorial left side give a more dispassionate appraisal of how well your words are working.

The Second Look

Here's a short checklist that identifies the most common first-draft flaws. The list synthesizes the main points of theory covered in Steps 1 through 7. Checking your first drafts against these questions will develop your editorial talents.

A POST-FIRST-DRAFT QUIZ

(You should be able to answer every question *Yes*)

The Essential Lyric Framework

1. Have I kept to one simple idea that can be summarized in a short sentence?
2. Are the essentials of the plot in my mind put down on the paper? (The audience knows only what the lyric states.)
3. Does my first verse pass the Who-What-When-Where test?
4. Does the plot move forward in each verse?
5. Did I choose the ideal form for my plot?
6. Does the bridge—in an AABA or a V/C lyric—contrast to the other sections in some manner?
7. Is the chorus of a verse/chorus song a reasonable outcome of its verses?
8. Is my title a synopsis of my lyric?
9. Did I put the title in the appropriate place and make it identifiable to a listener on first hearing?
10. Have I built to a satisfactory emotional payoff?
11. Does my lyric express a universally understood meaning?
12. Was I careful not to preach or moralize concerning the rightness or wrongness of anyone's personal conduct?
13. Can I *hear* several recording artists singing these words?

Managing the Viewpoint, Voice, Time Frame, and Setting

1. In a first-person lyric, did I put the singer in an attractive light and avoid such unappealing qualities as anger, sarcasm, and self-pity?
2. Does my third-person camera-eye lyric show some universal truth about the human condition?
3. Have I maintained a definite and consistent thinking lyric or talking lyric?
4. In a talking lyric, did I keep the language conversational?
5. Do my verb tenses match my time frame?
6. Have I made the setting of the story clear—barroom, bedroom, or boardroom?
7. In changing time frames or settings, did I make the change obvious to the ear?

Applying the Top-Ten Writing Principles

1. Do personal pronouns show the listener who owns the thoughts or actions?
2. Did I give each pronoun (*it, this, they*) a clear antecedent? (The listener links the closest noun to the pronoun.)
3. Have I maintained a consistent language style throughout?
4. Have I kept my tone consistent?
5. Did I eliminate clutter words such as *just, very, a lot, really, sort of,* and so on?
6. Have I avoided reversing the natural order of words (such as *upon your smile I still depend*)?
7. Did I delete any clever homonym that has to be *read* to be understood? (Chairman of the *bored* or *thyme* on my hands.)
8. Did I avoid trendy expressions that will date my lyric, such as: *where's the beef, chill out?*

A Rundown of Rhyme

1. Did I maintain the rhyme scheme I established in the first verse throughout subsequent verses?
2. Was I careful not to repeat my chorus end rhymes in my verse or bridge?
3. Did I weed out any tricky rhyme that calls attention to itself?
4. Are the sounds of rhymes varied enough? (Too many of one sound such as *-a-* tend to be boring.)
5. Did I rhyme only those words I want to emphasize?

Fitting Words to Music

1. Do the accents of my words fall when sung the way they fall when spoken: e-TER-nal-ly, not e-TER-nal-*LY*?
2. Do the important words fall on the important (accented or high) notes? (Not "along THE way" but "ALONG the WAY")
3. Have I matched the punctuation of my lyric lines to the music's commas, question marks, and periods?
4. Did I make sure not to give the singer too many successive -p- or -s- words? (They create a popping or hissing sound).
5. Is there space for the singer to breathe? And phrase?
6. Did I give the singer open vowel words to sing on notes that are held at the end of phrases? (On high notes open -i-, -a-, and -o- vowels are easier to sing than -e-.)
7. Do the words and music express a compatible emotion?

To take your lyric to the limit, polish until you can give every question a *yes* answer.

To begin the editing process, check your first draft against the quiz to be sure that you haven't missed any potential pitfall. If all the major elements are in place, then you can do some fine tuning such as deleting clutter words, upgrading your verbs, or emphasizing key words at the end of a line.

When you've completed a draft that's ready to leave the house, be sure to add the copyright notice at the bottom of each lyric sheet, followed by the year and your name: © 19— by Jane Doe. That shows the world you already claim professional status.

As your grasp of technique gets firmer, you'll be able to dispense with both the focus sheet and first-draft quiz because the questions will have become an instinctive part of your creative process. Before long you'll automatically keep the viewpoint and tone consistent and intuitively sense when to vary a string of "cherry" words with some "apricots."

Meanwhile, you've got two writing aids to keep you focused and help you to polish your first draft.

A Word on Lyric Collaboration

You may have noticed from the copyright credits throughout the book that every lyric selected to illustrate good writing lists one author. That is no accident: Too many heads spoil the sense.

With the exception of the lyrics by a few highly professional teams such as Marilyn and Alan Bergman and Betty Comden and Adolph Green, most first-rate lyrics are produced by one focused writer. What teachers have discovered in group writing projects is borne out daily on top-40 radio: lyrics created by committee tend toward incoherence.

Although this week's number one record may bear six writer credits, sales figures are no barometer of quality. The subject under discussion here is not how to produce a hit record, but how to write a coherent lyric. Unfortunately, the former often exists without the latter.

Your having read this far would seem to indicate a desire to become a first-rate lyricist. Then why not develop your talent to its fullest, on your own?

The Ultimate Goal

In this workbook, as in my classes, the ultimate objective is to express your ideas in your unique voice. Your voice will resonate loud and clear as you learn to write with simplicity and conviction.

Now let's get under way.

ASSIGNMENT NO. 1
An AAA Lyric with a Changing Time Frame

The Purpose:
To help you master a major song form.

The Assignment:
Write an AAA lyric of at least three but no more than four verses. Choose a subject that lends itself to changing time frames; for example, the morning, noon, and night of your character's workday ("By the Time I Get to Phoenix"), the phases of a relationship ("The First Time Ever I Saw Your Face"), the stages of a life ("It Was a Very Good Year"). As you change time frames, announce it clearly to the listener as in the above examples. The lyric may also establish and change a setting but it's not required.

Your title can either be imbedded in a closing refrain such as "Blowin' in the Wind" and "The Times They Are A-Changin' " or placed in the first line of the verse, as in the first three songs given. A refrain is optional. The subject matter is yours to choose.

The Warmup:
For background study, you'll find sixteen AAA songs including three of the five just cited in the songbook *Great Songs of the Sixties,* Quadrangle Books. Another source of dozens of AAA lyrics is *Writings and Drawings by Bob Dylan,* Knopf. To further reinforce your understanding of how the form works, reread the AAA section of Stage One's Step 2, which starts on page 22. If you happen to own recordings of any AAA songs, play and analyze the relationship between form and content.

The Example:
The following student lyric illustrates the way in which form and content are different aspects of the same thing. In fact, the concept of "Girls Night" seems inconceivable in any form but the AAA:

GIRLS NIGHT
(Final Draft)

A

In a teenager's bedroom in Pittsburgh
We whiled many hours away.
The stereo sang the songs of the Beatles,
We'd hang on each word they'd say.
We were Katie and Sue, my best friends, and me,
Life seemed so complicated then.
I'd say, "If Frank doesn't call I'll just die!"
Then he would, and I didn't; we'd laugh and we'd cry
And lift our Pepsis and propose a toast

Refrain
To GIRLS NIGHT and friendships that mean the most,
To GIRLS NIGHT.

A

In a studio apartment in Manhattan
Picking at salads and sipping chablis,
The music was Manilow, mellow and sweet,
A happy night for us three:
Kate'd just been promoted, and I'd sold my first song,
And Susie had something to tell:
She said "I've decided to marry Ted,"
And Katie and I could've dropped over dead!
We lifted our glasses in a toast instead

Refrain
To GIRLS NIGHT and friendships that mean the most
To GIRLS NIGHT.

A

In a split level house up in Larchmont
Katie had us out for the night.
Jack was off fishing—his annual trip,
So the timing and mood were just right.
It was three kids and two divorces later—
(But then who's keeping score?)
Katie announced she had had an affair
And Susie and I were so glad we were there,
And we lifted our coffee cups and drank a toast

Refrain
To GIRLS NIGHT and friendships that mean the most
To GIRLS NIGHT.

A

Well, Katie has run off to Paris,
Sue and Ted moved South near her dad,
And I'm here in Hollywood writing this song
And missing old friends—what good times we had!
We've promised to meet at the Plaza for tea
The year that we're seventy-eight.
As befitting our age we'll wear hats and white gloves
And we'll cry and we'll laugh and remember past loves
And tip our teacups and propose a toast

Refrain
To GIRLS NIGHT and friendships that mean the most
To GIRLS NIGHT, To GIRLS NIGHT, To GIRLS NIGHT.

The Analysis:

Barbara Klee made her lyric do everything the AAA does best: introduce characters, change settings and time frames, and illustrate a universal truth: abiding friendships ballast life's passages. Her title resounds in the refrain as clearly as her clinking wine glasses.

You'll recognize at the opening of each verse the repetitive device of anaphora signaling the change of settings. The toast, a repetitive *motif,* underscores the passing decades as it re-echoes from verse to verse. All three repetitive tools—the titled refrain, anaphora, and the motif—contribute to both the clarity and unity of the song.

The writer applies other binding devices that make for memorability. Alliteration: "the *s*tereo *s*ang the *s*ongs," "*d*ropped over *d*ead," "sp*l*it-*l*evel house up in *L*archmont," "*t*ip our *t*eacups"; assonance: "prop*o*se a t*o*ast," "p*i*cking . . . s*i*pping"; the specificity of salads and chablis and the allusions to the Beatles and Manilow vivify the scenes with what author Tom Wolfe calls "status details."

Virtually all these major effects were in place in the first draft of "Girls Night." Just a few minor flaws needed revision.

First Draft Critique:

The original names of the friends were Sally and Sue (sometimes Suzie); they were similar both in sound and character, so the listener could easily confuse them. Sally became Katie.

While Sue and Katie were acquiring promotions, husbands, and children, the singer lacked biographical details. She needed an identity of some kind. The rewrite turned her into a songwriter.

You'll remember from Step 6 how to use a spondee (TUMTUM) to emphasize a word in midline that you want stressed. Well, in the first verse of the first draft, the writer unintentionally stressed a word that she didn't want to call attention to: " . . . lift our BEER CANS and propose a toast. . . ." It called attention to itself for no purpose. The substituted *PEPsis* slips by unnoticed as it should.

Unlike the first three verses, the fourth lacked a setting and thereby diminished the lyric's unity. The final draft remedied the flaw: "I'm here in Hollywood."

Because of the writer's strict and unnecessary adherence to her dominant meter (TUMtata TUMtata TUMtata TUM), some lines sounded cluttered: "The stereo sang [out] the songs of the Beatles." "If Frank doesn't [ask me out] (call) I'll just die!" Deleting the bracketed words made the writing more emphatic.

Other lines needed a change of emphasis: "In a living room WAY up in Larchmont" put the stress on a function word instead of a content word. The revision emphasized the important word: "in a split level HOUSE up in Larchmont." Similarly, another line stressed the first half of a two-syllable verb, "We lifted our glasses and TOASTed instead," which is weaker than emphasizing the complete noun: "We lifted our glasses in a TOAST instead."

Perhaps the most significant improvement was one of verb tense. The original toast mistakenly used the past tense: "To girls night and friendships that MEANT the most." Although the singer is indeed looking back *(we lifted, we'd lift)* the toast itself should ring out in present tense as the friends pronounced it. Implicit in "to girls night" is "here IS to girls night" and therefore to "friendships that MEAN the most."

Summing Up:

Feel free to apply Barbara Klee's top-line device that made years roll clearly by in

"Girls Night." By applying her technique you can make your passage of time just as evident.

You have now got all the background theory and guidelines you need. Relax. Take a walk. Let your right brain go about its business. An idea will soon strike. When you're ready to jot down some random thoughts, turn to the next page.

Assignment No. 1
An AAA Lyric With a Changing Time Frame

Brainstorming/Clustering Space
(Put down random thoughts rapidly without censoring anything. Cluster any key word that needs developing or focusing. List potential titles as quickly as they come to you.)

THE FOCUS SHEET

Who is singing? _____male; _____ female; _____ either; _____ duet

What is the Viewpoint of lyric?
_____ First person (emphasis on "I").
_____ Second person (emphasis on "you"). If yes, is singer addressing _____ a particular you; _____ the collective you; _____ an absent person, place, or thing.
_____ Third person (emphasis on "he/she/they"). If yes, _____ is it an omniscient camera-eye view lyric? _____ or a singer-singee connection lyric?

What is the Voice? _____ thinking _____ talking.
Does the Voice change? _____no; _____yes.
If yes, in what line did you make it evident? _____

What is the Time Frame?
_____ The Nonspecific Present (one moment's feeling)
_____ The Habitual Present (an ongoing condition)
_____ The Particular Present (a one-time action)
_____ The Past (first-person reflection)
_____ The Past (third-person narrative)
_____ Historical Present (a past event told in present tense)
_____ The Future
_____ Does time move during the lyric? _____ no; _____ yes.
   If yes, how did you make it clear to the listener? _____

Does the lyric have a Setting? _____ no; _____ yes.
If yes, where: _____

Does the setting change? _____ no; _____ yes.
If yes, in what line did you show the change? _____

Did you imply a setting by using the word "here"? _____ no; _____ yes.
If yes, where do you picture "here"? _____
How does the lyric convey that setting?_____

What is the (one) Tone of the lyric?
_____ self-assertive (I Will Survive)   _____ reflective (Private Dancer)
_____ tongue-in-cheek (Short People)   _____ ironic (Send in the Clowns)
_____ wistful (The Way We Were)   _____ romantic (Endless Love)
_____ playful (Dress You Up)   _____ (specify other) _____

What is the relationship between singer and singee? _____
In what line did you show that relationship? _____

What is the lyric's basic form? _____ AAA; _____ AABA; _____ V/C?

Synopsize the lyric in one short sentence: _____

What is the universal situation or emotion with which you expect millions to identify? _____

What is the song's title? _____
(It should sum up your idea be identifiable after one hearing.)

First-Draft Page for Assignment No. 1
An AAA with a Changing Time Frame

One-Sentence Plot Synopsis: _____

_____

_____
(Title)

_____
_____
_____
_____
_____
_____
_____
_____
_____
_____
_____
_____
_____
_____
_____
_____
_____
_____
_____
_____
_____
_____
_____
_____
_____
_____
_____
_____
_____
_____
_____
_____
_____
_____

Date _____

Revision of AAA with Changing Time Frame

_____
(Title)

_____
_____
_____
_____
_____
_____
_____
_____
_____
_____
_____
_____
_____
_____
_____
_____
_____
_____
_____
_____
_____
_____
_____
_____
_____
_____
_____
_____
_____
_____
_____
_____
_____
_____
_____
_____
_____

© 19 _____   Date _____

ASSIGNMENT NO. 2
An AABA in the Particular Present

The Purpose:

This assignment unites two important songwriting elements—a major form and a popular time frame.

The Assignment:

Write an AABA lyric whose scenario takes place in one setting and reflects one specific moment—the particular now time frame. Design a plot in which the singee is present and the singer is thinking. The needs of your story will determine the length of your lyric, that is, whether it evolves into the classic AABA or the extended AABABA.

The Warmup:

To refresh your understanding of how the form works, read over the section on the AABA starting on page 26. When you've got a title, decide where you'll put it—at the top of the A or its last line.

A word on title placement. Sometimes beginning lyricists get overly conscientious when writing a top-line title. After opening both the first A and the second A with the title, they feel duty-bound to also start the third A with the title. You're not breaking any "rules" if you don't. If you plan to end the song with your title, omitting it from the opening line of the last verse will leave more room to build your plot to a climax. A perfect example of what I mean is the AABA "When Sunny Gets Blue."

For an example of the thinking lyric with the singee present, look back to "Fool If I Don't" on page 56. Remember that the goal is to make the listener aware that the singee is there, but the singer is thinking.

The Example: "Midnight Mood" has already illustrated the power of the particular present fused to a talking Voice. Here's another illustration of the AABA in the particular present, only this time a woman is thinking.

GOOD MORNING, GOODBYE

A   *He wakes with a start*
    His feet hit the floor
    He fumbles with buttons
    And heads for the door
    I stare at the ceiling
    And swear I won't cry
    As he whispers, "GOOD MORNING, GOODBYE"
    It's always, "GOOD MORNING, GOODBYE."

A   *I know that he has*
    To get home to his wife
    I know I'm not part of
    That part of his life
    He says to be patient
    I tell him I'll try
    But meanwhile, "GOOD MORNING, GOODBYE."
    It's always, "GOOD MORNING, GOODBYE."

B *Some days I feel like a villain*
And some days I feel like a fool
But mostly I feel like a lady in love
Who wished they'd change the rules.

A *His wife must be asking,*
"Where have you been?"
Will she believe
His story again?
Would I rather be her
Hearing the lies
Instead of "GOOD MORNING, GOODBYE"?
No, I'll take "GOOD MORNING, GOODBYE,"
I'll live with "GOOD MORNING, GOODBYE."

© 1983, By Brian Sitts. Used with permission.

The Analysis:

Simple and pared to the bone. This was Brian Sitts' first (workshop) draft—without a word out of place, without an extra syllable in sight. That of course doesn't mean that he didn't polish a lot at home to get a presentable first draft.

"Good Morning," which predates the release of "Saving All My Love for You," reflects both its theme and its form, but gives us a closeup of the darker side of the triangle.

This lyric illustrates the reason to choose the AABA when you want to dramatize one moment that goes from something, through something, to something. Like the very best AABAs, this one doesn't end until the last line.

Did you notice that the singer refers to her lover as *he* (third person), rather than the more common *you* (second person)? The lyric thereby establishes an emotional distance between the singer and singee—a subtle contribution to its effectiveness. Using the third person also guarantees that the listener will immediately know that the singer is thinking, rather than talking. Bear this choice in mind when you consider how you'll treat your singee—as *you* or *he* or *she*.

One reading isn't enough to catch all this lyric's fine features. Stop a minute and reread it aloud to hear how many sonic patterns you can identify before I point them out.

That's what I mean by a strong start that puts us right into the action. As in "All Over But the Leaving," Brian Sitts again uses alliteration and anaphora to emphasize form and meaning. First, a design of pronoun reversal *he/he/I; I/I/he:* The first verse's pattern of *He wakes/He fumbles/I stare/I swear* is inverted in the second A to *I know/I know/He says.* . . .

Without elbowing the listener, alliteration subtly links chains of thought: *feet/ floor/fumbles, start/stare/swear, wife/where/will/would, part/part/patient.* The whole fabric of the lyric is backstitched with sound motifs that outline the design: *I know/I know; not part of that part; some days/some days; I feel like/I feel like/I feel like; I'll take/I'll live.*

The bridge, a model of variation, contrasts with the verses three ways: from rising rhythm to falling rhythm; from four-foot lines to three-foot lines; from reacting to the moment to contemplating the future.

Every line is a reasonable outcome of the one before and flows easily into the next. The title couplet—the last two lines of each A—alters slightly as the story develops. Remember this device. It's one more way to emphasize likeness through difference.

Study this lyric—its rhythms, its rhyme scheme, its repetitional devices. Let it serve as a model AABA—which it is.

Summing Up:

If your aim is to write a pop song—rather than a cabaret song—then think record. By that I mean, ask yourself if your AABA could turn into a three-minute (roughly) recording. The classic AABA sometimes needs a little stretching. The verse/chorus is elastic: you just keep repeating the chorus section until you're ready to fade. A fairly wordy AABA, such as "One Hundred Ways" (147 words) became a hit by being sung through only once. If you write a leaner lyric like "Out Here on My Own," or "When I Need You," for example, you'll probably find it necessary to reprise the bridge. So decide if the bridge lyric bears repeating as in "Out Here," or if your story would benefit from new words the second time around as in "When I Need You."

This assignment may possibly be your first experience in writing an AABA. If you've been weaned on the sound of a repetitive hood chorus, I recommend a little AABA conditioning. You might check out two of Linda Ronstadt's albums of standards, "What's New?" and "Lush Life." They're both bulging with AABAs. Playing those albums and any other recordings you may own of songs listed on pages 27-28 will program your unconscious with the shape and sensibility of the form and thereby help prevent a "chorus-like" section from unwittingly intruding into your AABA.

Assignment No. 2
An AABA in the Particular Present

Brainstorming/Clustering Space
(Put down random thoughts rapidly without censoring anything. Cluster any key word that needs developing or focusing. List potential titles as quickly as they come to you.)

THE FOCUS SHEET

Who is singing? _____ male; _____ female; _____ either; _____ duet

What is the Viewpoint of lyric?
_____ First person (emphasis on "I").
_____ Second person (emphasis on "you"). If yes, is singer addressing _____ a particular you; _____ the collective you; _____ an absent person, place, or thing.
_____ Third person (emphasis on "he/she/they"). If yes, _____ is it an omniscient camera-eye view lyric? _____ or a singer-singee connection lyric?

What is the Voice? _____ thinking _____ talking.
Does the Voice change? _____ no; _____ yes.
If yes, in what line did you make it evident?

What is the Time Frame?
_____ The Nonspecific Present (one moment's feeling)
_____ The Habitual Present (an ongoing condition)
_____ The Particular Present (a one-time action)
_____ The Past (first-person reflection)
_____ The Past (third-person narrative)
_____ Historical Present (a past event told in present tense)
_____ The Future
_____ Does time move during the lyric? _____ no; _____ yes.
    If yes, how did you make it clear to the listener? _____

Does the lyric have a Setting? _____ no; _____ yes.
If yes, where: _____

Does the setting change? _____ no; _____ yes.
If yes, in what line did you show the change? _____

Did you imply a setting by using the word "here"? _____ no; _____ yes.
If yes, where do you picture "here"? _____
How does the lyric convey that setting? _____

What is the (one) Tone of the lyric?
_____ self-assertive (I Will Survive)   _____ reflective (Private Dancer)
_____ tongue-in-cheek (Short People)   _____ ironic (Send in the Clowns)
_____ wistful (The Way We Were)   _____ romantic (Endless Love)
_____ playful (Dress You Up)   _____ (specify other) _____

What is the relationship between singer and singee? _____
In what line did you show that relationship? _____

What is the lyric's basic form? _____ AAA; _____ AABA; _____ V/C?

Synopsize the lyric in one short sentence: _____

What is the universal situation or emotion with which you expect millions to identify? _____

What is the song's title? _____
(It should sum up your idea be identifiable after one hearing.)

**First-Draft Page for Assignment No. 2
An AABA Set in the Particular Present**

One-Sentence Plot Synopsis: _____
_____

_____
(Title)

_____
_____
_____
_____
_____
_____
_____
_____
_____
_____
_____
_____
_____
_____
_____
_____
_____
_____
_____
_____
_____
_____
_____
_____
_____
_____
_____
_____
_____
_____
_____
_____
_____
_____
_____

Date _____

Revision of AABA Set in the Particular Present

_____
(Title)

_____
_____
_____
_____
_____
_____
_____
_____
_____
_____
_____
_____
_____
_____
_____
_____
_____
_____
_____
_____
_____
_____
_____
_____
_____
_____
_____
_____
_____
_____
_____
_____
_____
_____
_____

© 19 _____   Date _____

ASSIGNMENT NO. 3
A Verse/Climb/Chorus with a One-Word Title

The Purpose:

To design a top-40 product by fusing a commercial title to the most commercial song form.

The Assignment:

Write a verse/chorus lyric featuring a strong, compelling, memorable, provocative, platinum record, Grammy-winning, one-word title. No limp, forgettable abstractions like Time, How, You, Then, Love. Pick a concrete noun or action verb to grab your listener's ears. "The" is not allowed. And no names, please. Your word should flash in the mind like a neon sign: Voyeur/Voyeur/Voyeur, Pressure/Pressure/Pressure, Diamonds/Diamonds/Diamonds.

The verse/chorus/bridge form has become virtually a formula. Writing with a climb instead of the predictable bridge will give your song a fresher contour. Shape the lyric this way: Verse/climb/chorus/verse/climb/chorus.

The Warmup:

If your radio dial is normally set to a top-40 station, you're familiar with this form from such hits as the Pointers' "I'm So Excited," and Madonna's "Open Your Heart." But it wouldn't hurt to review the function of the climb on page 40.

Now for the title part. Remember the one-word title exercise you did in step one? Check back to see if it says "write me!" If it doesn't excite you, then you'll have to go on a title hunt.

Obviously, we get ideas more readily when we're looking. So look—in the newspaper, magazines, at TV commercials, in the dictionary, the thesaurus. When you're outdoors, scour billboards, highway signs, bus ads and store windows. All you need is one compelling word—one, of course, that suggests to you a plot with universal appeal.

Doing any of the above could produce a half-dozen titles. But in the unlikely event that all these devices fail, brainstorming will surely turn up something.

The Example:

Here's a perfect example of both the form and the type of title that can put you on the charts. An eight-bar verse leads into an eight-bar climb which leads into an eight-bar chorus. Then the three parts repeat. I recommend that you let this lyric be your matrix. The song came about when the team was asked to write a shuffle for a recording project. To get the feel of the rhythm, start saying DAdaDAda/DAdaDAda/DAdaDAda/DAdaDAda over a few times in a slow four till it gets you moving your head side to side like a pendulum.

MANHANDLED

Verse   *Oh baby, when I'm good, I'm good,*
              But when I'm bad I'm better.
              I'm a fire without a match,
              Waiting for someone to set her.

Climb	*Oooh——don't want a guy who's big on talk—* *A lot of words that don't pay off.* *Words are not my stuff,* *Lip service isn't enough.* *I want to be*
Chorus	*MANHANDLED tonight* *Tied up in the arms of someone holding me tight.* *MANHANDLED tonight* *By the man who can handle me right.*
Verse	*Oh baby, can you measure up* *To all my expectations?* *If your bite's as good as your bark,* *I'll show you my appreciation.*
Climb	*Oooh, don't want a guy who's big on cool,* *Cool is not my style.* *Hot blooded wins by a mile.* *I want to be*
Chorus	*MANHANDLED tonight* *Tied up in the arms of someone holding me tight.* *MANHANDLED tonight* *By the man who can handle me right.*

The Analysis:

If you closed your eyes as someone read you the lyric, I bet you could *see* each of the separate six sections stream across your mind's movie screen because the opening line of each is outlined by a repeated pattern of sound: The verses both start with "Oh, baby" and the climbs both begin with "Ooooh, don't want a man who's big on _____." The chorus, like the majority of choruses, repeats exactly. Good writing reinforces structure through repetition.

Like all well-conceived verse/chorus lyrics, the chorus is the natural outcome of the thought . . . AND THAT IS WHY I SAY: "I want to be manhandled tonight. . . ." And the title is of course a precise summation of the song's plot.

Here's a writer who delights in word play—from her opening line, a "borrowing" from Mae West, to her fresh title concept, manhandled/handled by a man. She follows those with the paradoxical accident-about-to-happen line *fire without a match,* the layered meaning of "lip service," the fun of reversing the cliché, "his bark is worse than his bite," and the antithesis of "cool/hot (blooded)."

When you hear the familiar music business cry *send us a hit single,* a lyric like "Manhandled" is what's wanted. It typifies what's meant by commercial: it's simple, direct, clear, memorable, and universal in its appeal. In addition to those essentials, "Manhandled" is also fresh, playful, and well-crafted.

Summing Up:

Like all pros, Arline Udis doesn't wait around hoping the muse will come calling. Arline summons her muse every morning by sitting down to write. She can write on demand, write under pressure, write for a situation, write for an artist. And of course, she can rewrite. It's her determination to take a lyric to the limit that zoomed her career from her first class assignment to her first song contract in less than two years.

Success is not a mysterious process. It's simply a matter of practice and determination. To make sure you're on the right (commercial) track, be sure your title will lead you to express a viewpoint that will appeal to millions.

Assignment No. 3
A Verse/Climb/Chorus with a One-Word Title

Brainstorming/Clustering Space

(Put down random thoughts rapidly without censoring anything. Cluster any key word that needs developing or focusing. List potential titles as quickly as they come to you.)

THE FOCUS SHEET

Who is singing? _____ male; _____ female; _____ either; _____ duet

What is the Viewpoint of lyric?
_____ First person (emphasis on "I").
_____ Second person (emphasis on "you"). If yes, is singer addressing _____ a particular you; _____ the collective you; _____ an absent person, place, or thing.
_____ Third person (emphasis on "he/she/they"). If yes, _____ is it an omniscient camera-eye view lyric? _____ or a singer-singee connection lyric?

What is the Voice? _____ thinking _____ talking.
Does the Voice change? _____ no; _____ yes.
If yes, in what line did you make it evident?

What is the Time Frame?
_____ The Nonspecific Present (one moment's feeling)
_____ The Habitual Present (an ongoing condition)
_____ The Particular Present (a one-time action)
_____ The Past (first-person reflection)
_____ The Past (third-person narrative)
_____ Historical Present (a past event told in present tense)
_____ The Future
_____ Does time move during the lyric? _____ no; _____ yes.
     If yes, how did you make it clear to the listener? _____

Does the lyric have a Setting? _____ no; _____ yes.
If yes, where: _____

Does the setting change? _____ no; _____ yes.
If yes, in what line did you show the change? _____

Did you imply a setting by using the word "here"? _____ no; _____ yes.
If yes, where do you picture "here"? _____
How does the lyric convey that setting? _____

What is the (one) Tone of the lyric?
_____ self-assertive (I Will Survive)   _____ reflective (Private Dancer)
_____ tongue-in-cheek (Short People)   _____ ironic (Send in the Clowns)
_____ wistful (The Way We Were)   _____ romantic (Endless Love)
_____ playful (Dress You Up)   _____ (specify other) _____

What is the relationship between singer and singee? _____
In what line did you show that relationship? _____

What is the lyric's basic form? _____ AAA; _____ AABA; _____ V/C?

Synopsize the lyric in one short sentence: _____

What is the universal situation or emotion with which you expect millions to identify? _____

What is the song's title? _____
(It should sum up your idea be identifiable after one hearing.)

First-Draft Page for Assignment No. 3

One-Sentence Plot Synopsis: _____

_____

_____
(Title)

_____

_____

_____

_____

_____

_____

_____

_____

_____

_____

_____

_____

_____

_____

_____

_____

_____

_____

_____

_____

_____

_____

_____

_____

_____

_____

_____

_____

_____

_____

Date _____

Revision of Verse/Climb/Chorus

_____
(Title)

_____
_____
_____
_____
_____
_____
_____
_____
_____
_____
_____
_____
_____
_____
_____
_____
_____
_____
_____
_____
_____
_____
_____
_____
_____
_____
_____
_____
_____
_____
_____
_____
_____
_____
_____
_____
_____
_____
_____

© 19 _____   Date _____

ASSIGNMENT NO. 4
A Lyric with a Question Title

The Purpose:

First, to apply a classic attention-getting device to lyric writing. And secondly, to increase your creative output by thinking in terms of categories. For example, a song form has already acted to springboard you into three lyrics. This time, a title will trigger your lyric. The next one will employ a common theme; and so on.

The Assignment:

From "Which twin has the Toni?" to "Have you driven a Ford lately?" advertising copywriters often pose questions to sell products. So do songwriters: "Why Can't We Be Friends?" "Who Put the Bomp (in the bomp-ba bomp-ba bomp)?" "Where Have All the Flowers Gone?" "Would Jesus Wear a Rolex?"

As these titles demonstrate, questions can address any subject, be asked in any tone, and work in any song form. The title may appear only once in the opening line ("What Are You Doing the Rest of Your Life?") or be restated relentlessly in the chorus ("Why Don't We Do It in the Road?").

The Warmup:

The toughest part of the assignment may be to think of the question. Perhaps you've got a few stored in your title file waiting to be written. But if your mind's a blank, brainstorming can be the quickest route to "eureka!"

Here's a technique to access your imaginative right brain. Try dividing your brainstorming page into five sections headed Who, What, When, Where, Why. Then, starting from the first word—and without censoring yourself—write down as fast as you can every question that springs to mind. Keep going till you run out of ideas, then move to the next word, and so on. Something is bound to turn up before you finish the last W.

But just in case you're "titleless" after brainstorming, you might find inspiration in *The Complete Lyrics of Cole Porter*. Among the memorable questions he asked are *"What Is This Thing Called Love?" "Why Can't You Behave?" "Where Is the Life That Late I Led?" "Who Wants to be a Millionaire?" "Weren't We Fools?" "After You, Who?"*

No particular caveats come with this assignment, except the reminder to "prove your title."

The Example:

Here's a case of the content dictating the verse/chorus form.

HAVE YOU SEEN MY GUY?

Verse *I met him at the unisex barber.*
He was sittin' in the very next chair.
I thought he was an absolute knockout.
He had the most remarkable hair.

Verse *He wore the greatest dangle-down earrings.*
A dagger and a skull and a bomb.
'N' on his arms his sexy tattoos said:
"Death Before Dishonor" and "Mom."

Chorus

HAVE YOU SEEN MY GUY?
He's so hot I want to die.
HAVE YOU SEEN MY GUY?
He's the zapple of my eye.
He's a thriller, he's a killer way beyond compare,
The guy with the purple leather motorcycle jacket
And the incandescent technicolor hair.

Verse

He changed his name from Spencer to Spider.
I love him 'n' he's terribly tough.
He wants to get a job in a rock band.
Writin', playin', singin', 'n' stuff.

Verse

He took me for a ride on his Harley;
We did some window shopping at Flip.
He really is a man of the eighties—
He's so punky, funky, hunky, 'n' hip.

Chorus

HAVE YOU SEEN MY GUY?
He's so hot I want to die!
HAVE YOU SEEN MY GUY?
He's the zapple of my eye.
He's a thriller, he's a killer way beyond compare,
The guy with the purple leather motorcycle jacket
And the incandescent technicolor hair.

Verse

He took a scarlet magical marker
'N' wrote his number on the back of my hand.
He said next time he'd take me to heaven,
'N' then he split; and in the rain the number ran.

Verse

'N' now my life's a total disaster.
Oh where, Oh where, Oh where can he be?
I'm des-per-ate-ly seeking my baby,
That's why I'm on the cable TV
Askin' everybody

Chorus

HAVE YOU SEEN MY GUY?
He's so hot I want to die.
HAVE YOU SEEN MY GUY?
He's the zapple of my eye.
He's a thriller, he's a killer way beyond compare
The guy with the purple leather motorcycle jacket
And the incandescent technicolor hair.

The Analysis:

That's putting the Who, What, When, and Where in the first two lines! Just as the second verse should do, this one fills us in with more facts. And because Jim Morgan is a lyricist who sees the scene before his eyes, we get plenty of visual detail. And we remember the details because the specifics land at the end of lines for emphasis: *barber/chair/knockout/hair, earrings/jacket* and so on.

Knowing all the "rules" of writing, Morgan has earned the right to bend or break them. Here he flouts the caveat to choose the timeless over the timely as he plays punk trendiness for all it's worth. And when he feels the need, he even makes up words ("zapple" and "hunky").

He supports his light-hearted tone with close rhymes (thriller/killer) (punky/funky/hunky), and the teenage flair for melodrama (des-per-ate-ly seeking/total disaster).

Although not a musician, he has a composer's instinct for rhythmic variation, which is how he designs lyrics that collaborators find easy to set. Take, for example, the contrast between the basic eighth-note feel of the verses (cherry/cherry/cherry words) with the half-note feel of the title's drawn-out (kum-quat) words Seeeeen Myyyyyy Guyyyyy.

In the chorus' second half, he recycles the verse's rhythm, only this time with effective trochaic overkill with three non-stop bars of cherry-words: *PURple LEATHer MOTorCYcle JACKet AND the INcanDEScent TECHniCOLor HAIR.*

Summing Up:

Nothing beats the instant familiarity of a common expression to title a song: from "What's New?" to "What Have You Done for Me Lately?" On the off chance that the warmup suggestions yield nothing that gets you excited, check out Eric Partridge's *A Dictionary of Catch Phrases* for a question that hasn't yet topped the charts.

Before you plunge in to write, let your title simmer. Walk around with it for a day or two. Let your unconscious take over. When you go to bed, file a request to your dreaming mind to come up with a plot treatment. Sleep on it—which, translated, really means let your imaginative right brain take over. The song's form will reveal itself.

Write only when you're ready.

Assignment No. 4
A Lyric with a Question Title

Brainstorming/Clustering Space

(Put down random thoughts rapidly without censoring anything. Cluster any key word that needs developing or focusing. List potential titles as quickly as they come to you.)

THE FOCUS SHEET

Who is singing? _____ male; _____ female; _____ either; _____ duet

What is the Viewpoint of lyric?
_____ First person (emphasis on "I").
_____ Second person (emphasis on "you"). If yes, is singer addressing _____ a particular you; _____ the collective you; _____ an absent person, place, or thing.
_____ Third person (emphasis on "he/she/they"). If yes, _____ is it an omniscient camera-eye view lyric? _____ or a singer-singee connection lyric?

What is the Voice? _____ thinking _____ talking.
Does the Voice change? _____ no; _____ yes.
If yes, in what line did you make it evident?

What is the Time Frame?
_____ The Nonspecific Present (one moment's feeling)
_____ The Habitual Present (an ongoing condition)
_____ The Particular Present (a one-time action)
_____ The Past (first-person reflection)
_____ The Past (third-person narrative)
_____ Historical Present (a past event told in present tense)
_____ The Future
_____ Does time move during the lyric? _____ no; _____ yes.
If yes, how did you make it clear to the listener? _____

Does the lyric have a Setting? _____ no; _____ yes.
If yes, where: _____

Does the setting change? _____ no; _____ yes.
If yes, in what line did you show the change? _____

Did you imply a setting by using the word "here"? _____ no; _____ yes.
If yes, where do you picture "here"? _____
How does the lyric convey that setting? _____

What is the (one) Tone of the lyric?
_____ self-assertive (I Will Survive)   _____ reflective (Private Dancer)
_____ tongue-in-cheek (Short People)   _____ ironic (Send in the Clowns)
_____ wistful (The Way We Were)   _____ romantic (Endless Love)
_____ playful (Dress You Up)   _____ (specify other) _____

What is the relationship between singer and singee? _____
In what line did you show that relationship? _____

What is the lyric's basic form? _____ AAA; _____ AABA; _____ V/C?

Synopsize the lyric in one short sentence: _____

What is the universal situation or emotion with which you expect millions to identify? _____

What is the song's title? _____
(It should sum up your idea be identifiable after one hearing.)

First-Draft Page for Assignment No. 4
A Lyric with a Question Title

One-Sentence Plot Synopsis: _____

_____

_____
(Title)

_____

_____

_____

_____

_____

_____

_____

_____

_____

_____

_____

_____

_____

_____

_____

_____

_____

_____

_____

_____

_____

_____

_____

_____

_____

_____

_____

_____

_____

_____

_____

Date _____

Revision of Lyric with a Question Title

_____
(Title)

_____

_____

_____

_____

_____

_____

_____

_____

_____

_____

_____

_____

_____

_____

_____

_____

_____

_____

_____

_____

_____

_____

_____

_____

_____

_____

_____

_____

_____

_____

© 19 _____   Date _____

ASSIGNMENT NO. 5
A Breakup Song in Second-Person Viewpoint

The Purpose:

To help you generate more plot concepts from categories. You've already worked from three forms and a title. This time the category is a common theme. One of the most common is breaking up.

The Assignment:

Write a present-tense lyric in which the singer is in the act of breaking up with a love partner.

Breakup songs cover all the phases of disaffiliation: analyzing the relationship ("You Don't Bring Me Flowers"), finding clues that may lead to the breakup ("You've Been Talkin' in Your Sleep"), the confrontation ("How Am I Supposed to Live Without You?"), the one-more-time request ("Touch Me in the Morning"), and of course the actual act of leaving ("You're Moving Out Today").

There's also the *goin' out of my head/can't smile without you* aftermath of a breakup. But that's another theme: an I-can't-get-over-you song.

Because there is no more compelling way to write than to put your character in the thick of a dialogue with a singee, put your breakup in the present tense. The Voice: talking. The Who, the Where and the Why are in your hands. So is its form.

The Warmup:

Stephen Sondheim has written two of the theater's most riveting breakup songs: the caustic "Could I Leave You" from *Follies* and "We Do Not Belong Together" from *Sunday in the Park with George*. The former exemplifies the use of *meaningful sequence* in plot development. The latter is a duet of rare poignancy. Both these lyrics are worth study from the standpoint of song design.

Now for the plot. Decide who's leaving whom—and why? Make the lovers' parting spring from a reason you can empathize with. Brainstorm for a breakup motive. List all the possible reasons you can imagine—jealousy, incompatibility, infidelity, and so on. List-making is a powerful aid to increasing your conceptual ability.

Consider the setting. Where are they? Again, make a list of all the places you can picture for the lovers' final scene. Or maybe it's a farewell phone call.

Finally, be sure every line reflects the way we talk.

The Example:

This lyric resulted from a workshop assignment to write words to music. Each writer received a cassette with an Italian hit song performed and written by Umberto Tozzi. (Tozzi was the lyricist/composer/artist of the Italian hit "Gloria," which—with an English lyric by Trevor Veitch—became an American success for Laura Branigan.)

Students were to define what the music was saying to them and then write a lyric that matched that emotion. One student perfectly captured the hard edge and raw passion of the melody. Like many Euro-Pop hits, the music structure differs somewhat from our classic AAA, AABA, Verse-Chorus forms. We could label it AABABA. Treating the music as an augmented AABA, the writer put his title and the substance of the plot in the A sections and repeated the lyric of the bridge. He designed the lyric as a woman's song.

NO REASON TO STAY

A *Watch if you want while I clean out my closet,*
Gonna pack up my bags and put down a deposit
On a place of my own where I won't need your blessing.
Gotta make a new start and I guess today is the day.
I've got NO REASON TO STAY.

A *Why should I live by the rules that you've broken?*
Tell me why in the world I should leave myself open
To the hurt that I feel when you want me to hold you?
Tell me why I should act out the role you want me to play?
I've got NO REASON TO STAY.

B *I know you've heard it before*
And so you're bound to ignore me now.
You'll make a promise and then
You'll think you have me again somehow.
But you see I've gotten stronger
And I won't take it anymore.
This time, I'm gonna walk out tall.
This time, I won't fall back on you.

A *Here is your key and the string that it's tied to;*
It reminds me too much of the ways I was lied to—
Of the nights when I spent more time crying than sleeping—
Of the gifts that you gave me to keep me from running away.
I've got NO REASON TO STAY.

B *I know you've heard it before*
And so you're bound to ignore me now.
You'll make a promise and then
You'll think you have me again somehow.
But you see I've gotten stronger,
And I won't take it anymore.
This time—I'm gonna walk out tall.
This time, I won't crawl back to you.

A *You can look up my name in the book when you're lonely.*
We can talk if you like, but don't call if you only
Want to ask me again how on earth I could go.
If you don't have the answer, you know why I needed to say
I've got NO REASON TO STAY.

© 1983, by Brian Sitts. Used with permission.

The Analysis:

The lyric grabs our attention with its opening challenge: "Watch, if you want. . . ." and we're hooked. A nonstop explosion of hurt and anger ticks off the reasons for finally packing her bags and calling it a day. The singer builds a convincing case; and because her action sounds justified, we can identify with her.

The most striking element of the lyric is a consistent (apocopated) rhyme pattern that links key words and unifies each A section: *blessing/guess; hold you/role; sleeping/keep; go,(If)/know.*

The writer employs many forms of repetition for emphasis: in the first verse, the verb sequence of *gonna pack/gotta make;* in the second, underscoring *why—Why should I live/Tell me why/Tell me why;* in the third, echoed words strengthen opening lines—*Of the nights/Of the gifts.* In the bridge we hear two more instances: *You'll make/You'll think; This time/This time.* And in the last A, there's a more subtle sound linkage, the alliterated *-l-* in *look/lonely/like.*

You'll notice that the reprise of the bridge contains an intensification of emotion: *won't fall back on you; won't crawl back to you.*

Did you hear how the writer varied the meter by changing the end punctuation on three occasions from end-stopped to run-on lines? In the first, second, and fourth A, the thought expressed in the second line spills over into the next line. This non-stop emotional outpouring contributes to our sensing the singer's agitated state.

Clearly, each word was chosen with care, but the writing never gets slick. For example, genuine feeling takes priority over perfect rhyme: we hear unstressed (*broken/open*) and diminished rhyme (*hold/role*) ring out with conversational naturalness.

Summing Up:

Thrusting the singer into the act of leaving—rather than having her merely think about doing it or talk about doing it—infuses "No Reason to Stay" with immediacy. You can make the second-person talking Voice do the same for your breakup song.

Let your plot develop in your unconscious. Give it lots of incubation time. Then believe in your characters. If *you* do, so will your listener.

Assignment No. 5
A Breakup Song in Second-Person Viewpoint

Brainstorming/Clustering Space

(Put down random thoughts rapidly without censoring anything. Cluster any key word that needs developing or focusing. List potential titles as quickly as they come to you.)

THE FOCUS SHEET

Who is singing? _____ male; _____ female; _____ either; _____ duet

What is the Viewpoint of lyric?
_____ First person (emphasis on "I").
_____ Second person (emphasis on "you"). If yes, is singer addressing _____ a particular you; _____ the collective you; _____ an absent person, place, or thing.
_____ Third person (emphasis on "he/she/they"). If yes, _____ is it an omniscient camera-eye view lyric? _____ or a singer-singee connection lyric?

What is the Voice? _____ thinking _____ talking.
Does the Voice change? _____ no; _____ yes.
If yes, in what line did you make it evident?

What is the Time Frame?
_____ The Nonspecific Present (one moment's feeling)
_____ The Habitual Present (an ongoing condition)
_____ The Particular Present (a one-time action)
_____ The Past (first-person reflection)
_____ The Past (third-person narrative)
_____ Historical Present (a past event told in present tense)
_____ The Future
_____ Does time move during the lyric? _____ no; _____ yes.
If yes, how did you make it clear to the listener? _____

Does the lyric have a Setting? _____ no; _____ yes.
If yes, where: _____

Does the setting change? _____ no; _____ yes.
If yes, in what line did you show the change? _____

Did you imply a setting by using the word "here"? _____ no; _____ yes.
If yes, where do you picture "here"? _____
How does the lyric convey that setting? _____

What is the (one) Tone of the lyric?
_____ self-assertive (I Will Survive)   _____ reflective (Private Dancer)
_____ tongue-in-cheek (Short People)   _____ ironic (Send in the Clowns)
_____ wistful (The Way We Were)   _____ romantic (Endless Love)
_____ playful (Dress You Up)   _____ (specify other) _____

What is the relationship between singer and singee? _____
In what line did you show that relationship? _____

What is the lyric's basic form? _____ AAA; _____ AABA; _____ V/C?

Synopsize the lyric in one short sentence: _____

What is the universal situation or emotion with which you expect millions to identify? _____

What is the song's title? _____
(It should sum up your idea be identifiable after one hearing.)

First-Draft Page for Assignment No. 5
A Breakup Song in Second-Person

One-Sentence Plot Synopsis: _____

_____

_____
(Title)

_____

_____

_____

_____

_____

_____

_____

_____

_____

_____

_____

_____

_____

_____

_____

_____

_____

_____

_____

_____

_____

_____

_____

_____

_____

_____

_____

_____

_____

Date _____

Revision of Breakup Song in Second Person

_____
(Title)

_____
_____
_____
_____
_____
_____
_____
_____
_____
_____
_____
_____
_____
_____
_____
_____
_____
_____
_____
_____
_____
_____
_____
_____
_____
_____
_____
_____
_____
_____
_____
_____
_____
_____
_____
_____
_____

© 19 _____   Date _____

ASSIGNMENT NO. 6
A Third-Person Camera-Eye View

The Purpose:

To use the camera-eye Viewpoint to illustrate a truth about human nature or society.

The Assignment:

Becoming a camera enables you to say things about the world around you that neither first person nor second person permits. When you're writing from the omniscient third person the singer maintains anonymity—giving the facts without passing judgment.

You can choose either to show us a truth like the fact that today's teenagers have inherited a tough world ("Jack and Diane"), or to paint a portrait of a recognizable archetype as in "Old Hippie," which illustrates that some former Sixties activists, now middle-aged, feel ill at ease in this decade. Depending on your purpose, either name your character(s) (as in "Eleanor Rigby") or make your title characterize him ("Nowhere Man") or her ("Valley Girl").

Put your lyric into the habitual present time frame to reinforce the ongoing nature of the situation.

The Warmup:

Refer to the Third Person diagram on page 52 for some camera-eye songs to study. Look back over "Sue and John," a classically simple AAA on page 24. This time re-examine it from the aspect of the omniscient third person to see how the writer achieved her effects.

A tip on form: Both the verse/chorus form ("She's Leaving Home" and "Jack and Diane") and the AAA form ("16th Avenue") are good frameworks for your statement because they lend themselves to multiple character sketches, moving time frames, and changing settings. The AABA is the least likely to serve your purpose.

Before you begin to write, be sure that you have devised a scenario for your individual singee that is characteristic of not just of one, but of millions.

The Example:

To illustrate an axiom in three one-act scenes, Maureen Sugden picked the AAA, the natural framework.

DYING ON THE VINE

*Every day like clockwork, provided that the weather's fine
Martha takes her lunch to the playground down the block.
She's a first-rate secretary who's just turned thirty-nine.
Tossing bread crumbs to a pigeon, she's soon feeding half the flock.
The laughter of the children feeds the ache behind her breast.
She has measured out her life with coffee spoons and single beds.
Now, too late, she feels the need that will not be expressed:
To lean down and touch her lips to her own children's shining heads.
"I want someone else's life," she says. "I get no joy from mine.
Like a flower past its prime, I am DYING ON THE VINE."*

Laurie's dryer's broken; she's hanging laundry on the line—
White flags wave surrender in the sultry summer breeze.
Above the screen door's flapping she can hear the baby whine
While the three-year old, just toilet-trained, stands clinging to her knees.
So she falls back on the dream that's always rescued her before;
Limousines and beaded gowns, lobster tails on silver trays,
Men who light your cigarette, then whisk you out the door
To a moonlit beach where whisper-soft calypso music plays.
"I want someone else's life," she says. "I get no joy from mine.
Like a flower past its prime, I am DYING ON THE VINE."

Waking up at poolside, Miranda takes a sip of wine.
Her watch says four more hours until dinner on the yacht.
She has spent each morning shopping, and the men here are divine.
She's got everything—why be concerned with everything she's not?
But it's funny how your mind works when you've time upon your hands.
She's been feeling something vaguely wrong—a dread without a name.
Hummingbird in constant flight, she drinks and never lands,
Though she longs for solid ground, she fears she'll always be the same.
"I want someone else's life," she says. "I get no joy from mine.
Like a flower past its prime, I am DYING ON THE VINE."

The Analysis:

As "Cat's in the Cradle" shows us that the apple doesn't fall far from the tree, and "Harper Valley PTA," illustrates that people in glass houses shouldn't throw stones, "Dying on the Vine" dramatizes that the other man's grass is always greener. It's interesting that the writer illustrated an axiom by using a different common expression.

The lyric's design is unique: I know of no other lyric in which each verse—*a tableau vivant*—serves as the foil for the subsequent one. The verses' cumulative effect underscore the irony.

Maureen Sugden etches her vignettes on our memory with action verbs and Kodak words: *Tosses bread crumbs to a pigeon; hanging laundry on the line; white flags wave surrender; three-year old clinging to her knees.*

The technicolor documentary comes with a stereo sound track: *the laughter of the children, the screen door's flapping, the baby's whine, whisper-soft calypso music.* Who needs a video?

The image of *lobster tails on silver trays* deserves mention both for its visual impact and its musicality. Like a Chardin still life, the crusty matte-red shells on a shiny metal surface make a striking contrast in colors and textures. The manner in which the words create their special sonic effect requires some analysis.

If you slowly say *lobster tails on silver trays* you can probably pinpoint the repeated sounds that please the ear; the ER in lobstER and silvER and the T—S in TailS and TrayS. But the patterns of consonants are more intricate than that: one is a linear motif of LRTS/LRTS which you can see this way:

LobsteRTailSsiLveRTrayS

The second pattern counterpoints the first in a motif of reversed consonants SRTL/LTRS that you can see like this:

LobSteRTaiLssiLverTRayS

All the elements combine to make a memorable line.

And the names—(spinster) Martha, (housewife) Laurie, (playgirl) Miranda. Perfect casting. When christening your characters (and towns, and streets, and bars) be careful to make both the sound and connotation of the name reflect the characteristics you want to emphasize.

Summing Up:

In case you're feeling "idea-less," I recommend a browse through a book of axioms. *(The Concise Oxford Dictionary of Proverbs* is a good one to own.) You'll find dozens of concepts for a lyric statement; for example, judge not, that ye be not judged, or when poverty comes in the door, love flies out the window. Some idea is bound to jump off the page.

Assignment No. 6
A Third-Person Camera-Eye View

Brainstorming/Clustering Space

(Put down random thoughts rapidly without censoring anything. Cluster any key word that needs developing or focusing. List potential titles as quickly as they come to you.)

THE FOCUS SHEET

Who is singing? _____male; _____ female; _____ either; _____ duet

What is the Viewpoint of lyric?
_____ First person (emphasis on "I").
_____ Second person (emphasis on "you"). If yes, is singer addressing _____ a particular you; _____ the collective you; _____ an absent person, place, or thing.
_____ Third person (emphasis on "he/she/they"). If yes, _____ is it an omniscient camera-eye view lyric? _____ or a singer-singee connection lyric?

What is the Voice? _____ thinking _____ talking.
Does the Voice change? _____no; _____yes.
If yes, in what line did you make it evident?

What is the Time Frame?
_____ The Nonspecific Present (one moment's feeling)
_____ The Habitual Present (an ongoing condition)
_____ The Particular Present (a one-time action)
_____ The Past (first-person reflection)
_____ The Past (third-person narrative)
_____ Historical Present (a past event told in present tense)
_____ The Future
_____ Does time move during the lyric? _____ no; _____ yes.
If yes, how did you make it clear to the listener? _____

Does the lyric have a Setting? _____ no; _____ yes.
If yes, where: _____

Does the setting change? _____ no; _____ yes.
If yes, in what line did you show the change? _____

Did you imply a setting by using the word "here"? _____ no; _____ yes.
If yes, where do you picture "here"? _____
How does the lyric convey that setting?_____

What is the (one) Tone of the lyric?
_____ self-assertive (I Will Survive)   _____ reflective (Private Dancer)
_____ tongue-in-cheek (Short People)   _____ ironic (Send in the Clowns)
_____ wistful (The Way We Were)   _____ romantic (Endless Love)
_____ playful (Dress You Up)   _____ (specify other) _____

What is the relationship between singer and singee? _____
In what line did you show that relationship? _____

What is the lyric's basic form? _____ AAA; _____ AABA; _____ V/C?

Synopsize the lyric in one short sentence: _____

What is the universal situation or emotion with which you expect millions to identify? _____

What is the song's title? _____
(It should sum up your idea be identifiable after one hearing.)

First-Draft Page for Assignment No. 6
A Third-Person Camera-Eye View

One-Sentence Plot Synopsis: _____

_____

_____
(Title)

_____

_____

_____

_____

_____

_____

_____

_____

_____

_____

_____

_____

_____

_____

_____

_____

_____

_____

_____

_____

_____

_____

_____

_____

_____

_____

_____

_____

_____

_____

Date _____

Revision of Third-Person Camera-Eye View

_____

(Title)

© 19 _____   Date _____

ASSIGNMENT NO. 7
A Verse/Chorus Lyric with a Simile or Metaphor Title

The Purpose:
To practice figurative language and to exercise your verse/chorus muscles.

The Assignment:
Write a verse/chorus lyric that features either a simile or a metaphor in the title. You'll remember from Step 5 that a simile states a comparison; it likens two dissimilar things by saying one thing is like another, as in Bob Seger's hit "(I'm) *Like* a Rock"—a person is like a rock. A metaphor treats something as if it actually were something else, as in Paul Simon's "I *Am* a Rock"—a person *is* a rock.

So you have a choice: a simile title such as "It Was Almost *Like* a Song," or a metaphor title such as "You *Are* Music." In a simile, the comparison is stated; in a metaphor it's implied.

The Warmup:
If you've already got a title, then you're all set to go. If you don't, try to generate one by free-association in a two-step process. First, start with an important content word that springs to mind; for example, it could be *you, life, men, time, love,* and so on. Let's illustrate with *love.*

Put your chosen word, in this case *love,* on the left side of your brainstorming page. On the right side of the page quickly list all the things you could liken *love* to. Here, for example, are a few metaphors that have served lyricists well:

LOVE	is/is like	a sea voyage
	is/is like	a game of chance
	is/is like	the weather
	is/is like	a song
	is/is like	a journey
	is/is like	a play

Keep going till you run out of comparisons. Step two: Go back and pick the simile/metaphor you like best. Using that as your nucleus word, start to cluster for associations. Here, from a class exercise is one student's five-minute clustering from the word *journey.*

As you see, it triggered two titles: "You've Got the Green Light Tonight," and "Love's a Two-Way Street."

If your first clustering nets nothing interesting, pick a second metaphor word, and so on, until clustering triggers a title that excites you. Once you've got your title, the main thing to remember about figurative language is *don't overdo it*: remember, a metaphor should *make* a point, not *be* the point. Before you start to write, review the metaphor guidelines beginning on page 93.

The Example:

This student example evolved from this assignment and earned for the writer her first publishing contract and record.

SLY LIKE A FOX

Verse

*You think I'm your vixen
You play your tricks
And I come.
You think I can't resist a man
So handsome.
You figure you can win.
You can get yourself in to me.
But the closer you come
The clearer it is I see.*

Chorus

*That you are SLY LIKE A FOX,
Clever and charming,
You are SLY LIKE A FOX,
Smooth and disarming,
You are SLY LIKE A FOX
With that sweet way of talking,
You are SLY LIKE A FOX,
Patiently stalking your prey.*

Verse

*Baby, we're through—
I've had enough o' you, so leave me alone.
Never comin' back, gonna cover my track,
Gonna disconnect my phone.
Don't send flowers,
Or wait for me hours to show.
You're trying to trap me,
But everything's telling me no!—*

Chorus

*That you are SLY LIKE A FOX,
Clever and charming,
You are SLY LIKE A FOX,
Smooth and disarming,
You are SLY LIKE A FOX
With that sweet way of talking,
You are SLY LIKE A FOX,
Patiently stalking your prey.*

Bridge	*I've gotten wise,*
	I see behind your eyes.
	There's no more time to wait,
	I'm getting out before it's too late.

Chorus	*'Cause you are SLY LIKE A FOX,*
	Seductive, deceiving,
	SLY LIKE A FOX,
	You had me believing, but
	You're SLY LIKE A FOX,
	Crafty and cunning,
	You are SLY LIKE A FOX,
	That's why I'm running away.

(repeat chorus to fade)

The Analysis:

With a simple simile the writer portrays the wily ways of a handsome womanizer—rather like the singee in "You're So Vain"—only more so.

Regine Urbach avoided the trap of overdoing the metaphor. She used just a few associated theme words to augment the title: *vixen, stalking, prey, trap, crafty, cunning.* That's all it took. The rest of the language is literal: *"don't send flowers . . . gonna disconnect the phone. . . ."*

You may have noticed that some of the lines in the second verse appear longer than corresponding lines in the first. That's because they were shaped by a composer/lyricist who felt a need to vary the eighth notes in the first verse (cherry words) to sixteenth notes (huckleberry words) in the second verse. It works.

The chorus' rhyme pattern is fresh with *talking/stalking* and *cunning/running* sounding like interior rhymes. The last line of the first two choruses satisfies the ear with its book-end pinging *PAtiently stalking your PREY.* The song's final line illustrates the technique of putting the payoff at the end of the final chorus: *. . . that's why I'm running away.* The *aWAY* echoes back to both the PREY and the -A- sounds of the bridge's *wAit/lAte* and brings a sense of emotional closure.

Incidentally, the writer was aware that her title was ungrammatical—that it should be "Sly *as* a Fox." She simply preferred the effect of *like.* When you know the rule, and your instinct says break it, honor your instinct.

Summing Up:

A final reminder on the subject of not carrying figurative language too far: if your metaphor becomes improbable, your lyric becomes unbelievable. Make your metaphor true to life.

Assignment No. 7
A Verse/Chorus Lyric with a Simile/Metaphor Title

Brainstorming/Clustering Space

(Put down random thoughts rapidly without censoring anything. Cluster any key word that needs developing or focusing. List potential titles as quickly as they come to you.)

THE FOCUS SHEET

Who is singing? _____ male; _____ female; _____ either; _____ duet

What is the Viewpoint of lyric?

_____ First person (emphasis on "I").

_____ Second person (emphasis on "you"). If yes, is singer addressing _____ a particular you; _____ the collective you; _____ an absent person, place, or thing.

_____ Third person (emphasis on "he/she/they"). If yes, _____ is it an omniscient camera-eye view lyric? _____ or a singer-singee connection lyric?

What is the Voice? _____ thinking _____ talking.

Does the Voice change? _____ no; _____ yes.

If yes, in what line did you make it evident?

What is the Time Frame?

_____ The Nonspecific Present (one moment's feeling)

_____ The Habitual Present (an ongoing condition)

_____ The Particular Present (a one-time action)

_____ The Past (first-person reflection)

_____ The Past (third-person narrative)

_____ Historical Present (a past event told in present tense)

_____ The Future

_____ Does time move during the lyric? _____ no; _____ yes.

If yes, how did you make it clear to the listener? _____

Does the lyric have a Setting? _____ no; _____ yes.

If yes, where: _____

Does the setting change? _____ no; _____ yes.

If yes, in what line did you show the change? _____

Did you imply a setting by using the word "here"? _____ no; _____ yes.

If yes, where do you picture "here"? _____

How does the lyric convey that setting? _____

What is the (one) Tone of the lyric?

_____ self-assertive (I Will Survive)   _____ reflective (Private Dancer)

_____ tongue-in-cheek (Short People)   _____ ironic (Send in the Clowns)

_____ wistful (The Way We Were)   _____ romantic (Endless Love)

_____ playful (Dress You Up)   _____ (specify other) _____

What is the relationship between singer and singee? _____

In what line did you show that relationship? _____

What is the lyric's basic form? _____ AAA; _____ AABA; _____ V/C?

Synopsize the lyric in one short sentence: _____

What is the universal situation or emotion with which you expect millions to identify? _____

What is the song's title? _____

(It should sum up your idea be identifiable after one hearing.)

First-Draft Page for Assignment No. 7
A Verse/Chorus Lyric with a Simile/Metaphor Title

One-Sentence Plot Synopsis: _____

_____

_____
(Title)

_____
_____
_____
_____
_____
_____
_____
_____
_____
_____
_____
_____
_____
_____
_____
_____
_____
_____
_____
_____
_____
_____
_____
_____
_____
_____
_____
_____
_____
_____
_____
_____
_____
_____
_____
_____
_____

Date _____

Revision of A Verse/Chorus Lyric with a Simile/Metaphor Title

_____
(Title)

_____
_____
_____
_____
_____
_____
_____
_____
_____
_____
_____
_____
_____
_____
_____
_____
_____
_____
_____
_____
_____
_____
_____
_____
_____
_____
_____
_____
_____
_____
_____
_____
_____
_____
_____
_____
_____

© 19 _____   Date _____

ASSIGNMENT NO. 8
A First-Person Reflection or a Persona Song

The Purpose:

To stimulate your imagination and to stretch your plot skills to write a story song.

Many pop lyricists turn inward for song ideas. And frequently their plots are confined to a current personal concern: freeing up from a dependent relationship, getting over an affair, dealing with casual sex. It's amazing how writers can recycle the same obsession under different guises; the title's different, and the style, and the genre—but the theme's the same: *when am I gonna be me?*; or, *I can't get over you*; or, *just another one-night stand.*

But despite the range of treatments of a single theme, such a narrow range of subject matter—oneself—restricts creative growth. The more you can write outside yourself, to a given subject, to a particular title, for a specific character, and on demand, the greater your potential for a successful career.

The Assignment:

You have a choice: 1) Write a first-person, past-tense story song with a beginning, middle, and end, or 2) A persona song.

If you choose the first option, make your first-person singer a generic *Everyman* character with whom anyone can identify, such as the singer of "The Piña Colada Song" who was tired of his lover and answered a personals ad; or like the train passenger who met up with a "Gambler" and got some useful philosophy.

If you pick the second option, then you must characterize your singer in some specific manner as to occupation ("Private Dancer," "Wichita Lineman") or unique circumstance ("Ode to Billy Joe").

Whichever you choose, be sure that your meaning, either stated or implied, will be of interest to the general public.

The Warmup:

If writing a story doesn't come naturally to you, this assignment might give you a small anxiety attack. But consider it a growth experience!

Reading fiction can be good preparation. Musing about characters in exotic locales takes you out of yourself. If you're not reading something you can draw upon, you could look through *TV Guide* for synopses of film plots that could spark an idea.

Reflective songs such as "Same Old Lang Syne," "The Old School," and "Class Reunion" might give you a jumping off place. Possibly you own albums of artists who specialize in stories: Bruce Springsteen, John Conlee, or Harry Chapin. In "Mail Order Annie," for example, Chapin took on the persona of a pioneer farmer picking up his mail-order bride at the railroad depot.

In most story songs the first line contains both the word "I," and the What and the Where of the situation: "I was tired of my lady. . . ." "On a train bound for nowhere, I . . . ."

If you're temporarily plotless, you might generate an idea by brainstorming for opening line settings: "I was on the 7:59 from Great Neck. . . ." "On a Greyhound headed for Memphis, I. . . ."

The Example:

This lyric evolved from a student's desire to write a song within a song.

KISS ME, CARMEN
(Final draft)

Verse

I was hiding down in Mexico
In a dark and dingy hole,
Drinking up all the whiskey in sight
With the money I just stole.
When a beautiful Spanish lady
Walked in and ordered a drink
I said "What's your name, senorita?"
She said, "Carmen," and gave me a wink.

Climb

Well, from drinking we went to dancing,
And then she took me home.
I was inspired by passion
As I sang her this song.

Chorus

KISS ME, CARMEN
Kiss me over and over and over and over again
KISS ME, CARMEN
And help me forget
A lifetime of crime
And the price that they've put on my head.

Verse

In the morning I woke up at Carmen's
With a gun shoved next to my head.
The sheriff was standing there laughing,
As his deputy dragged me from bed.
When they took me out in handcuffs,
What I saw made my blood run cold:
The sheriff walked over to Carmen
And handed her pieces of gold.

Climb

At first I swore I'd get even
With the woman who did me wrong,
But I remembered the taste of her kisses
And I cried as I sang this song:

Chorus

KISS ME, CARMEN
Kiss me over and over and over and over again
KISS ME, CARMEN
And help me forget
A lifetime of crime
And the price that they've put on my head.

Verse

Now I'm lying in this dirty jailhouse—
Bars of moonlight on the ground
Trying hard to fall asleep
When I hear a familiar sound:
Somewhere a prisoner's singing,
Other prisoners start singing along—
As I slowly make out the words
I laugh—then I join in the song:

Chorus

KISS ME, CARMEN
Kiss me over and over and over and over again
KISS ME, CARMEN
And help me forget
A lifetime of crime
And the price that they've put on my head.

The Analysis:

By using two fictional archetypes—the anti-hero and the *femme fatale*—Noel Cohen created a persona for his singee as well as for his singer. Then he made the song-within-a-song chorus develop from the passionate plea of one man seduced to the baleful ballad of many men betrayed.

A story song demands that every change in time frame and setting be made evident to the ear. On that point, the final draft of "Carmen" scores 100 percent; after the first lines establish the Who, What, and Where, transitional statements outline successive sections: *from drinking we went to dancing . . . in the morning I woke up at Carmen's . . . Now I'm lying in this dirty jailhouse. . . .*" That's the way to do it—simple, direct, and clear.

Like all good stories, "Carmen" has a beginning, "muddle" and end. The line "the price that they put on my head" subtly foreshadows Carmen's future treachery. The coupling of visual verbs *shoved/laughing/dragged/walked* with specific nouns *gun/head/bed/pieces of gold* brings the scenes to life. And with the memorable image *bars of moonlight,* the lyricist puts us right into the jailhouse cell.

"Kiss Me, Carmen" exemplifies Aristotle's theory that a convincing improbability is always preferable to an unconvincing possibility. A jail full of men hoodwinked by the same Delilah is an unlikely situation, but the lyricist convinced us. The story satisfies on another level: seeing our anti-hero behind bars reassures us that justice is more than poetic—that bad guys, however romantic, will end up where they belong.

First Draft Critique:

At the lyric's debut reading, "Carmen" 's ironic closing chorus delighted the class. All the plot ingredients were there in the initial draft; just a few loose lines needed to be nailed down.

The key trouble spot was the second verse, which required a stronger link to the climb. Here's the original:

Well, the next thing I remember
Was the sound of breaking wood
The sheriff was standing there laughing
But I did not feel that good:
As they dragged me out in handcuffs
I saw a sight made my blood run cold
There was my Carmen, next to a lawman
He was counting out pieces of gold.

The writer saw the scene clearly in his head, but he didn't transfer it clearly to the paper. He failed to take into consideration, for example, that his chorus interrupted the narrative. The second verse had to give the listener a clear back-at-Carmen's-place link to the climb. The original line "The next thing I remember . . ." didn't do the job. But "in the morning I woke up at Carmen's . . ." did.

Similarly, the first draft's *sound of breaking wood* told the listener nothing. The writer thought he'd conveyed the picture of a nightstick hitting the bandit's head. But that's asking the listener to interpret the plot, rather than to follow it.

Then there was the confusion of "*they* dragged me out." Who was they? As far as we had heard, there was just one man, the sheriff. The writer presumed we could see the scene he visualized: a sheriff with his deputy.

Next, the vagueness about Carmen being paid the gold. The fact that Carmen was "*next to* a lawman" and the lawman was "*counting out* pieces of gold" lacks the precise meaning the writer intended to convey—that the sheriff was paying her. The revision inserts the missing verb, "*walked over to . . .*" as it upgrades "*counting out*" to "*handed her. . . .*" Now the writer's intended meaning is unmistakable.

Summing Up:

Clear writing results from transferring plot details from your head to the paper. To be sure that you've accomplished that goal, give yourself the necessary emotional distance from your first draft. As always, put it away for a while. Then when you pick it up—a day or two later—you'll have gained enough perspective to look at your words as if you'd never seen them.

The first requirement of your job as editor is to forget everything you know about the plot. Imagine as you read over your first draft that you're hearing (seeing) the story for the first time. If any word, or phrase, or line causes your eye to stumble—even for a split second—you've hit a plot hole that needs repaving.

Assignment No. 8
A First-Person Reflection or a Persona Song

Brainstorming/Clustering Space

(Put down random thoughts rapidly without censoring anything. Cluster any key word that needs developing or focusing. List potential titles as quickly as they come to you.)

THE FOCUS SHEET

Who is singing? _____male; _____ female; _____ either; _____ duet

What is the Viewpoint of lyric?
_____ First person (emphasis on "I").
_____ Second person (emphasis on "you"). If yes, is singer addressing _____ a particular you; _____
the collective you; _____ an absent person, place, or thing.
_____ Third person (emphasis on "he/she/they"). If yes, _____ is it an omniscient camera-eye view
lyric? _____ or a singer-singee connection lyric?

What is the Voice? _____ thinking _____ talking.
Does the Voice change? _____no; _____yes.
If yes, in what line did you make it evident?

What is the Time Frame?
_____ The Nonspecific Present (one moment's feeling)
_____ The Habitual Present (an ongoing condition)
_____ The Particular Present (a one-time action)
_____ The Past (first-person reflection)
_____ The Past (third-person narrative)
_____ Historical Present (a past event told in present tense)
_____ The Future
_____ Does time move during the lyric? _____ no; _____ yes.
If yes, how did you make it clear to the listener? _____

Does the lyric have a Setting? _____ no; _____ yes.
If yes, where: _____

Does the setting change? _____ no; _____ yes.
If yes, in what line did you show the change? _____

Did you imply a setting by using the word "here"? _____ no; _____ yes.
If yes, where do you picture "here"? _____
How does the lyric convey that setting?_____

What is the (one) Tone of the lyric?
_____ self-assertive (I Will Survive)   _____ reflective (Private Dancer)
_____ tongue-in-cheek (Short People)   _____ ironic (Send in the Clowns)
_____ wistful (The Way We Were)   _____ romantic (Endless Love)
_____ playful (Dress You Up)   _____ (specify other) _____

What is the relationship between singer and singee? _____
In what line did you show that relationship? _____

What is the lyric's basic form? _____ AAA; _____ AABA; _____ V/C?

Synopsize the lyric in one short sentence: _____

What is the universal situation or emotion with which you expect millions to identify? _____

What is the song's title? _____
(It should sum up your idea be identifiable after one hearing.)

First-Draft Page for Assignment No. 8
A First-Person Reflection or a Persona Song

One-Sentence Plot Synopsis: _____
_____

_____
(Title)

_____
_____
_____
_____
_____
_____
_____
_____
_____
_____
_____
_____
_____
_____
_____
_____
_____
_____
_____
_____
_____
_____
_____
_____
_____
_____
_____
_____
_____
_____
_____
_____
_____
_____

Date _____

Revision of A First-Person Reflection or a Persona Song

_____
(Title)

_____
_____
_____
_____
_____
_____
_____
_____
_____
_____
_____
_____
_____
_____
_____
_____
_____
_____
_____
_____
_____
_____
_____
_____
_____
_____
_____
_____
_____
_____
_____
_____
_____
_____
_____

© 19 _____   Date _____

ASSIGNMENT NO. 9
A List Song

The Purpose:

To practice the Top-Ten Principle of Specificity.

The Assignment:

Write a lyric whose main feature is a series of rhymed specifics in a particular category. For example, in "Let's Do It," Cole Porter argues that every species of human and animal falls in love and mates, so why don't you and I? The broad category is *everything that mates* from the realistic *Finns/penguins in flocks* to the fanciful *cuckoos in clocks.*

Although the majority of list songs aim to amuse, they also can stir deeper emotions. "Thanks for The Memory," "These Foolish Things" and "Traces," as their titles suggest, use specificity to recall shared intimate moments.

All three major music forms have proven workable as the framework for a list song: The AAA ("Friendship," "The Ballad of the Shape of Things"); the AABA ("I Can't Get Started," "That's Entertainment"); and the Verse/Chorus ("Fifty Ways to Leave Your Lover," "You're Moving Out Today"). Choose the structure that best expresses the emotion you want to evoke in your listener.

The effectiveness of a list song stems from the freshness of its (usually) perfectly rhymed allusions and from the arrangement of those particulars in ascending order of charm, wit, or wistfulness—as the case may be. If you aspire to be a latter day Noel Coward, then make your rhymes perfect all the way through. In an otherwise perfectly rhymed lyric, one off-rhyme can't help but call attention to itself as careless writing. It would be rather like a tailor starting with elegant glen plaid suiting and then failing to match the plaid at the seams.

The Warmup:

For high style and artful rhymes, the list songs of Noel Coward, Cole Porter, and Stephen Sondheim are your best role models. Luckily, Coward's and Porter's gems have been collected between book covers in *The Lyrics of Noel Coward* and *The Complete Lyrics of Cole Porter.* But until Stephen Sondheim's works are similarly compiled, you'll have to seek out his lapidary examples in the original cast albums of his Broadway shows, such as *Follies,* which contains "I'm Still Here" and "Could I Leave You?" and *Company* ("The Little Things You Do Together").

Here are a few additional list songs for study: "To Keep Our Love Alive," "I'm Hip," "Come Back to Me," "The Things We Did Last Summer," "How About You?" "They're Either Too Young or Too Old," "I Remember It Well," "My New Celebrity," "I'm Going to Hire a Wino to Decorate Our Home," and "Anything You Can Do I Can Do Better."

The Example:

You've already been treated to Francesca Blumenthal's list-song closeup of the New York singles scene, "Museum." Now she shows how one lovelorn woman handles the lulls between lovers.

BETWEEN MEN
(Third draft)

When some women end a love affair
They frequently go to pot,
And pills, and gin, and Haagen Dazs,
And lie around a lot.
But when this heart of mine's about to break
It's not uppers or downers or fudge carmel ripple I take:

BETWEEN MEN, I take French conversation,
How to roll sushi, or unroll a tent.
BETWEEN MEN, I've learned reincarnation
And sexual styles of the Orient.
Plus real estate, belly dance, scuba, ceramics (but not sten),
When? BETWEEN MEN.

BETWEEN MEN, I have studied hypnosis
And how to save someone who seems to be choking.
And then—I learned self-diagnosis;
And five times I signed up for giving up smoking.
I've done EST, biofeedback, volleyball, yoga, and Zen.
What then? BETWEEN MEN.

It's amazing how good I've gotten
So skillful, so sexy, so wise,
Now when things start looking rotten
How time flies!

BETWEEN MEN—I've learned takeoff and landing,
Maintaining Cadillacs, building a shelf;
BETWEEN MEN—I have grown so outstanding
I think I am falling in love with myself.

So if things fly apart, well, me and my heart say: Amen!
Between dates and divorces
I don't play the horses,
I marshall my forces,
And sign up for courses.
So the next guy who gets me is gonna get more than a ten!
Now I'm torn between Ronnie and Roger and Johnny
And Bryan and Barry and Ben—
Which, it's clear to me, is the best way to be
BETWEEN MEN!

The Analysis:

The *go to pot* wordplay in the introductory verse announces that we're going to be amused. Part of the lyric's fun comes from the freshness of the concept and part from its execution. We laugh at the incongruous matings of *sushi* and *tent* linked by variations on a verb (*roll/unroll*).

A series of disparate subjects—real estate, belly dance, scuba, and ceramics—points up the singer's eclectic taste and shows us she'll try anything once. Well, almost anything; by her shunning *sten,* she decidedly doesn't want to be dictated to. The writer skillfully makes the character likable: we identify with her as she flunks giving up smoking and admire her learning the Heimlich maneuver to save potential choking victims.

Another aspect of our pleasure resides in the use of the species instead of the genus: *gin* and *Haagen Dazs,* for example, are each an aspect of something bigger—overindulging in liquor and "bingeing" on sweets. We're always more entertained by the particular than by the general. Similarly, *takeoff and landing* are elements of learning to fly; in addition to the charm of their specificity, takeoff and landing can be taken on another level—as a metaphor for the beginning and end of a love affair.

Like all well-written lyrics, "Between Men" takes us from something, through something, to something: the courses have wrought a transformation in the singer. To build to her climax the writer stretches the final stanza with a four-line rhyme, overstates the case with three sets of suitors, and tops it off with a twist on the title.

First Draft Critique:

The first draft had the concept in place and most of the main ingredients. It was just a matter of rearranging some details and polishing a few rough edges.

This is the second half of the original first verse:

> *But when my heart is bored, or breaking*
> *It's not some substances I'm taking.*
> *Between lovers and live-ins and dates and divorces*
> *I'm taking courses.*

Not bad. But not as good as it should be—and did become. First of all, the present progressive verb tense, *I'm taking* is wrong: the action is not going on now. In a lyric that aspires to charm sophisticated cabaret audiences an ungrammatical construction sounds tacky—unless of course it's been clearly done for effect. Correcting the verb from *taking* to *take* further enhances the lyric: *take* now sets up a parallel construction showing what the singer *doesn't* do, followed by the echoed verb, what the singer does do: " . . . I take French conversation." (The *divorces/courses* pairing will be put to better use in the climax.)

List songs are all about creating pictures with specificity; *some substances* lies there imageless. The second draft upgraded *substances* with some particulars: "It's not uppers or downers or heavenly hash. . . ." Better. But *hash* sounds dated; the third draft delivered *fudge caramel ripple*—timeless.

The last stanza of the original draft lacked a climax:

> *If I had to, I'd do it all, all over again*
> *Between you and me, baby, I've worked myself up to a ten*
> *And I've done it all—BETWEEN MEN.*

That first line's got itosis: Does *it* refer to all the courses she's taken or all the men she's been taken by? That's what I call a lazy line—the writer's grown tired, and in an effort to get the lyric finished, has settled for a quick rhyme for *men.*

Instead of building to a real payoff, the lyric just ends. The song's opening led us to expect more of a finish. The first draft was not exciting enough to elicit enthusiastic applause. Also, having the singer simply assert that she's a "ten"—without any evidence to back it up—makes her lose some of her charm—and thereby some audience identification.

In the third draft 'he writer came up with the validation for her character's claim to a double-digit rating—she has six men to choose from! Now we have cause for applause. We're eager to cheer the singer's turnaround from *nebbish* to *femme fatale.* Our applause says "Hooray for you!" And by extension, hooray for me, 'cause if you can undergo such a metamorphosis, so can I.

Summing Up:

If being specific doesn't come naturally—and it doesn't for many writers—consider the list song your practice field. You may also feel uneasy with the demand for the perfect rhyme. Small wonder, it's a fast-vanishing art. If you need a little encouragement, turn back to page 16 and reread "You're a Jerk," a lyric written by a student brought up on rock and roll. Once he got into the assignment, he not only had a great time, he found a comedic voice he didn't know he had.

Assignment No. 9
A List Song

Brainstorming/Clustering Space
(Put down random thoughts rapidly without censoring anything. Cluster any key word that needs developing or focusing. List potential titles as quickly as they come to you.)

THE FOCUS SHEET

Who is singing? _____ male; _____ female; _____ either; _____ duet

What is the Viewpoint of lyric?

_____ First person (emphasis on "I").

_____ Second person (emphasis on "you"). If yes, is singer addressing _____ a particular you; _____ the collective you; _____ an absent person, place, or thing.

_____ Third person (emphasis on "he/she/they"). If yes, _____ is it an omniscient camera-eye view lyric? _____ or a singer-singee connection lyric?

What is the Voice? _____ thinking _____ talking.

Does the Voice change? _____ no; _____ yes.

If yes, in what line did you make it evident? _____

What is the Time Frame?

_____ The Nonspecific Present (one moment's feeling)

_____ The Habitual Present (an ongoing condition)

_____ The Particular Present (a one-time action)

_____ The Past (first-person reflection)

_____ The Past (third-person narrative)

_____ Historical Present (a past event told in present tense)

_____ The Future

_____ Does time move during the lyric? _____ no; _____ yes.

If yes, how did you make it clear to the listener? _____

Does the lyric have a Setting? _____ no; _____ yes.

If yes, where: _____

Does the setting change? _____ no; _____ yes.

If yes, in what line did you show the change? _____

Did you imply a setting by using the word "here"? _____ no; _____ yes.

If yes, where do you picture "here"? _____

How does the lyric convey that setting? _____

What is the (one) Tone of the lyric?

_____ self-assertive (I Will Survive)   _____ reflective (Private Dancer)

_____ tongue-in-cheek (Short People)   _____ ironic (Send in the Clowns)

_____ wistful (The Way We Were)   _____ romantic (Endless Love)

_____ playful (Dress You Up)   _____ (specify other) _____

What is the relationship between singer and singee? _____

In what line did you show that relationship? _____

What is the lyric's basic form? _____ AAA; _____ AABA; _____ V/C?

Synopsize the lyric in one short sentence: _____

What is the universal situation or emotion with which you expect millions to identify? _____

What is the song's title? _____

(It should sum up your idea be identifiable after one hearing.)

First-Draft Page for Assignment No. 9
A List Song

One-Sentence Plot Synopsis: _____

_____

_____
(Title)

_____
_____
_____
_____
_____
_____
_____
_____
_____
_____
_____
_____
_____
_____
_____
_____
_____
_____
_____
_____
_____
_____
_____
_____
_____
_____
_____
_____
_____
_____
_____
_____
_____
_____
_____
_____

Date _____

Revision of A List Song

_____
(Title)

—————————————————————————————————————
—————————————————————————————————————
—————————————————————————————————————
—————————————————————————————————————
—————————————————————————————————————
—————————————————————————————————————
—————————————————————————————————————
—————————————————————————————————————
—————————————————————————————————————
—————————————————————————————————————
—————————————————————————————————————
—————————————————————————————————————
—————————————————————————————————————
—————————————————————————————————————
—————————————————————————————————————
—————————————————————————————————————
—————————————————————————————————————
—————————————————————————————————————
—————————————————————————————————————
—————————————————————————————————————
—————————————————————————————————————
—————————————————————————————————————
—————————————————————————————————————
—————————————————————————————————————
—————————————————————————————————————
—————————————————————————————————————
—————————————————————————————————————
—————————————————————————————————————
—————————————————————————————————————
—————————————————————————————————————
—————————————————————————————————————
—————————————————————————————————————

© 19 _____   Date _____

ASSIGNMENT NO. 10
A Protest Song

The Purpose:

There are two purposes: first, to give you an opportunity to express your feelings about one of the many ills of contemporary life; and second, to underscore the power of lyrics to influence society in a positive way.

The Assignment:

Write a lyric that will stir the public's conscience on a particular matter of concern to you. The subject matter could range from vivisection to AIDS. Like the subject, the viewpoint, time frame, and form are your choice. The lyric's tone will of course evolve from the effect you seek. It might be ironic like "Dirty Laundry," playful like "Merry Little Minuet," or caustic like "Jack and Diane."

The Warmup:

First look back at that self-quiz you took on page 142 to see if you listed anything you can now turn into a lyric. If you hadn't filled in all ten blanks, this is the ideal time to finish the exercise.

If the exercise nets nothing, there's always the front page and the human interest sections of your newspaper.

The Example:

While watching a telecast of "60 Minutes," Jim Morgan came up with a song concept complete with title, "Dirty Little Secret." The drama of a true-life tragedy detailed on the program stimulated Jim to tackle a touchy theme that has had virtually no treatment by lyricists.

DIRTY LITTLE SECRET

What a pretty little picture
What a pretty little scene
What a pretty little dwelling
On a lawn that's lush and green.
There's an average looking family
And they're standing in a line
Father, mother, two cute children
Johnny's eight and Mary's nine.
It's a pretty little snapshot—
One could point to it with pride
As a model of a middle-income
Home where they reside, but
A DIRTY LITTLE SECRET's locked inside.

Yes, they've got a nasty problem
It recurs the moment when
Mary spills a glass at dinner—
There's a pause and once again
Father's temper is exploding
Like it has at times before
Now his daughter's got some bruises
And she's huddled on the floor.
Then he says he wants to make up
And he takes her to the den
Mom and Johnny overhear it
'Cause the walls are pretty thin, as
The DIRTY LITTLE SECRET strikes again.

In the morning all is over;
Things are tense, but otherwise
Everything is back to normal
They avoid each other's eyes.
Father dashes to the office,
Johnny rushes to his class,
Mother dresses Mary's bruises
And she wishes this would pass.
Trapped by fear and economics
They can't go—they have to stay.
Mom and Mary do the dishes
Then they both kneel down to pray that
The DIRTY LITTLE SECRET goes away.

And life goes on,
And their hopes begin to climb
But everything repeats itself
From time to time
To time to time to time.

Now the pretty little picture
Has a pretty picket fence
For you see, it's six years later
In our series of events
Johnny's old enough for high school,
Mary's old enough to date.
Father's set an early curfew—
She's eleven minutes late.
She comes rushing up the driveway
Now her key is in the door
And her father's there to meet her
And he knocks her to the floor, as
The DIRTY LITTLE SECRET strikes once more.

And he's ranting and he's raving
And he's saying "You're a tramp!"
And her head is on the carpet
Which is turning red and damp.
Father takes her to her bedroom
Johnny hears, and starts to run
To the cab'net in the rec room
Where his father keeps the gun;
Johnny kicks the bedroom door down
And his father starts to shout,
Johnny aims . . . (Three shots)
And the DIRTY LITTLE SECRET now is out.

Police call voice:
"Car number seven, report to 392 Maple. Reports of gunshots.
Use caution."

Radio announcer:
". . . who resides at 392 Maple Street was arrested tonight on a charge of
patricide. If convicted, the charge carries a mandatory sentence of life
imprisonment."

There's another dirty secret
It's the ugliest of all
It's that those who hurt their children
Were abused when they were small.
It's a vicious little cycle,
Which will endlessly unfold
And the innocent will suffer
If it festers uncontrolled.
So if a DIRTY LITTLE SECRET
Makes your life a living hell
There's a simple way to end it:
Tell
Tell (whispered).

The Analysis:
Because he so clearly pictures in his mind every detail of his story, Jim Morgan can vivify it for his listener. He writes like a film director: from an establishing shot of the family on the lawn, his camera dollies inside for a closeup of the first explosive scene at the dinner table.

He smoothly segues to a morning-after montage of the family beginning its day. Maneuvering his lens to a shot of the picket fence—a new addition to the landscape—he establishes the passage of time. Then he moves inside and narrows his focus on Mary as she rushes, key in hand, toward the front door.

His camera darts from bedroom to rec room to bedroom as a volley of percussive sounds—kicking, shouting, shooting—climaxes the drama.

"With names changed to protect the innocent," as they say, the writer fictionalized a real tragedy as a means to deliver his lyric's important message: tell.

Although "Dirty Little Secret" ends with the taking of a life, the lyric in no way recommends or condones murder as a justifiable solution. On the contrary, the voice-over narrator specifies the penalty of life imprisonment for the crime. The double tragedy points up the moral of the tale—that long-term concealment of such brutality can beget a far greater crime.

Summing Up:

Neither child abuse nor incest is your everyday top-40 topic. But no subject matter need be off-limits—to an adventurous lyricist. The execution, however, is everything.

As you weigh potential ideas and review the range of treatment options, consider the perspective of the third-person camera-eye view combined with the historical present time frame. The fusion of the two can give your close-up lens a unique vantage point.

If you have a hard time coming up with a subject, perhaps you can draw inspiration from such social documentaries as "Brother, Can You Spare a Dime," "Allentown," and "Goodnight Saigon."

Assignment No. 10
A Protest Song

Brainstorming/Clustering Space

(Put down random thoughts rapidly without censoring anything. Cluster any key word that needs developing or focusing. List potential titles as quickly as they come to you.)

THE FOCUS SHEET

Who is singing? _____male; _____ female; _____ either; _____ duet

What is the Viewpoint of lyric?
_____ First person (emphasis on "I").
_____ Second person (emphasis on "you"). If yes, is singer addressing _____ a particular you; _____ the collective you; _____ an absent person, place, or thing.
_____ Third person (emphasis on "he/she/they"). If yes, _____ is it an omniscient camera-eye view lyric? _____ or a singer-singee connection lyric?

What is the Voice? _____ thinking _____ talking.
Does the Voice change? _____no; _____yes.
If yes, in what line did you make it evident? _____

What is the Time Frame?
_____ The Nonspecific Present (one moment's feeling)
_____ The Habitual Present (an ongoing condition)
_____ The Particular Present (a one-time action)
_____ The Past (first-person reflection)
_____ The Past (third-person narrative)
_____ Historical Present (a past event told in present tense)
_____ The Future
_____ Does time move during the lyric? _____ no; _____ yes.
If yes, how did you make it clear to the listener? _____

Does the lyric have a Setting? _____ no; _____ yes.
If yes, where: _____

Does the setting change? _____ no; _____ yes.
If yes, in what line did you show the change? _____

Did you imply a setting by using the word "here"? _____ no; _____ yes.
If yes, where do you picture "here"? _____
How does the lyric convey that setting?_____

What is the (one) Tone of the lyric?
_____ self-assertive (I Will Survive)   _____ reflective (Private Dancer)
_____ tongue-in-cheek (Short People)   _____ ironic (Send in the Clowns)
_____ wistful (The Way We Were)   _____ romantic (Endless Love)
_____ playful (Dress You Up)   _____ (specify other) _____

What is the relationship between singer and singee? _____
In what line did you show that relationship? _____

What is the lyric's basic form? _____ AAA; _____ AABA; _____ V/C?

Synopsize the lyric in one short sentence: _____

What is the universal situation or emotion with which you expect millions to identify? _____

What is the song's title? _____
(It should sum up your idea be identifiable after one hearing.)

First-Draft Page for Assignment No. 10
A Protest Song

One-Sentence Plot Synopsis: _____

_____

_____

(Title)

_____

_____

_____

_____

_____

_____

_____

_____

_____

_____

_____

_____

_____

_____

_____

_____

_____

_____

_____

_____

_____

_____

_____

_____

_____

_____

_____

_____

_____

Date _____

Revision of A Protest Song

_____
(Title)

_____
_____
_____
_____
_____
_____
_____
_____
_____
_____
_____
_____
_____
_____
_____
_____
_____
_____
_____
_____
_____
_____
_____
_____
_____
_____
_____
_____
_____
_____
_____
_____
_____
_____
_____
_____
_____
_____

© 19 _____   Date _____

Get the Self-Assignment Habit

The sole way to learn to write is to write—and review and rewrite, and then to repeat the process—over and over. That means you must constantly come up with new ideas.

To keep the ideas coming, stockpile *song starters*. By song starters I mean any kind of verbal snippet that appeals to you. It might be a book title, an axiom, advertising slogan, overheard remark, newspaper headline, a phrase from a novel or poem, a billboard blurb, an anchorman's signoff, a current slang expression. Sources are infinite.

Be constantly on the alert for that phrase that could lead you into a lyric. Jot it down and immediately file it away in some organized manner. Your song starter supply will also provide insurance against those dry periods—known as writer's block—when your imagination seems to have gone on a permanent vacation.

Become a title collector. There is no better way to start a lyric than with a memorable title. To get you into the title-first habit and help keep your ideas organized, the Appendix provides pages to store your cache of song starters: one-worders, antonyms, place names, colloquial expressions—and whatever original categories you may dream up.

Keep your creative motor running. It's the secret of successful songwriting.

A RECAP OF STAGE FOUR

When you've completed these ten assignments, you will have written in each of the three main song forms, in each of the three Viewpoints, and in both Voices. You will also have manipulated Time Frames and Settings, dealt with figurative language, and consciously accessed your right and left hemispheres.

Having done all that, it is likely that you will have acquired a new degree of technical facility with words and become a better writer than you were when you first opened this book.

Now you've had a taste of what the pros do every day. Stage Five will detail the next three steps to success.

How To Move Onward And Upward

Link by link,
Making the connections. . . .
All it takes is time and perseverance
With a little luck along the way. . . .
STEPHEN SONDHEIM

Starting a Songwriting Workshop

Well, that's the basics—the theory, the principles, and the techniques on which to build a strong foundation of craft. Now comes the real work to develop your writing talent. It's not an overnight process. Lyric writing proficiency results from practice, and professional feedback, and more practice.

To help speed your progress, nothing beats joining a professional workshop. The discipline of a weekly assignment and the insights gained from constructive criticism combine to accelerate creative growth.

If you're lucky enough to live in a major music center—New York, Atlanta, Nashville, or Los Angeles—you'll find a wide variety of workshops to pick from. And as songwriting as a career continues to grow in popularity and prestige, you may discover that your community college or local Y offers songwriting courses. But should there be no available workshops in your area, don't despair. Simply form your own. It's easier than you may think. With this book—designed to serve both as a course/workbook for the reader and a textbook/guideline for a group—you've got the instructor. So actually all you need to start a workshop are a few fellow songwriters.

Rounding Up a Peer Group

Perhaps at this moment you are the only budding lyricist you know. But that's only a temporary situation. Since the odds are good that any given group of twenty-five people contains at least one amateur lyricist or composer, it should be no major task to round up a nucleus of eager songwriters. To get under way, all you need are two or three.

How do you find fellow songwriters? Depending on the extent of music activity in your area, you could post a notice in music schools, colleges with music departments, recording studios, record stores, and the like. And chances are that you'll turn up a few interested writers by placing an ad in your local paper, the newsletter of the local musicians union, or your community college paper.

For the sake of moving ahead to guidelines on conducting a local workshop, let's imagine that you've already assembled a small peer group. Now come decisions about the when, the where, and the how of your sessions.

THE WORKSHOP STRUCTURE

Make a Commitment

Start with a commitment: expect regular attendance and completed assignments from one another as if you'd registered at a college and paid tuition. In fact, contributing a nominal fee to a kitty that could be applied to future expenditures would give each member more than a symbolic investment in your group.

"Timetable" the workshop; decide on a specific number of weeks as well as a particular day, time, and place to meet. To underscore your sense of purpose, give your group a name—The Songwriters Association of _____ (fill in the blank). You could even print a schedule of workshop meetings with an agenda of assignments. In fact, any printed matter—such as flyers, business cards, a newsletter—confers an air of professionalism on group activities. Like "dressing for success," the sooner you behave like a professional, the faster you become one.

Where, When, and How Many?

I suggest that you start with one weekly two- to three-hour session for ten or twelve weeks. The group's size will dictate the length of the session; a group of six to ten people requires more feedback time than a group of four or five. Then, depending on the success of the first "course," you could follow it with "beyond the basics" sessions for ongoing feedback.

Where to hold your meetings? The most likely spot is a member's living room or dining room. (A round table confers equal status on all and permits comfortable note-taking.) But if it's possible, I recommend a member's office or small conference room as the ideal site. The nonsocial ambience acts as a reminder to everyone that this is a *work*shop, not a coffee klatch.

The Format

Where do you begin? Right at the beginning of the book. Review Steps 1-7 slowly and thoroughly. This is the bulk of songwriting theory. Even though everyone might have already read these sections, it can take two or three readings to assimilate all the ideas covered in Stages One and Two. So spend a generous amount of time going over them, taking turns analyzing and discussing the various points.

To reinforce the theory, complete the exercises. I recommend that you do them independently at home and then evaluate one another's work in class. Even such a seemingly easy assignment as picking one-word song titles and writing a synopsis of their plots reveals a lot about the writer's approach to lyrics: the group's reaction will show class members whether or not they're on the right track. You may find it fun to do some exercises in class, setting a timer for five minutes to come up with a particular example.

When you get to Step 2's song forms, I advocate devoting a full session to each of the three major forms. Assign each member to bring in on cassette several songs in the form under discussion along with enough typed lyric sheets for everyone. (You can choose from the book's suggestions, or use other recordings that you own.) As you listen to the music, follow along with the lyric, noting all the form's special features, variations, and potential hazards. Mastering song forms is simply a matter of focused listening.

You'll probably want to allow half the initial course time—five to six weeks—to absorb theory. That will leave the other half for the actual writing, and rewriting, of complete lyrics. When all the members of the group feel they understand when to pick which form, how to handle Viewpoint, Voice, Time Frame, and Setting, and how to avoid the pitfalls common in figurative language, you can move on to the assignments in Stage Four.

Do them in sequence. Three to five assignments would seem to be a reasonable number to cover during the initial workshop. In my basics class I require assignments to be typed and accompanied by a focus sheet. Letting a lyricist stumble over scribbled rough drafts from a notebook acts to condone slipshod writing. Conversely, if a writer is obliged to type his words on paper, he'll exert a greater effort and write with more care. And filling out a focus sheet makes him confront his thinking process—a step toward coherence.

Remember to provide time for rewrites. You can either make the polishing of the previous week's lyric a regular part of next week's assignment, or save up the rewrites for the last session.

Becoming a Critic

Insightful, constructive criticism is of course essential to a successful workshop. You may wonder how a beginning writer can competently criticize the work of others.

Effective criticism demands the ability to distinguish good writing from bad writing. You've now got the means to develop that ability: Stages One and Two pinpoint the main elements that result in successful and unsuccessful lyrics. When you begin to internalize the principles of good writing you'll be able to identify—as a lyric hits your ear—the particular principle that's being violated. The more you absorb songwriting theory, the better critic you'll become.

From analyzing thousands of students' class assignments I've learned a few dos and don'ts of effective criticism. The following guidelines will help you to create a nurturing atmosphere and foster the acceptance of one another's uniqueness.

THE CRITIQUE GUIDELINES

Support Each Writer

The broad spectrum of lyric styles represented in the book—pop, country, R&B, dance, cabaret, and theater—is characteristic of every class I've ever taught. It is therefore likely to be characteristic of any workshop anywhere. Unfortunately, many professional critique sessions in New York, Nashville, and LA focus narrowly on the writing of "hits." Innovative, off-beat, nonmainstream voices can thus be discouraged and sometimes even permanently stilled because a writer has been branded "uncommercial."

Make it your practice to encourage a diversity of styles and to base the criticism of a lyric solely on the writer's avowed intention rather than on some trendy top-40 stereotype.

The Three Questions

Back in the 18th century the German poet, dramatist, and philosopher Goethe defined the three key questions that underpin all literary criticism:

1. What is the writer's intention?
2. Is it a viable premise?
3. How close did the writer come to achieving his or her intention?

In other words, if the lyric is supposed to be funny, are we laughing? If it's designed to teach five-year olds good nutrition, is the vocabulary and style appropriate? If the song has been conceived as a country ballad, does the plot, setting, and general ambiance ring with rural authenticity? The fundamental question is, "Does it work on its own terms?"

Presenting the Song: The Ground Rules

A performed song is an instant experience: it requires no introduction. But a critique session is another matter: there are a few facts that "critiquers" need to know, along with a few they should *not* be told. Here are my ground rules for presenting a song:

1. *Identify your intention.* What's the targeted genre: dance, gospel, rock, country, top-40, cabaret, and so on. The listener must know the writer's purpose in order to give an appropriate reaction. As a case in point, a writer presented to the class a song he announced was to be the opening number of a topical revue. With its minor key, wistful lyric, and slow ballad-like tempo it bombed as a curtain raiser—although it worked as an anywhere-else song. Intention is all.

2. *Identify the singer's gender.* If a lyric is designed for a singer of the opposite sex from the reader, say so. Critiquers quite naturally assume that a lyric read by a male writer is intended for a male singer—unless told otherwise.

3. *Set up special material.* When a lyric's been written for a particular context—a play, revue, TV theme—give a one-sentence setup.

4. *Never tell the title.* If you've done the job right, the group will tell you the title.

5. *Do not apologize, defend, or explain.* Simply read the lyric, or play the demo. This develops a professional manner in the writer and saves precious class time.

A Song Is an "Ear Product"

A lyric is designed not for the eye, but for the ear. This makes it mandatory to present a song in a way that exposes every ambiguity and verbal glitch. In my classes, lyric sheets—if distributed at all—are laid face down where they remain while the song is being performed. Looking at a lyric as you hear it read is about as productive as taking a shower with your clothes on; it doesn't allow the job to get done.

The point is what did we *HEAR?* Did we *hear* "until the last stair" or "until the last stare" or "until the last dare"? Scanning a lyric sheet as the song is performed prevents the writer from learning what he needs to know: Are my words working? Perhaps listeners get the intended meaning only because they *saw* the words, whereas they might have been totally confused had they merely *heard* them. And how will a writer know if the title comes across? Or if the form makes a clear impression? Did the listeners identify the title and form because their ears told them or because their eyes read the words on the printed page?

I remember a class being puzzled at a line in a satirical song about costly cosmetics: it sounded like this: "There's no denying/That a race increases is the latest craze." The words in the second line didn't make sense to the group. And if class members who listen more intently than the average audience can't understand a line, it's pretty unlikely that record listeners will. If we'd been looking at a lyric sheet as the lyric was read, the writer would never have learned that her words, *"erasing creases* is the latest craze" fused in the audience's ears. But because her words got an ear test, and failed, the lyricist got the chance to revise a line that didn't work.

After the song's been tested aurally, a lyric sheet may facilitate further analysis. But the most useful criticism comes from reacting instantly to what's been heard rather than from poring over what's been typed.

What to Listen For: The Main Elements

Title. Is the title immediately apparent? Or are two memorable phrases competing for the title? A well-conceived title echoes in the listener's mind. And finally, does the title sum up what the song is truly about? Some don't; all should.

Form. Is the song form obvious? Listeners should be able to visualize clear shapes streaming by as the lyric is read or the melody is played. If verses, bridges, and choruses produce vague rather than sharp outlines on the mind's picture screen, the writer needs to review song forms. Here again, looking at a lyric sheet proves nothing; just because a writer labels four lines "the chorus" doesn't make it *sound* like a chorus. And of course the key question is: does the form both support and enhance the lyric's purpose?

Development. Is there a satisfactory emotional conclusion? Some wrapup line or implied meaning? There should be.

Universality. Does the lyric strike a common chord? That is, is it about characters you recognize in situations you readily understand? Would you want to hear the lyric again and again? That's what makes *popular* songs.

Run Down the Top-Ten Writing Principles

As the first draft streams by your ear, you'll also be asking yourself the question: does the lyric embody or ignore the principles of good writing? To help you identify any broken "rules," here's a synopsis of Step 4's top-ten principles:

Simplicity. Keep to a single idea and eliminate subplots. A simple plot can be summarized in one short sentence.

Clarity. Include key pronouns to identify who is doing the talking or thinking. Make clear to the ear any shift in viewpoint, voice, time frame, or setting.

Compression. Make every word carry meaning. Unnecessary adjectives and adverbs weaken the emotional impact.

Emphasis. Prefer one-syllable words and active verbs. Place content words—verbs and nouns—at the end of lines.

Consistency. Keep to a unified language style and emotional tone.

Coherence. Place ideas in ascending order of importance and maintain a logical chronology from line to line.

Specificity. Prefer the particular to the general and the concrete to the abstract. Try to show an emotion, rather than tell it.

Repetition. Satisfy the listener's need to recognize the familiar: repeat important words and/or lines for emphasis—especially the title.

Unity. Treat plot details with a length appropriate to their importance. Weave the elements of time, action, and place into a harmonious whole to create a single general effect.

Genuine Feeling. Write about situations and emotions you understand. There is no substitute for sincerity.

If the lyricist has employed all these principles, the first draft is ready for polishing. Then the Post-First-Draft Quiz on pages 158-59 can serve as a checklist for the fine-tuning process.

THE CRITIQUE PROCEDURE

The Moderator

Just as a quiz show needs an emcee, a songwriting workshop needs a moderator—someone who'll keep to the agenda, initiate the critique, control the long-winded, squelch the hypercritical, and wrap up the session. Perhaps each member could rotate as moderator. It's more likely however that the person who most enjoys responsibility will instinctively assume the position. Ideally, the moderator will combine insightful criticism with emotional support.

Before making any negative comments, the moderator should first acknowledge the lyric's assets. The critique could begin with some observations like "There's no doubt that that's an AABA," or "What a distinctive title!" or "What a fresh metaphor!" After noting all the good points, then identify the lyric's central flaw: Perhaps it's a contradictory tone, or an unsympathetic singer, or a lack of payoff.

First Things First

Take notes. As the first draft is being read I jot down any word or phrase that sticks out—anything ambiguous or inconsistent with the lyric's central tone, style, or content. Initially, I verify the title by asking the group what they think the song is called; hearing conflicting responses shows the writer that the title needs clarification.

Next I deal with form by confirming with the writer that what I heard matched the intention. Then I generally give an overall impression of the lyric, pointing out where some word called attention to itself or confused me, or why, perhaps, I was let down by an unfulfilled expectation. Finally, referring to my jottings, I take up the particular "burrs" I'd noted during the reading.

Treating the "Private" Lyric

Striking the common chord is essential to successful lyric writing; without universality, there's no song to sing. But sometimes a beginning songwriter will produce a private idea that's otherwise well executed. To immediately pronounce the lyric "too personal" would be to invalidate all the writer's good work and weaken her self-confidence. In cases of private scripts I've made it a practice to comment favorably on the matters of the title, form, clarity, consistency, and development of the lyric before mentioning its lack of universality. That way the writer gets enough positive reinforcement to leave the session feeling she's done more right than wrong.

Get a Show of Hands

It's helpful to lyricists to "see" where the words go wrong. Here's a little device that pinpoints the trouble spots. When I've heard, for example, an awkward shift in time frames, or the viewpoint shuttle between second and third person, I ask the writer to reread the lyric from the top and request listeners to raise a hand at the point at which they're confused. As hands start shooting up, the writer gets visible evidence of where the words don't work.

After identifying the key problem(s) for revision, the moderator can then open the critique to pertinent comments, guiding the group to ground its criticism in songwriting principles. For example, avoid remarks like "I want to hear some visual imagery in the lyric." That is not constructive criticism, but personal taste, and as such, valueless. Legions of songs have made it to the status of standards without one image to their names. More useful would be an observation like "the second verse paraphrases what I'd already heard in the first verse, and I don't understand what caused the breakup." Now the lyricist knows what to do.

Effective Communicating: Use Nonevaluating Language

Successful communication of all kinds—parent/child, husband/wife, boss/employee, teacher/student—is rooted in nonjudgmental language. Taking a cue from the psychotherapist Carl Rogers, try to frame comments in "I/Me" messages:

> I didn't understand the line . . .
> I couldn't tell when the chorus started.
> For **me**, the lyric seemed to end abruptly.

Such remarks, which simply state how the lyric affects the speaker, are nonthreatening to the writer. "You/Your" messages, on the other hand, are judgmental. Avoid comments like:

> **Your** meter is boring.
> **You** always write about losers.
> **Your** words don't sing very well.

Even praise can be judgmental. In dispensing praise, a speaker puts himself on a superior plane and thereby makes the recipient feel uneasy and defensive. Refrain from making comments like:

> **You've** finally stopped being hung up on the same theme.
> Congrats! **You've** gotten out of that rhythmic rut.
> **You're** really getting good at persona songs.

That's the old backhanded compliment.

One final point: Good critiquing, like good parenting, does not advise. Rather it identifies the problem, and then lets the owner of the problem do the solving. Criticism that makes suggestions ("You should show how the singer is lonely instead of just stating it") or offers solutions ("If I were you I'd turn the whole lyric into a phone call") tends to inhibit the writer's growth. When a group member thinks he or she has a solution to the stated problem, it could be offered like this: "You might want to try the viewpoint in third person."

In concluding each critique, it would be helpful for the moderator to soften any overly critical comments by a group member, reaffirm the lyric's assets, and recap the key points for revision. This summing up promotes the feeling of emotional closure.

Words and Music: Separate and Equal

As your workshop thrives, *music-ready* lyrics will be getting set with tunes. So your group will be giving feedback on melodies as well as lyrics. Every tune deserves to get the same thoughtful response that you'll give to a lyric.

The same fundamental question applies: How close did the composer come to achieving his intention? If it's a dance tune, does it make you want to dance? If it's an AAA song, does the verse bear numerous repetitions? If it's an AABA ballad, does the bridge contrast enough to the A sections? If it's a verse/chorus song, can you all hum the chorus title line after hearing it once?

Use Everyday Terms

Group members who lack a background in music theory may feel unqualified to comment (especially negatively) on a tune. But anyone can express in everyday terms why and where a melody confuses or disappoints. The same show-of-hands technique that pinpoints a lyric's trouble spots can reveal a tune's shortcomings. Then the composer, like the lyricist, will know where and how to revise until the tune gets the green light for a lyric.

Lyrics First

Sometimes a member will bring a completed self-penned song to present for feedback. My recommendation is to critique the words and music separately—lyric first. There's a good reason: Often a self-contained writer prematurely sets an unready lyric. Then, when the criticism calls for a reshaping of the lyric, the writer finds that the words are so fused to the tune that revision is virtually impossible. I encourage all lyricist/composers to try to hold off firming up a melody to their words until the lyric has gone through the complete cycle of feedback/rewrite/feedback. When all the wrinkles have been ironed out, *then* laminate the music. This procedure has proven to make for a much better-crafted song.

No rhyme before its time.

SUMMING UP

As every professional knows, writing is all about rewriting. Step 13 will give you a dry run of a critique session and its results—the rewrites.

A Guided Critique Session

Now that you've got some guidelines, let's try a practice critique.

In your actual workshop you'll of course be reacting to lyrics your ear has heard. In this simulated session you'll be working under the handicap of reacting to lyrics your eye has seen. To try to offset this drawback, the first drafts will appear without announcing the title in full caps and without the labels of verse, chorus, and bridge.

First drafts come in all degrees of readiness for music: some require only a minor touchup, others need a major overhaul. In this dry run, a student lyric will illustrate each extreme.

How We'll Proceed

I'll give you the gender of the targeted singer plus any other information necessary to explain the writer's intention. As you read the lyric, try to pretend (in a great leap of imagination!) that the words are hitting your ear instead of your eye. It would be ideal if someone could read you the lyrics.

The objective is to get an instant impression—as you would if the words were being read or sung. So scan the lyric without pausing over any line. After you've read it, cover it with a piece of paper to prevent taking a second look.

Then, based on the three fundamental questions of criticism discussed in the last step, decide how close the writer came to achieving his or her professed intention.

Next consider the lyric's main elements listed on page 242. Are you certain of its title? And its form? Did the lyric build to a satisfactory end? Was it about believable people in a recognizable situation?

Using the Top-Ten Principles Checklist (pages 242-43), see how well the lyric stacks up against this standard of good writing. If the lyric passes the first level of criteria then move along to level two, fine-tuning. The Post-First-Draft Quiz on pages 158-59 will refresh your memory on small points that could possibly be improved. For example, were all the *its* clear to you? Did any rhyme call attention to itself?

Then consider how you would express your reactions to the writer. Ready? Here we go.

LYRIC EXAMPLE #1:

This song is part of a musicalized biography of Mae West. Imagine Mae West in a slinky red satin dress singing directly to the audience with her come-up-and-see-me-sometime swagger:

*I wanna do a lot of shameless things
And I don't care who's keepin' score.
I want my cup to runneth over,
Then let it runneth over some more.
I want all the diamonds in Solomon's mines
And I want Solomon as well.
I want all the pleasures of heaven
And all the excitement of hell.
'Cause nothin' succeeds like excess, you bet,
Nothin' so relieves my stress.
Nothin' gives me so much pleasure ever
As havin' too much of a real good thing.
So pile it on,
I ain't settlin' for less
'Cause nothin' succeeds like excess.
I wanna climb to the top of Pike's Peak
And then go a step or two higher.
I wanna make love mornin', noon, 'n' night
And never even perspire.
I wanna be admired by kings and holy men,
And do everything that's taboo.
I wanna have it all.
And I want the leftovers too.
'Cause nothin' succeeds like excess, you bet
Nothin' so relieves my stress,
Nothin' gives me so much pleasure ever
As havin' too much of a real good thing.
So pile it on,
I ain't settlin' for less.
'Cause nothin' succeeds like excess.*

First, can you identify the song's title? And its form? I would guess yes, because each was well conceived. It's clearly a verse/chorus lyric. The writer distinguished the verse from the chorus two ways: by a contrast in rhythm and by putting specific facts in the verse and a general statement in the chorus. The verse also fulfills the guideline *and that is why I say:* "Nothing Succeeds Like Excess." The title's "unmistakable-ness" stems partly from its framing the chorus at the top and bottom; additionally, it has the advantage of being Oscar Wilde's well-known wordplay on the adage nothing succeeds like success.

Can you imagine Mae West singing these words? I certainly can. So the lyricist scores three important points: a memorable title that summarizes the lyric's content, an appropriate form, and a language style consistent with his character.

So now we can move on to the top-ten writing principles. What do you think? Is it simple? Definitely. Clear? Absolutely. Consistent in tone? Yes. Coherent? Yes. Specific? It certainly is; the writer might have said "want to climb the highest mountain" and "want all the jewels in the world" but the specificity of "diamonds in Solomon's mines," and "Pike's Peak" lift it out of the vague and into the memorable.

Did repeated elements make the lyric easy to follow? Definitely: first, the title flashes four times; many lines are strengthened with echoes—*I want/I want; Nothin'/Nothin'/Nothin';* the Biblical borrowing, *"my cup runneth over"* (plus allusions to Pike's Peak and Solomon's mines) creates instant familiarity. Is the lyric unified? I'd say so. That's a strong first draft. Now we can get a little tough.

Turn back and reread the first draft; this time be attentive to details.

Fine Tuning

Does anything bother you? I'll tell you what bothers me—flab. The lyric flunks *Compression:* it's larded with superfluous words.

Bearing in mind that closeness creates strength of effect, mentally delete any word, phrase, or line that doesn't carry its semantic weight. Let's start with the opening line: read it aloud. Of what use is *a lot of?* None. Those three words, by coming between *wanna do* and *shameless things* weaken the thought.

And what about the fourth line's *let it?* Say the line without those two words. Hear how much more emphatic it sounds? Skip down to *I want to be admired by kings and holy men.* How does it hit your ear? To me its rhythm sounds limp. And the verb *admired* is far too tame for the title. Think for a minute how you would improve the line.

And what about the chorus? I'd say that to gain impact, it needs to lose weight.

Before Moving On
Exercise #35
Here's the chorus. Tighten it up. Cross out every unnecessary word, phrase, or line. Be brave.

> *'Cause nothin' succeeds like excess, you bet*
> *Nothin' so relieves my stress*
> *Nothin' gives me so much pleasure ever*
> *As havin' too much of a real good thing*
> *So pile it on,*
> *I ain't settlin' for less*
> *'Cause nothin' succeeds like excess.*

The Final Draft

In his revision, Alan Knee performed radical surgery, leaving the lyric lean and forceful. Here's the slimmed-down version. This time the title and form are identified. To appreciate the full benefit of weight loss, become Mae West. Now read the lyric aloud with gusto:

NOTHING SUCCEEDS LIKE EXCESS
(Final Draft)

Verse *I wanna do shameless things.*
Don't care who's keepin' score.
Want my cup to runneth over,
Then runneth over some more.
Want all the diamonds in Solomon's mines
And Solomon as well.
Want all the pleasures of heaven
And all the excitement of hell.

Chorus *'CAUSE NOTHIN' SUCCEEDS LIKE EXCESS.*
Nothin' so relieves my stress.
So pile it on, I ain't settlin' for less
'CAUSE NOTHIN' SUCCEEDS LIKE EXCESS.

Verse *I wanna climb to the top of Pike's Peak,*
Then go a step or two higher.
Make love mornin', noon, 'n' night
And never even perspire.
Wanna be desired by popes and kings,
Do everything that's taboo.
I'm a woman who wants it all,
And all the leftovers too.

Chorus *'CAUSE NOTHIN' SUCCEEDS LIKE EXCESS.*
Nothin' so relieves my stress.
So pile it on, I ain't settlin' for less
'CAUSE NOTHIN' SUCCEEDS LIKE EXCESS.

What a difference! Did you make as many cuts as the writer? I'll take a guess you made fewer; novice editors tend to cut with caution. But now that you've got audible proof that less is more, next time you'll be braver.

Hear how the first verse gained impact by losing twelve words? Now the singer's got some room to interpret; for example, she can sing *shaaamelesss things;* similarly, by cutting out *let it,* the second *runneth over* gets the stress it deserves.

The chorus now packs a wallop. Losing all that flab allows the four successive -ess- rhymes to punch up the point.

In the second verse the writer did some fine fine-tuning: Upgrading *holy men* to *popes* and placing *kings* at the end of the line makes a sound improvement two ways—in emphasis—from DUMdaDUM to DUM, and in singability—from the flat -eh- of *men* to the richer short -i- of *kings.* And listen to how some small changes made a big difference: By adding the noun *woman,* replacing the limp *have* with the forceful *want* (thus linking them with alliteration), and echoing *all,* the writer transformed two ordinary lines, *I want to HAVE it ALL / And I WANT the LEFTovers TOO,* into two dynamic ones—*I'm a WOMan who WANTS it ALL / And ALL the LEFTovers TOO.*

With its deletion of forty-eight (!) words, the final draft of "Nothing Succeeds Like Excess" proves that, in lyrics, nothing succeeds like excision.

LYRIC EXAMPLE #2

This lyric was designed as a top-40 dance song for "an assertive female artist."

> *Kamikaze, you've been lettin' your lovin' slide,*
> *Kamikaze, now we're in for a bumpy ride.*
> *Kamikaze, you've been lettin' me down too fast,*
> *Kamikaze, be careful or we're gonna crash.*
> *Used to be, used to be,*
> *Your eyes were all over me.*
> *Now I find, now I find,*
> *I'm out of sight and out of mind.*
> *You were burning hot,*
> *Now you're turning cold,*
> *Love me, love me not.*
> *Is it yes or no?*
> *Kamikaze, you've been lettin' your lovin' slide*
> *Kamikaze, now we're in for a bumpy ride*
> *Kamikaze, you've been lettin' me down too fast,*
> *Kamikaze, be careful or we're gonna crash.*
> *Ooh-ooh-ooh*
> *Up too high not to come dow-own.*
> *Ooh-ooh-ooh*
> *Up too high not to come dow-own.*
> *You were burning hot,*
> *Now you're turning cold,*
> *Love me, love me not.*
> *Is it yes or no?*
> *Kamikaze, you've been lettin' your lovin' slide.*
> *Kamikaze, now we're in for a bumpy ride.*
> *Kamikaze, you've been lettin' me down too fast,*
> *Kamikaze, be careful or we're gonna crash.*

There's no mistaking the "Kamikaze" title or the verse/chorus format. And we can almost hear the hard-edge rhythmic groove. So the title, form, and genre work. That's a good start.

Employing repetitive devices *(used to be/used to be)*, slurring *(dow-own)*, nonsense syllables *(ooh-ooh-ooh)*, antithesis *(burning hot/turning cold)* and an axiom *(out of sight out of mind)* all add to the lyric's colloquial quality. Those are the sounds of a natural lyricist at work.

But on occasion, even natural lyricists lose their focus. Now to the downside. You'll remember a Step 1 essential: a memorable title that resounds with one meaning and summarizes the essence of the lyric's statement. The word *kamikaze* (kahm-a-kah-zee) refers to a World War II Japanese plane or pilot in a suicide attack. Used figuratively, kamikaze becomes a metaphor for self-destruction. Does the lyric's plot fit the title's meaning? No. The title demands a plot about a singee who is committing slow suicide in some way—perhaps with drink or drugs. But what we hear is a lyric about a neglectful lover.

When a first draft suffers from a malady as fatal as a mismatch of title and plot, forget the rest of the flaws. Nothing can be gained by pointing out further glitches to the lyricist. In the course of the editing, most of them will end up on the cutting room floor anyway. At this point simply be sure the writer understands the lyric's central problem and how to fix it. There're two approaches: either rewrite the plot to match the existing title, or retitle the expressed plot. Because the writer wanted to keep *Kamikaze,* she revised the plot.

KAMIKAZE
(Draft #2)

Chorus
KAMIKAZE, be careful or you're gonna crash
KAMIKAZE, goin' too high too fast
KAMIKAZE, doncha play dangerous games
KAMIKAZE, you're gonna go down in flames.

Verse
Pull yourself together and look me in the eye
Too much heavy drinking leads to fuzzy thinking
Don't you know you've started on a downhill slide
Better stop in your tracks before it's too late
Better clean up your act right away.

Chorus
KAMIKAZE, be careful or you're gonna crash
KAMIKAZE, goin' too high too fast
KAMIKAZE, doncha play dangerous games
KAMIKAZE, you're gonna go down in flames.

Verse
You're cruisin' the fast lane
And it's startin' to show, takin' its toll
You gotta look up, slam on the brakes
Or you'll go over the edge, outta control
Always racing on red alert
Change your pacing, or you'll get hurt like a

Chorus
KAMIKAZE, be careful or you're gonna crash
KAMIKAZE, goin' too high too fast
KAMIKAZE, doncha play dangerous games
KAMIKAZE, you're gonna go down in flames.

Bridge
You'll burnout, burnout, burnout, burnout
You're outta line
Watch out, watch out, watch out, watch out
You're outta time, all outta time

Verse

You're up in outer space
Get yourself right back down to earth
Plant your feet here on the ground
And hold on for all you're worth
Better cool out and don't look back
Better rule out the fast track

Chorus

KAMIKAZE, be careful or you're gonna crash
KAMIKAZE, goin' too high too fast
KAMIKAZE, doncha play dangerous games
KAMIKAZE, you're gonna go down in flames.

The second draft brings some cohesion. But in curing one problem, the revision creates two others. First, did you spot the inconsistency? The lyric's new central flaw occurs in the second verse where the pilot analogy takes a nosedive. We now hear *fast lane, brakes,* and *over the edge* as if a kamikaze were a drag car racer: the notorious mixed metaphor. That's a simple revision; just make all the comparisons on the right side of the metaphor equation "planelike."

Second point: Something essential is missing. Where did the relationship go between the singer and singee? In draft one they were troubled lovers—a universal theme; in this draft the singer is a faceless voice berating an unidentified boozer. How many singers (and listeners) will want to identify with lecturing an alcoholic? By labeling the singee's dangerous habit, the writer lost much of the lyric's universality. And with its cold judgmental tone, the singer becomes a shrew. The writer can easily regain audience identification by making the singee's problem less specific and the singer's tone more caring.

To recap, the lyricist should both unify the figurative language of the second verse and reestablish the singer/singee connection. Then she could polish the chorus a bit. It's pretty good, but it could be better. Did you notice that its opening line, although provocative, gives the effect before the cause? The chorus will gain coherence by simply reversing the order of the first two lines. And here's a minipoint: "crash" is superfluous; "go down in flames" says it all and in color.

Let's see what the third draft brings.

KAMIKAZE
(Draft #3)

Verse

You're the king of the ni-ight,
And you know everyone at every ba-ar.
That faraway look in your ey-es
Is tellin' me you've gone much too fa-ar.
You're gettin' wired,
It's time to slow down.
I'm gettin' tired
Of being around
'Cause like a

Chorus	*KAMIKAZE, you've been flyin' too high, too fast.*
	KAMIKAZE, takin' too many chances.
	KAMIKAZE, you've been playin' in a dangerous game,
	KAMIKAZE, you're gonna go down in flames.

Verse	*We had dreams, we had passion—*
	Yesterday, we had it al-l.
	Here you are with a fatal attraction—
	It's keeping you bouncing
	Off the wal-ls.
	You're gonna burnout
	Anyday
	It's gonna turn out
	To be too late
	'Cause like a

Chorus	*KAMIKAZE, you've been flyin' too high, too fast.*
	KAMIKAZE, takin' too many chances.
	KAMIKAZE, you've been playin' in a dangerous game.
	KAMIKAZE, you're gonna go down in flames.

Bridge	*Hold on, hold on, hold on to me,*
	And don't let go.
	Watch out, watch out, oh doncha see
	You're losin' control.
	A midcourse correction is what you need.
	Change your direction, come back to me.

Chorus	*KAMIKAZE, you've been flyin' too high, too fast.*
	KAMIKAZE, takin' too many chances.
	KAMIKAZE, you've been playin' in a dangerous game.
	KAMIKAZE, you're gonna go down in flames.

This draft shows the lyricist's developing skills as a rewriter: she can confidently let go of the mediocre and replace it with something better.

"Kamikaze" is *kaming* together: the metaphors are now consistent with the title, and the singer appealingly tempers her warning with caring support—major improvements. And by deleting *heavy drinking*, the singee's fatal attraction can be interpreted as alcohol, or drugs, or gambling (even Mafia connections), which instantly broadens the lyric's appeal.

Fine Tuning

Since the writer has corrected the central flaws, we can now address the small ones. The third draft is virtually music ready, but the "readier" the better. What points do you think need polishing? A few things bother me in the area of coherence, tone, and emphasis. Here they are in order of importance, starting at the bridge.

It's more logical to first warn someone to *watch out* and then to suggest he *hold on,* rather than vice versa. Also in the bridge, *midcourse correction* sounds like a command from ground control to cockpit. The phrase, encased as it is within the line *you're losin' control/A midcourse correction is what you need* re-injects that judgmental tone.

The chorus now flows logically and builds well, saving its strongest thought for last. But it sounds a bit crowded: it would gain punch by losing some words—specifically each *you've been* and the second and fourth *kamikaze*.

Backing up to the first verse, the principle of emphasis needs some attention. Remember, strong writing results from placing the stress on nouns and verbs. Here we hear a preposition stressed, *AT every bar*. Similarly, in the same line, the stress falls inappropriately on *everyONE*, rather than *EVeryone*. Although the lines *It's time to slow down* and *Of being around* are presumably rhythmic mates, they're unequal in speed; the latter moves appropriately fast, but the former is slowed by the butting of *it's* and *time*. Remedy: some faster-moving words.

Let's see how the writer applied the analysis.

KAMIKAZE
(Final Draft)

Verse
You're the king of the ni-ight,
You know every club, every ba-ar.
And that faraway look in your ey-es,
Is tellin' me you've gone much too fa-ar.
You're gettin' wired,
Ya better slow down.
I'm gettin' tired
Of being around
When you're a

Chorus
KAMIKAZE, flyin' too high too fast,
Takin' too many chances.
KAMIKAZE, playin' in a dangerous game,
You're gonna go down in flames.

Verse
All the dreams, all the passion,
Yesterday, baby, we had it al-l.
Now ya got a fatal attraction—
It's keeping you bouncing off the wal-ls.
You're gonna burnout
Any day.
It's gonna turn out
To be too late
'Cause you're a

Chorus
KAMIKAZE, flyin' too high too fast,
Takin' too many chances.
KAMIKAZE, playin' in a dangerous game,
You're gonna go down in flames.
KAMIKAZE, flyin' too high too fast,
Takin' too many chances.
KAMIKAZE, playin' in a dangerous game,
You're gonna go down in flames.

Bridge	*Watch out, watch out,*
	Oh can't ya see
	You're outta control.
	Hold on, hold on,
	Hold on to me
	And don't let go.
	I'll come to the rescue
	And show you what love can do.
Chorus	*KAMIKAZE, flyin' too high too fast,*
	Takin' too many chances
	KAMIKAZE, playin' in a dangerous game,
	You're gonna go down in flames.

(Repeat chorus to fade)

© 1985, Lyric by Jan Kramer/Music by Jim Maresca

Right from the start you can hear the superiority of the revised second line that now places the emphasis on key nouns: *And you know every CLUB, every BA-ar.* Listen to the way the writer speeded up the sixth line with *ya better slow down: ya better* not only sings faster than *it's time to, better* also links the two *gettin*'s with assonance.

The chorus, having jettisoned the extra weight, can now fly right along. As you may have noted, the lyric gained music in this draft. In the process the collaborators chose to double the second chorus for effect. The bridge's shape was also slightly altered (for the better) enabling the lyricist to create a fresh accent with the light rhyme of *rescue/do.*

The second verse lightens the rhythmically leaden *We had dreams/We had passion,* to *All the dreams/All the passion,* and simplifies the third line to *Now ya got a fatal attraction.*

The tone of the final draft is warmed considerably by the singer's concern for the singee. "Kamikaze," with its well-mated tune and state-of-the-art demo, is now ready to compete in the pop marketplace.

It's not how you start, it's how you finish.

SUMMING UP

The successful final drafts of "Nothing Succeeds Like Excess" and "Kamikaze" illustrate the invaluable contribution of constructive feedback.

Songwriting talent is raw material that needs to be shaped, and honed, and polished. The growth process begins as you learn to distinguish good writing from bad. It gains momentum as you perfect editing skills.

There is no better way to speed the development of those skills than by exercising them regularly in the supportive atmosphere of your own local workshop.

Now a look ahead to the marketplace.

Joining The Pros

As you continue to perfect your craft, you'll need to do two more things: expand your musical contacts and learn how to market your product.

Just as a workshop creates the supportive atmosphere in which to develop your talent, a songwriting association provides the services to advance your career.

National, Regional, and Local

Where do you find a songwriting association? That depends of course on where you live. You could bus to one if you live around New York, Nashville, or LA. But even if you're located far from a music mecca, your area may boast one of the more than sixty local and regional songwriting associations that dot the country. Check the Appendix to see.

If you lack a nearby support group, my advice—again, like starting a workshop—is to form a group of your own. Thousands of beginning lyricists and composers around the country have found that forming a songwriting association put them on the express lane to professionalism.

Success in songwriting, as in virtually everything else, depends on making connections. So the sooner you begin to link yourself to the pros the faster your career will take off. We'll talk more about forming a local association in a minute, but first let's look over the services available at the national organizations. Most supply some kind of long-distance aid and comfort.

There are two basic types of songwriter organization—the service association and the performing rights society. We'll start with the service groups because they'll be the most helpful at this stage of your career. (The addresses and phone numbers for all branches of the following groups are listed by state in the Appendix).

THE SERVICE GROUPS

THE SONGWRITERS GUILD OF AMERICA (SGA). Formerly called the American Guild of Authors and Composers, the Guild has for over fifty years championed and protected the rights of the songwriter. Founded in 1931 by a group of successful songwriters, its earliest services were designed to benefit the achieved lyricist and composer, services including the industry's finest writer/publisher contract, a royalty collection plan, copyright renewal service, a catalog administration plan, and the administration of estates. These membership benefits are unique to the Guild—the first and most prestigious of the service organizations.

In the early 1970s the Guild added new programs to aid and educate the beginning writer—songwriting workshops, song critiques, a collaborating service, and Ask-a-Pro, a question-and-answer rap with industry professionals. Today each of the Guild offices in New York, Nashville, and Hollywood offers these programs to enhance your knowledge of the craft and business of songwriting.

THE NASHVILLE SONGWRITERS ASSOCIATION INTERNATIONAL. NSAI is another important organization whose membership spans the country. In addition to their local activities, NSAI travels with weekend miniseminars to its regional vest-pocket satellites in cities from Pittsburgh to LA. To learn if there's a local NSAI Workshop Group near you, call their Nashville headquarters.

NSAI produces three annual programs: the Spring Songwriting Symposium, the Summer Seminar, and the Hall of Fame Award Ceremony. If country music is your genre, your agenda should include visits to these Nashville events. They offer unique opportunities to meet new collaborators, get professional critiques on your songs, and make important industry contacts.

THE LOS ANGELES SONGWRITERS SHOWCASE. LASS is a nonprofit service organization for songwriters sponsored by BMI and founded in 1971 by Len Chandler and John Braheny. Its most visible program is a weekly interview/showcase/critique session that brings new songwriters and their songs to the attention of the music industry.

LASS's general membership services include career counseling, song critiques, workshops, interview tapes, and all manner of trade discounts. The Professional Membership Division features such services as private pitch sessions—a means for their out-of-town, as well as local professional members to get songs auditioned before top industry record and film producers. A monthly publication, *Musepaper,* features news of current music business activities, interviews with industry pros, and articles on craft. Subscribing to *Musepaper* (available to nonmembers) provides an inexpensive link to the pop marketplace.

LASS produces California's major songwriter event of the year: Songwriters Expo, an annual two-day series of song critiques, seminars, and panels on all aspects of songwriting, held every fall in Los Angeles.

THE NATIONAL ACADEMY OF SONGWRITERS. The Hollywood-based NAS is a nonprofit membership organization dedicated to educating, assisting, and protecting songwriters. Its membership benefits include a song registration service, group legal service, US copyright registration service, hotline, song critiques, monthly seminars, publishers' workshops, a lead sheet service, and songwriting courses. The Professional Membership Division offers various song marketing plans, including Songpitch and Songlink, in which the songs of pro members are presented to the marketplace.

Many of its services, such as an 800-number hotline, song critiques, discount books, and the bimonthly newspaper *SongTalk*—extend to its out-of-town members.

These are the four national songwriter service groups. Contact each for a brochure of their services and a schedule of current seminars, workshops, and special events. Membership in any one of them will enhance your career. Budget permitting, join them all. They are your main pipelines to professionalism.

THE PERFORMING RIGHTS SOCIETIES

The three performing rights societies—ASCAP, BMI, and SESAC—collect and distribute royalties due their writer and publisher members from radio, TV, and concert performances. Every professional lyricist, composer, and music publisher belongs to one of the three organizations.

In addition to their prime functions, both ASCAP and BMI sponsor free songwriting workshops that are open to all writers without regard for their affiliation—or lack of it.

The New York headquarters of the ASCAP Foundation, the society's educational arm, conducts two annual ten-week workshops—one for pop writers and one for theater writers. Admission to both of these workshops is by audition tape.

ASCAP's theater workshop is presided over by Charles Strouse, composer of such Broadway successes as *Applause* and *Annie.* The fifteen writing teams (or self-contained lyricist/composers) selected to participate must already be at work on a musical theater project. During the course of the workshop each team gets to present six numbers from that work in progress. Criticism—given by a panel of superstar professionals—provides invaluable insights to the writers for the development of their projects. Applications for the fall workshop are accepted in July and August. Address your inquiry to Bernice Cohen, Director of Musical Theater Activities, in New York.

ASCAP's East Coast Pop Workshop is moderated by pop/theater writer and artist Rupert Holmes. Like the theater "workshop," these ten-week sessions are essentially high-class critiques paneled by a stellar cast of top music publishers, artists, and record producers. From the hundreds of applicants to the spring workshop, twenty-five participants are accepted. For particulars, contact the Public Relations Department in New York.

When you feel that your writing has achieved a high degree of professionalism in your chosen genre—pop or theater—by all means apply to the appropriate ASCAP workshop. Participating in these programs will give your career a major boost, since the sessions provide an opportunity to meet other emerging writers and make important industry contacts.

Also check out ASCAP's regional offices in Nashville and Los Angeles. They too sponsor workshops on such specialties as writing country songs and film scoring.

Since 1961, BMI's esteemed Musical Theater Workshop and Librettist Course have helped nurture budding Broadway writers. These free programs, each of which runs for two years, are conducted by a team of achieved Broadway writers groomed by the late Lehman Engel. These are *workshops* in the true sense of the word: weekly assignments demand a continuous output of writing that is critiqued against high theatrical standards. For application information, contact Allan Becker at BMI's New York headquarters.

When you decide to affiliate with a performing rights society, you become, in effect, an ASCAP writer, or a BMI writer, or a SESAC writer. Membership in one society excludes (simultaneous) membership in another. So contact all three for membership information and, if possible, visit them to learn how they differ from one another. Then join the association you feel will best serve your career.

OTHER SIGNIFICANT ORGANIZATIONS

THE NATIONAL ACADEMY OF RECORDING ARTS AND SCIENCES—NARAS is a nonprofit organization formed in 1957 to foster leadership for artistic, educational, and technical progress in recording. In addition to presenting the Grammy Awards, they conduct seminars, provide scholarships, and publish a quarterly magazine *Pulse*. Although NARAS is essentially a professional organization of successful songwriters, musicians, recording artists, producers, and arrangers, it offers an associate membership to the preprofessional.

If you live near, or plan to visit, any of NARAS chapter cities—New York, Nashville, Atlanta, Chicago, Memphis, San Francisco, or Los Angeles—inquire about upcoming seminars. Attendance is open to nonmembers.

THE DRAMATISTS GUILD, founded in 1920, is a professional association of playwrights, composers, and lyricists. Their services include use of the Guild's seven contracts, counseling on all theatrical contracts, advice on dealings with producers, and an annual marketing directory. Headquartered in New York, the Guild maintains an 800 number to inform its national membership of the many symposia and weekend workshops held in major cities across the country. For anyone with theatrical interests, their renowned *Dramatists Guild Quarterly* alone makes an associate membership worth the fee.

THE MUSICAL THEATRE WORKS INC. is a nonprofit membership organization dedicated to the exploration and development of original music theater. MTW encourages the growth and development of new librettists and introduces the work of new composers and lyricists. MTW's biannual programs include: a Librettists' Workshop; a Lecture Series; a Works-in-Progress reading program; a Meet the Composer Series; and Production Showcases of new musical works.

REACH OUT, LINK UP

Now you've got an overview of the most significant organizations designed to protect, educate, and nurture the emerging pop and theater writer. Contact them. Join them. Link yourself to professionalism, even if it's a long-distance connection. And whenever you can, visit a major music center to get a first-hand taste of the marketplace at a Guild Ask-a-Pro, or an NAS SongTalk, or the LASS Expo.

Coming back home after the excitement of meeting music publishers and record producers can be frustrating. Now what do you do? How do you keep up your new contacts? And make more? How do you learn the ropes about demos, and contracts, and copyrights? How do you get there from here? Quite simply, the quickest way to narrow the gap between you and the music industry is to form a local songwriter association.

What Your Local Group Can Do

Consider some of the services and projects that your local (nonprofit) group could create for its members:

> A collaborators pool
> Educational seminars with top industry personnel
> Song critiques by visiting professionals
> An area songwriting contest
> Media support with free radio/TV announcements
> Discounts on studio time, tapes, and trade periodicals
> A local newsletter that links you to other associations

Sound good? You can make it all happen. Let's look at how a couple of writers went about it.

CSA: A Case History

In March, 1979, two Connecticut writer/performers, Don Donegan and Bill Ewing, decided it was time for local songwriters to band together for mutual support. They started the ball rolling by finding a club in New London to showcase their original songs and those of their friends. The weekly event was a great success for the club and the writers. With the fees the club owner paid them to produce the showcase, Don and Bill opened a bank account in the name of The Connecticut Songwriters Association (CSA). After getting some legal advice they drew up their own articles of incorporation and within a few months achieved nonprofit status.

Then CSA began to hold regular meetings. They started a monthly newsletter supported by local ads. They invited representatives of ASCAP, BMI, The Songwriters Guild, and New York music publishers and record companies to speak at their seminars. Services were slowly added: song critiques, a tape library, member trade discounts, and representation in Nashville.

As a result of group programs, members began to sign publishing contracts and get record cuts. With industry encouragement, some writers relocated to Nashville and LA to pursue their careers full time. Today CSA, with a roster of over 150 members, provides Connecticut's songwriting community with both local services and a link to the main marketplaces.

CSA's founders readily acknowledge that geography played a part in their success; proximity to New York makes it relatively easy to import major industry professionals. Yet new groups in such areas as Cleveland, Louisville, and Denver are finding equal success in attracting top pros to come to speak. The music industry is eager to encourage and train aspiring songwriters. After all, you are its future.

A Hotline Away

There's no reason in the world for any budding composer or lyricist anywhere to feel isolated from the music business mainstream. Information and assistance are only a hotline away. Thanks to the burgeoning songwriting self-help network, making it in the record business no longer requires packing up and moving to Hollywood. Today you can sign a publishing contract right at your desk in Hoboken or Houston.

SUMMING UP

A successful career in songwriting rests on three Ts—Talent, Technique, and Tenacity. You've got the talent. It is my hope that this book outlines all the techniques necessary to develop that talent to the utmost. The tenacity it takes to turn a hobby into a career is now in your talented hands.

APPENDIX

Anything you do,
Let it come from you.
Then it will be new. . . .
STEPHEN SONDHEIM

SONG STARTERS
(A title a day keeps writer's block away)

ANTONYM TITLES:
(Ex. "The Night We Called It a Day," "My Future Just Passed")

_____

_____

_____

_____

_____

_____

_____

_____

_____

COLLOQUIAL EXPRESSION TITLES (OR WITH TWIST):
(Ex. "Come What May," "Break It to Me Gently," "High Cost of Loving")

_____

_____

_____

_____

_____

_____

_____

_____

_____

_____

COLOR TITLES:
(Ex. "Blue Moon," "Little Green Apples," "Yellow Submarine")

_____

_____

_____

_____

_____

_____

_____

_____

_____

_____

ONE-WORD TITLES:
(Ex. "Witchcraft," "De-Lovely," "Maneater," "Muscles," "Songbird")

_____
_____
_____
_____
_____
_____
_____
_____
_____
_____

APOSTROPHE TITLES:
(Ex. "Skylark," "Willow, Weep for Me," "Mr. Sandman," "Moon River")

_____
_____
_____
_____
_____
_____
_____
_____
_____
_____
_____
_____

HEART TITLES:
(Ex. "Heartbreaker," "It's a Heartache," "Heart and Soul")

_____
_____
_____
_____
_____
_____
_____
_____
_____
_____

OVERHEARD EXPRESSIONS:
(Ex. "Anyplace I Hang My Hat Is Home," "My Heart Stood Still")

_____
_____
_____
_____
_____
_____
_____
_____
_____
_____
_____

BOOK TITLES:
(Ex. "I Never Promised You a Rose Garden," "Games People Play")

_____
_____
_____
_____
_____
_____
_____
_____
_____
_____
_____

FRIENDSHIP THEME:
(Ex. "Me and Bobby McGee," "You've Got a Friend," "That's What Friends Are For")

_____
_____
_____
_____
_____
_____
_____
_____
_____
_____

SONG STARTERS
(Start your own categories)

_____

_____

_____

_____

_____

_____

_____

_____

_____

_____

_____

_____

_____

_____

_____

_____

_____

_____

_____

_____

_____

_____

_____

_____

_____

_____

_____

_____

_____

_____

_____

_____

_____

_____

_____

_____

_____

_____

_____

ANSWERS TO PRACTICE CRITIQUES AND QUIZZES

STAGE I   HOW TO BUILD A SOUND STRUCTURE

Step 1   The Essential Lyric Framework
Answer to Practice Critique #1

My Critique: Despite its freshness and memorability, the title "Nitpick," works against the song. The real message of the lyric is a positive one, "Let's stop bickering." But the chorus, by emphasizing a negative sentiment three times, leaves the listener with the wrong impression: "we may pick away all the love we had." The line "I don't want to nitpick anymore" would work well as a last line for the first verse to lead into a chorus that reflects the message stated in second verse. That positive sentiment could be capsulized with a new title more in the vein of "Let's Kiss and Make Up" or "We Need Some Love Action." Make sure your title embodies the true sentiment of your song.

Answers to Step 1 Quiz
1. A genuine idea; a memorable title; a strong start; a payoff; the appropriate form.
2. Any of the following: antonyms, alliteration, days/months, colors, places, colloquialisms, altering the adage.
3. Any of the following: a question, a greeting, a request, a provocative statement, a time frame, a situation, a setting, an image, an occupation.
4. Attitudinal; Situational; Narrative (Story Song).
5. Scene Method; Imagery; Ironic Tension; The Return.

Step 2   The Major Song Forms
Answer to Practice Critique #2

My Critique: This potentially good AABA was ruined by a boring bridge that ignores the key principle of contrast. The continuing emphasis on the pronoun *I* and a meter and rhyme scheme identical to that of the A sections renders the varied content virtually imperceptible. Here's a bridge that does the job: it contrasts in pronouns, meter, rhyme, and content:

> *In your smile I find a sweetness*
> *That makes every day so fine*
> *In your touch I find completeness*
> *And I'm oh, so grateful you are mine.*

It was good to hear the sound of *your* and *you* and that fresh rhythm and rhyme scheme. These variations will make the return to the familiar cadence and rhyme scheme of the final A really pay off. Practicing the time-honored theory of making the elements of a bridge contrast those of the A sections will help insure your writing successful AABA songs.

268

Answers to Step 2 Quiz

1. a) ABAC; b) AAA; c) ABAB; d) AABA; e) verse/chorus.
2. The fifth and the seventh.
3. a) A refrain is a repeated line or two that occurs at the end of each verse of an AAA song, which also may contain the song's title. b) A chorus is the main section of a verse/chorus song; it capsulizes the lyric's central idea and virtually always contains its title.
4. a) Framing the top line or the last line of each verse. b) Framing the first or last line of each A section. c) Most effectively placed in the chorus' first line; less effectively in its last line.
5. In the AABA form, the bridge is an essential element; in the verse/chorus form, it's an optional one.
6. a) To serve as a contrast in the A sections. b) Any of the following: switch pronouns; flashback; flash forward; particularize with details; generalize.
7. To create tension by delaying the start of the chorus.

Step 3 Managing Viewpoint, Voice, Time Frame, and Setting

Answer to Practice Critique #3

My Critique: What's ailing "Mid-Love Crisis"? A case of split viewpoint. The writer lost his focus and suddenly switched from telling a story in third person to addressing the singee in second person. The cure of course is to unify the viewpoint: either put the entire lyric in third person by modifying the chorus or the entire lyric in second person by modifying the verse. If you suggested second person, you picked the stronger of the two solutions; the lyric will deliver more listener identification if we hear the singer talking directly to the singee. Here's a sample rewrite:

Verse
You're telling me it's over—
That you'd rather live alone.
You've got a need to test your wings
And fly off on your own.
You're longing for adventure
That this small town can't supply.
Changin' times have changed you
So you're tellin' me goodbye.

Now the viewpoint of the verse fits the viewpoint of the chorus. Jotting down your lyric's selected viewpoint at the top of your first-draft page will help insure that you stay focused.

Answers to Step 3 Quiz

1. The Viewpoint, Voice, Time Frame, and Setting.
2. a) A first-person lyric in which the singer has been given some particular identity, especially an occupation. b) Any of the following: "Wichita Lineman"; "Dirty Laundry"; "Private Dancer"; "Rhinestone Cowboy"; "King of the Road."
3. That the events portrayed reflect a pattern that is endlessly repeated and is of some social significance.
4. Talking.
5. The Moving Present.
6. The Habitual Present.
7. A transitional line that takes the listener from one place to the next.

STAGE II HOW TO MAKE YOUR WORDS WORK

Step 4 Applying the Principles to Avoid the Pitfalls
Answer to Practice Critique #4

My Critique: It's the principle of *coherence* that's being violated. The lyric fails to deliver the intended impact because the writer failed to put her thoughts in a logical sequence. The first verse establishes the intimate setting of *this bed;* then the second verse yanks the bedroom rug out from under the scene by shifting to the general *the house.* The setting then jumps back to the bed with *I press my pillow.* Linking the two references to *bed* would act to unify the lyric. The writer considered the critique and made this revision:

This bedroom's dark and empty
Without your kiss goodnight.
My heart is feeling weary
As I turn out the light.

This bed was once a haven
Now it's just a barren space
I pull your pillow close to me
As tears run down my face.

Now the two verses exert more feeling because the ideas arrive in a coherent sequence.

Answers to Step 4 Quiz
1. Clarity; Compression; Consistency; Coherence.
2. By making sure that the antecedent to *it* is the last noun heard before the *it.*
3. Place words with semantic weight—verbs and nouns—at the end of a line.
4. a) Alliteration and Assonance. b) *Sunny/summer/scene* are linked by the initial consonant -s- (alliteration). The vowel -o- unites *golden/glow* and the vowel -uh- further links *sunny* and *summer* (assonance).
5. Time, place, and action.

Step 5 Figuring Out Figurative Language
Answer to Practice Critique #5

My Critique: It's that old literal/figurative mixup. The writer ignored guideline #7 to give a figurative image a figurative setup. Although the conceit of a *menu of men* strains believability a bit, let's accept it as a viable lyric concept. To make it work, the writer must throw out his setup of *lunch/dinner*—as well as all such subsequent literal references as *waiter/table/waitin'/order*)—and cue in the listener at the outset that the singer's speaking metaphorically. A number of phrases spring to mind that would work simultaneously on two levels: *love diet/varied menu/only an appetizer/ the main course/dessert/fast food/junk food.* Of course, only a couple are needed to unify the lyric.

I'm sure you got as dizzy as I did trying to follow the lyric's crazy clock. The writer, after establishing the song's time frame as *now,* then set off a series of time bombs: a *couple of weeks have passed/last night/today/tonight/now/the very next day(!).*

"Menu of Men" illustrates what can happen if you ignore three precepts of effective lyric writing: give a figurative image a figurative setup, define your time frame, and make sure that your chorus holds up after the events of the second verse.

Answers to Step 5 Quiz

1. c; d; b; e; a.
2. "Your smile's a light at the end of the tunnel."
3. In a third form of pun, two meanings of a word are suggested simultaneously: "Macon Love."
4. Be sure your intended *double entendre* suggests two simultaneous levels of meaning—one of which is suggestive ("Who *came* at my command").
5. Mixing literal and figurative in the same thought or a series of linked ideas.

Step 6   You Got Rhythm
Answer to Practice Critique #6

My Critique: I'd be surprised if you felt moved. The culprit: the inappropriate limerick meter, whose light-hearted anapests contradict the weightiness of the subject, thereby rendering the words ineffective. This example of poor mating of sound and sense illustrates how your meter can either support or subvert your meaning.

Answers to Step 6 Quiz

1. Iambic pentameter
2. a) Ev́-'ry̆-oňe cǒn-/síd-eřed hǐm thě/ców-ařd ǒf thě/cóun-ty̆/;
   b) four c) falling.
3. a) Vary the placement of your stresses from line to line. b) Vary the end punctuation from end-stopped lines to an occasional run-on line. c) Vary the number of unstressed syllables within a foot.
4. In 4/4 time that would equal twelve 16th notes and one quarter note:

5. A spondee.

Step 7   A Rundown of Rhyme
Answer to Practice Critique #7

My Critique: The writer diminished the impact of the chorus by previewing its -a-end-rhyme scheme in the initial verse. First-rate lyrics save the chorus rhymes for the chorus and vary the remaining end rhymes. That's the lyric's central flaw. But two more "unsound" choices bored my ear. First, the dull thud of the identity *away/way* and then the recycling of *love* in the chorus. *Love* sounds fine in the verse with the emphatic *sure of/our love* mating, but its reappearance in the chorus must be ascribed to carelessness rather than purposeful repetition for emphasis. With a little work, the first draft could be much improved.

Answers to Step 7 Quiz

1. a-2; b-1; c-3; d-3; e-3; f-5

2. Every rhyme agent sets up the expectation to hear a perfect rhyme mate. Diminished rhyme, such as raunch/pawn, not only disappoints, it can cause confusion. Paunch? Pawned? Augmented rhyme (pawn/raunch), on the other hand, delivers what we expect—and more.

3. a) Bread/red. b) Pairings of different parts of speech are considered a superior rhyme; bread/red pairs a noun with an adjective, which is more unexpected than simper/whimper, which pairs a verb with a verb.

4. Feminine rhymes (such as singing/bringing).

5. b) For three reasons: (1) That succession of -s- words will sound like the singer's got loose dentures. (2) *Don't/stop*—a word combination that makes the mouth reform—is difficult to sing; all the words in the b) phrase, on the other hand, flow easily into one another without having to reform the mouth. (3) A line that ends with an open vowel like *me* enables the singer to hold the note. If you always "test-sing" your words as you write, you'll always write singable words.

A SONGWRITER'S BIBLIOGRAPHY

LYRICISTS AND COMPOSERS: THEIR WORK, THEIR LIVES

The Savoy Operas
By W.S. Gilbert
Macmillan, London (1983)

Thou Swell, Thou Witty
The Life and Lyrics of Lorenz Hart
By Dorothy Hart
Harper & Row, New York (1976)

The Complete Lyrics of Lorenz Hart
Edited by Dorothy Hart
Knopf, New York (1986)

The Lyrics of Noel Coward
The Overlook Press
Woodstock, New York (1975)

Lyrics
By Oscar Hammerstein II
Hal Leonard Books, Milwaukee (1985)

Lyrics on Several Occasions
By Ira Gershwin
Knopf, New York (1959)

Dancing in the Dark
Words by Howard Dietz,
An autobiography
Quadrangle/New York Times Book Co.,
    New York (1974)

The Complete Lyrics of Cole Porter
Edited by Robert Kimball
Knopf, New York (1983)

A Hymn To Him
The Lyrics of Alan Jay Lerner
Edited by Benny Green
Limelight Editions, New York (1987)

What the World Needs Now
by Hal David
Simon & Schuster, New York (1970)

American Popular Song
The Great Innovators 1900-1950
By Alec Wilder
Oxford University Press, New York (1970)

They're Playing Our Song
By Max Wilk
Atheneum, New York (1973)

How to Write a Song
As told to Henry Kane
Macmillan, New York (1962)

Harold Arlen: Happy With the Blues
By Edward Jablonski
Doubleday, New York (1961)

Our Huckleberry Friend
Life, Times and Lyrics of Johnny Mercer
Lyle Stuart, Secaucus, NJ (1982)

Their Words Are Music
By Lehman Engel
Crown Publishing, New York (1975)

Musical Stages (An Autobiography)
By Richard Rodgers
Random House, New York (1975)

273

I Should Care (An Autobiography)
By Sammy Cahn
Arbor House, New York (1974)

The Street Where You Live
(An Autobiography)
By Alan Jay Lerner
W.W. Norton, New York (1978)

The Stephen Sondheim Songbook
Introduction by Sheridan Morley
Chappell & Co. Ltd., London (1979)

Sondheim & Co.
By Craig Zadan
Harper & Row, New York (1986)

*Playwrights, Lyricists, Composers on
Theater*
Edited by Otis L. Guernsey Jr.
Dodd, Mead, New York (1974)

The Poetry of Rock
Edited by Richard Goldstein
Bantam Books, New York (1968)

Baby, That Was Rock and Roll
The Legendary Leiber and Stoller
Text by Robert Palmer
Harcourt Brace Jovanovich, New York
(1978)

The Beatles Illustrated Lyrics
Edited by Alan Aldridge
Delacorte Press, New York (1969)

How To Be a Successful Songwriter
As told to Kent McNeel and Mark Luther
St. Martin's Press, New York (1976)

In Their Own Words
As Told to Bruce Pollak
Collier Macmillan Publishing Co., New
York (1975)

Writings and Drawings
By Bob Dylan
Knopf, New York (1973)

ON CREATIVITY

The Brain Book
By Peter Russell
E.P. Dutton, New York (1979)

Whole Brain Thinking
Working From Both Sides of the Brain
By Jacquelyn Wonder and Priscilla
Donovan
Ballantine Books, New York (1984)

Centering Through Writing
By Margaret Hatcher
University Press of America, Lanthan,
Maryland (1983)

Writing the Natural Way
By Gabriele Lusser Rico
J.P. Tarcher, Louisiana (1983)

A Writer's Time
A Guide to the Creative Process
By Kenneth Atchity
W.W. Norton, New York (1986)

FOR WORDS
AND WORDPLAY

The Craft of Lyric Writing
By Sheila Davis
Writer's Digest Books, Cincinnati (1985)

Elements of Style
William Strunk Jr. and E.B. White
Macmillan, New York (1959)

The Songwriter's Rhyming Dictionary
By Sammy Cahn
Facts on File, Inc., New York (1983)

The Complete Rhyming Dictionary
Edited By Clement Wood
Doubleday, New York (1943)

Webster's New World Dictionary
The World Publishing Co.
New York and Cleveland

Roget's International Thesaurus
Thomas Y. Crowell Co., New York

*The Second Barnhart Dictionary
    of New English*
Harper & Row, New York (1980)

*Harper Dictionary
    of Contemporary Usage*
By William and Mary Morris
Harper & Row, New York (1985)

Fowler's Modern English Usage
By H.W. Fowler
Oxford University Press, New York (1985)

Pocket Dictionary of American Slang
Wentworth and Flexner
Pocket Books, New York (1960)

*Morris Dictionary
    of Word and Phrase Origins*
By William and Mary Morris
Harper & Row, New York (1962)

Familiar Quotations
By John Bartlett
Little, Brown & Co., Boston

*Handbook of Commonly Used
    American Idioms*
Edited by Adam Makkai, Ph.D.
Barron's Educational Series
Woodbury, NY (1984)

*The Concise Oxford Dictionary
    of Proverbs*
Edited by J.A. Simpson
Oxford University Press, New York (1982)

A Dictionary of Catch Phrases
By Eric Partridge
Stein & Day, New York (1986)

The Craft and Business of Songwriting
By John Braheny
Writer's Digest, Cincinnati (1987)

This Business of Music
By Shemel and Krasilowsky
Billboard Publishers, Inc. New York
    (1979)

*The Music Business
Career Opportunities and Self-Defense*
By Dick Weissman
Crown Publishers, Inc., New York (1979)

Songwriter's Market (An Annual)
(Where to Sell Your Songs)
Edited by Julie Wesley Whaley
Writer's Digest Books, Cincinnati (1987)

Musepaper (Monthly Newsletter)
Los Angeles Songwriters Showcase
P.O. Box 93759
Hollywood, CA 90093

Songwriter USA (Monthly Newsletter)
Rowpa Creative Concepts Inc.
7400 Powers Ferry Road, Suite 110
Atlanta, GA 30339

American Songwriter (Bi-monthly
    Magazine)
27 Music Square East
Nashville, TN 37203

Working For Yourself
(A Guide to Success for People Who
    Work Outside the 9-5 World)
By Phillip Namanworth and Gene Busnar
McGraw-Hill, New York (1980)

SONGWRITER'S
ORGANIZATIONS

Alabama

Muscle Shoals Music Association
P.O. Box 2009
Muscle Shoals, AL 35662
(205) 381-1442

Arizona

ASCAP
9200 North Central Avenue
Phoenix, AZ 85020
(602) 861-2128

Arizona Songwriters Association
P.O. Box 678
Phoenix, AZ 85001
(602) 841-6397

Tucson Songwriters Association
620 North 6th Avenue
Tucson, AZ 85705
(602) 624-8276

Arkansas

Arkansas Songwriters Association
P.O. Box 55128
Hillcrest Station
Little Rock, AR 72205
(501) 758-0126

California

The Songwriter's Guild of America (SGA)
6430 Sunset Blvd.
Hollywood, CA 90028
(213) 462-1108

National Academy of Songwriters (NAS)
6772 Hollywood Blvd.
Hollywood, CA 90028
(213) 463-7178

The Los Angeles Songwriters Showcase
(LASS)
P.O. Box 93759
Los Angeles, CA 90093
(213) 654-1666

ASCAP
6430 Sunset Blvd.
Hollywood, CA 90028
(213) 466-7681

BMI
6255 Sunset Blvd.
Hollywood, CA 90028
(213) 465-2111

SESAC
9000 Sunset Blvd.
Hollywood, CA 90069
(213) 274-6814

Central California Songwriters Association
1042 Pierce Drive
Clovis, CA 93612
(209) 299-6309

Santa Barbara Songwriters Guild
P.O. Box 2238
Santa Barbara, CA 93120
(805) 569-2533

California Copyright Conference
P.O. Box 145
North Hollywood, CA 91603
(213) 980-3357

NARAS (National Office)
303 Glenoaks Blvd.
Burbank, CA 91502
(213) 849-1313

NARAS
2731 Franklin Street
San Francisco, CA 94123
(415) 777-4633

NARAS
4444 Riverside Drive
Burbank, CA 91505
(213) 843-8253

Musicians Contact Service
6605 Sunset Blvd.
Hollywood, CA 90028
(213) 467-2191

Northern California Songwriters
Association
407 California Ave. #8
Palo Alto, CA 94306
(415) 327-8296

California Country Music Association
721 Cipriano Place
Monterey Park, CA 91754
(818) 289-4204

San Diego Songwriter's Guild
P.O. Box 270026
San Diego, CA 92128-0976
(619) 576-8132

Orange Entertainment Songwriter
Services Division
421 N. Tustin Ave.
Orange, CA 92667
(714) 633-8200

San Gabriel Valley Music
Box 396
West Covina, CA 91709
(no listing)

Santa Cruz Songwriters Guild
P.O. Box 76
Ben Lomond, CA 95005
(408) 338-2891

San Francisco Folk Music Center
885 Clayton Street
San Francisco, CA 94117
(415) 441-8910

Southern California Songwriters Guild
P.O. Box 723
Cypress, CA 90630
(no listing)

North Bay Songwriters Association
P.O. Box 6023
Santa Rosa, CA 95406
(707) 887-1445

Sacramento Songwriters Showcase
4632 U Street
Sacramento, CA 95817
(916) 456-3911

North County Songwriters Guild
13828 Tobiasson Rd.
Poway, CA 92064
(619) 748-5138

Colorado

ASCAP
3090 South Jamaica Court
Aurora, CO 80014
(303) 695-6754

Country Music Foundation
Box 19435
Denver, CO 80219
(303) 936-7762

Rocky Mountain Songwriters and
      Musicians
231 Harrison Street
Denver, CO 80206
(303) 355-7426

Connecticut

Connecticut Songwriters Association
P.O. Box 4137
Wallingford, CT 06492
(203) 389-5862

District of Columbia

Songwriters Association of Washington
      (SAW)
1377 K St. N.W. - Suite 632
Washington, DC 20005
(202) 682-7361

Black Music Association (BMA)
P.O. Box 63683
Washington, DC 20019
(no listing)

Florida

ASCAP
1065 N.E. 125th Street
North Miami, FL 33161
(305) 895-6390

Georgia

ASCAP
One Georgia Way, N.W.
Atlanta, GA 30339
(404) 952-8843

Atlanta Songwriters Association
1083 Austin Avenue, N.E.
Atlanta, GA 30307
(no listing)

NARAS
% Master Sound
1227 Spring Street N.W.
Atlanta, GA 30309
(404) 876-1644

Hawaii

Composers Workshop of Hawaii
P.O. Box 22368
Honolulu, HI 96822
(no listing)

Illinois

ASCAP
999 East Touhy
Des Plaines, IL 60018
(312) 827-7810

NARAS
P.O. Box 11614
Chicago, IL 60611
(312) 269-0393

American Music Conference
1000 Stokie Blvd.
Wilmette, IL 60091
(312) 266-7200

Chicago Music Coalition
P.O. Box 41069
Chicago, IL 60641
(no listing)

Chicago Songwriters Assoc.
1228 West Jarvis Avenue
Chicago, IL 60623
(no listing)

Indiana

Indianapolis Songwriters
P.O. Box 44724
Indianapolis, IN 46244-0724
(317)335-3269

Whitewater Valley Songwriters and
      Musicians
RR #4 Box 12
Liberty, IN 47353
(317) 458-6152

Kansas

Composers, Arrangers & Songwriters of
    Kansas
117 West 8th Street
Hays, KS 67601
(913) 625-9634

Kentucky

Louisville Area Songwriters Cooperative
P.O. Box 16
Peewee Valley, KY 40056
(503) 241-1645

Louisiana

ASCAP
3340 Severn Avenue
Metairie, LA 70002
(504) 889-0278

New Orleans Songwriters
2643 De Soto Street
New Orleans, LA 70119
(no listing)

Louisiana Songwriters
4775 Arrowhead St.
Baton Rouge, LA 70808
(no listing)

Maryland

ASCAP
One Parkway Drive building
7258 Parkway Dr.
Hanover, MD 21076
(301) 796-5222

Massachusetts

ASCAP
Ten Speen Street
Framingham, MA 01701
(617) 875-3515

Michigan

ASCAP
755 West Big Beaver Road
Troy, MI 48084
(313) 362-2444

Detroit Songwriters
2310 Highland
Detroit, MI 48206
(no listing)

Minnesota

ASCAP
7851 Metro Parkway
Bloomington, MN 55420
(612) 854-0763

Minnesota Songwriters Association
4949 Upton Ave. South
Minneapolis, MN 55410
(612) 872-1229

Missouri

ASCAP
Trade Center Building
300 Brookes Drive
Hazelwood, MO 63042
(314) 895-1830

Missouri Songwriters Association Inc.
3711 Andora Place
St. Louis, MO 63125
(314) 894-3354

Nevada

Las Vegas Songwriters Association
1650 Cookson Court
Las Vegas, NV 89115
(702) 452-0954

New York

The Songwriters Guild of America (SGA)
276 Fifth Avenue
New York, NY 10001
(212) 686-6820

ASCAP
One Lincoln Plaza
New York, NY 10023
(212) 595-3050

BMI
320 West 57th Street
New York, NY 10019
(212) 586-2000

SESAC
10 Columbus Circle
New York, NY 10019
(212) 586-1708

NARAS
157 West 57th St.
New York, NY 10019
(212) 245-5440

The Dramatists Guild
234 West 44th Street
New York, NY 10036
(212) 398-9366

Musical Theatre Works
440 Lafayette Street
New York, NY 10003
(212) 677-0040

Hudson Valley Songwriters
P.O. Box 176
Goshen, NY 10924
(914) 294-5756

The Songwriters Advocate (TSA)
47 Maplehurst Road
Rochester, NY 14617
(716) 266-0679

Snowbelt Songwriters Guild
RD #2 Box 438-B
Oswego, NY 13126
(315) 343-4269

Westchester Songwriter's Guild
P.O. Box 1256
White Plains, NY 10602
(914) 965-1867

North Carolina

Middle Atlantic Songwriters, Inc.
444 Rocky Run Road
Midway Park, NC 28544
(918) 353-2872

North Carolina Composers Association
P.O. Box 11163
Betabara Station
Winston-Salem, NC 27116
(919) 777-0148

Triad Songwriters Association
P.O. Box 24095
Winston-Salem, NC 27104
(no listing)

Ohio

ASCAP
3550 Curtis Blvd.
Eastlake, OH 44094
(216) 946-8828

Columbus Songwriters
3312 Petzinger Road
Columbus, OH 43227
(no listing)

Midwest Songwriter's Association
720 Forest Hill Road
Heath, OH 43056
(614) 323-0669

Ohio Songwriters Association
14614 Pearl Road
Strongsville, OH 44136
(216) 572-1124

Songwriter Workshop of Cleveland
2777 Lancashire Road Suite 4
Cleveland Heights, OH 44106
(no listing)

Oklahoma

Songwriters of Oklahoma
2001 Glen Eagle
Edmond, OK 73034
(405) 341-2996

Pennsylvania

ASCAP
Benjamin Fox Pavilion
Old York Road
Jenkinstown, PA 19046
(215) 885-2510

ASCAP
North Point Building
9800 McKnight Road
Pittsburgh, PA 15237
(412) 366-2345

Pennsylvania Association of Songwriters,
    Composers and Lyricists (PASCAL)
P.O. Box 4311
Allentown, PA 18105
(215) 433-6788

Black Music Association (BMA)
307 Broad Street
Philadelphia, PA 19112
(215) 732-2460

South Carolina

South Carolina Songwriters Association
P.O. Box 9266
Greenville, SC 29604
(803) 295-4246

Tennessee

The Songwriters Guild of America (SGA)
50 Music Square West
Nashville, TN 37203
(615) 329-1782

ASCAP
2 Music Square West
Nashville, TN 37203
(615) 244-3936

BMI
10 Music Square East
Nashville, TN 37203
(615) 259-3625

SESAC
11 Music Square South
Nashville, TN 37203
(615) 244-1992

NARAS
7 Music Circle North
Nashville, TN 37203
(615) 255-8777

NARAS
66 S. Front Street
Memphis, TN 38103
(901) 525-0621

Nashville Songwriters Association
    International (NSAI)
803 18th Avenue South
Nashville, TN 37203
(615) 321-5004

Memphis Songwriters
1922 Jermyn Ct.
Memphis, TN 38119
(no listing)

Tennessee Songwriters Association
214 W. Main Street, Suite 103
Hendersonville, TN 37075
(615) 824-4555

Texas

ASCAP
16990 Dallas Parkway
Dallas, TX 75248
(214) 248-8022

East Texas Songwriters
408 Haden Street
Tyler, TX 75701
(214) 597-0416

Texas Music Association
P.O. Box 1585
Mesquite, TX 75149
(214) 188-7689

Virginia

Southwest Virginia Songwriters
    Association
P.O. Box 689
Salem, VA 24153
(703) 380-2921

Washington

ASCAP
10740 Meridian Avenue North
Seattle, WA 98133
(206) 367-8316

Pacific Northwest Songwriters
P.O. Box 98324
Seattle, WA 98188
(206) 824-1568

Seattle Songwriters
770 E. Crestwood Ct.
Port Orchard, WA 98366
(no listing)

Wisconsin

Songwriters of Wisconsin
P.O. Box 874
Neenah, WI 54956
(414) 725-1609

Canada

Alberta Recording Industry Association
6916 82nd Avenue
Edmonton
CANADA T6 OE7
403/465-1311

Canadian Songwriters Association
135 York Street #204
Ottawa, Ontario
CANADA K1N 5T4

Open Door Music Society
1921 W. 4th Ave.
Vancouver, BC
CANADA V6J 1M7

Pacific Songwriters Association
944 Howe Street
Vancouver, BC
CANADA V6Z 1N9
(604) 683-7664

Performing Rights Organization of
    Canada Ltd. (PRO)
41 Valleybrook Drive
Ontario
CANADA M3B 2S6

The author is a consultant and teacher who, in addition to her New York workshops, conducts seminars at colleges and songwriting associations around the country. For information, contact:

SONGCRAFT SEMINARS
441 East 20th Street—Suite 11B
New York, NY 10010
(212) 674-1143

Move on.
Just keep moving on. . . .
Stephen Sondheim

SONG TITLE INDEX

(Page numbers in boldface italic indicate lyrics that appear either in their entirety or in excerpts.)

Abraham, Martin, and John, 50
Ac-cent-tchu-ate the Positive, 50, 149
After You, Who?, 183
Ain't Misbehavin', 27
Alfie, 17
Alice's Restaurant, 65
All Over but the Leaving, 67, *143*
Allentown, 231
Always on My Mind, 12
Amelia, 55
Annie's Song, 15, 25, 63
Anything Goes, 120
Anything You Can Do I Can Do Better, 56, 220
As Time Goes By, 27
At Seventeen, 65
Autumn Leaves, 20

Baby, It's Cold Outside, 15, 67
Bad, Bad Leroy Brown, 52, 65, 92
Ballad of the Shape of Things, 24, 220
Barcelona, 56
Beautiful Friendship, 15
Beautiful Girls, 32
Between Men, 48, *221*
Big Yellow Taxi, 24
Blow, Gabriel, Blow, 90
Blowin' in the Wind, 17, 23, 24, 161
Blue Moon, 14, 66, 90
Body and Soul, 7, 27
Born to Run, 48
Both Sides Now, 48
Bowler Hat, A, 24
Bridge Over Troubled Water, 24, 99
Broadway, *4*
Brother, Can You Spare a Dime, 231
Burnout, *41*
But Not For Me, 31
By the Time I Get to Phoenix, 13, 23, 67, 161

Cabaret, 27, 92
Cactus Tree, 23
Cajun Moon, 53
California Dreamin', 15, 24
California, Here I Come, 90
Call Me Irresponsible, 32
Can't Smile Without You, 190
Careless, 15
Cat's in the Cradle, 5, *62*, 198
Change Partners, 17
Changing, Changing, 48, *49-50, 83*
City of New Orleans, 89
Claire, 15, 50, 55
Class Reunion, 14, 67, 90, 212
Climb Every Mountain, 27, 50, 56
Come Back to Me, 220
Come in from the Rain, 10, 27, 50
Come Rain or Come Shine, 66
Come Saturday Morning, 66
Come What May, 44
Comedy Tonight, 91
Comin' In and Out of Your Life, 15
Could I Leave You?, 14, 190, 220
Coward of the County, 5, 14, 52, 65, 152
Crazy in the Night, 23

Day Off, The, *118*
Days of Wine and Roses, The, 32
Delilah, 152
Desolation Row, 23
Desperado, 17
Detente, 151
Diamonds, 89, 176
Diamonds Are a Girl's Best Friend, 84
Didn't We?, 32
Dirty Laundry, 48, 228
Dirty Little Secret, 52, 53, 65, 67, 84, *228-30*
Do That To Me One More Time, 15, 23

Do You Know the Way to San Jose?, 10
Do You Know Where You're Goin' To?, 28
Don't Cry Out Loud, 37
Don't It Make My Brown Eyes Blue, 27
Don't Rain on My Parade, 97
Dying on the Vine, 52, 63, *83*, 84, *197-98*

Easter Parade, 5
Ebony and Ivory, 93
Eleanor Rigby, 23, 24, 52, 65, 197
Empty Bed Blues, 20
Endless Love, 12, 63
Even Now, 66
Evening Star, 53, 54, 90
Every Breath You Take, 55
Every Little Kiss, 37
Everything That Glitters, 17, 37
Everything's Coming Up Roses, 5

Falling in Love with Love, 15
Fascinated By Your Freckles, *3*
Feelings, 15, 67, 101
Fifty Ways to Leave Your Lover, 220
First Time Ever I Saw Your Face, The, 23, 161
Fly Me to the Moon, 20, 32
Follow Your Heart, 67, 131, *132-33*
Fool If I Don't, Fool If I Do, 55, *56*, 67, 169
40-Hour Week for a Living, 53
Frankie and Johnny, 24, 65, 152
Friendship, 24, 220
From Time to Time, *40*

G. I. Jive, 115
Galveston, 50, 55, 78, 90
Gambler, The, 10, 35, 67, 212
Garden Party, 65

Gentle on My Mind, 13, 23, 119
Girls Night, 55, 65, 67, 84, *162-63*
Gloomy Sunday, 152
Gloria, 190
Go For It!, *36*
Goin' Out of My Head, 63, 190
Golden Ring, 65
Good Morning, Goodbye, 55, 67, *167-70*
Good Morning, Heartache, 50, 90
Goodbye, Yellow Brick Road, 84
Green Finch and Linnet Bird, 90
Guess Who I Saw Today?, 14, 15

Harmony, 91
Harper Valley PTA, 15, 24, 53, 198
Have You Never Been Mellow?, 37
Have You Seen My Guy?, 50, *183-84*
Heart Hunter, 52, *109*
Heart Thief, *6*
Heartbreaker, 41
Hello, 32, 35
Hello, Paris, 50, *51*
Here I Am, 7
Here You Come Again, 27
Here's That Rainy Day, 98
Hey, Big Spender, 50
Hey, Look Me Over, 32
Him, 10
Hound Dog, 92
How About You?, 220
How Am I Supposed to Live Without You?, 41, 63, 68, 190
How Do You Keep the Music Playing?, 100
100% Chance of Rain, 37
Hungry Heart, 89

I Am a Rock, 92, 204
I Am Woman, 63
I Can't Get Started, 27, 220
I Can't Smile Without You, 11
I Got Lost in His Arms, 15
I Got Rhythm, 118
I Have Dreamed, 34
I Like to Lead When I Dance, 92
I Made It Through the Rain, 41, 78, 99
I Never Do Anything Twice, 91
I Remember (Sky), 34, 90, *92*
I Remember It Well, 220
I Say a Little Prayer, 56, 63
I Walk the Line, 24
I Wanna Dance With Somebody, 37
I Want a Monster to Be My Friend, *152*

I Want Your Love, *42*
I Will Survive, 5, 7, 55, 59
I Write the Songs, 10, 89
I'd Like to Teach the World to Sing, 104
I'd Rather Leave While I'm in Love, 27
If Ever I Should Leave You, 13
If Ever You're in My Arms Again, 41
If I Had You, 27
If You Could Read My Mind, 67
If You Go Away, 66
I'll Be Around, 27
I'll Be in Love With You, *30*
I'll Never Love This Way Again, 37
I'm All Smiles, 48
I'm Going to Hire a Wino to Decorate Our Home, 220
I'm Hip, 220
I'm So Excited, 176
I'm So Tired, *3*
I'm Still Here, 14, 15, 220
In the Ghetto, 15, 52, 53, 63
In the Winter, 82
In the Year 2525, 66
It Might as Well Be Spring, 92
It Was a Very Good Year, 7, 13, 23, 161
It's All Over But the Leaving, *143*
It's So Nice to Have a Man Around the House, 104

Jack and Diane, 52, 197, 228
Johnny Can't Read, 52
Just Once, 38, 48, 119
Just One of Those Things, 120
Just the Way You Are, 27

Kamikaze, 63, *250-55*
King of the Road, 48
Kiss Me, Carmen, 48, 65, 67, *213-14*

Ladies of the Canyon, 23
Lady, 32
Last Dance, 67
Last Night When We Were Young, 66
Last Word in Lonesome Is Me, The, 101
Laura, 32
Lawyers in Love, 23
Leaving on a Jet Plane, 37, 54, 67
Let Me Pretend, *57*, 58, 59-60
Let's Call the Whole Thing Off, 56
Let's Do It, 220
Lick It Up, 152
Like a Rock, 94, 202
Little Boxes, 24

Little Priest, A, 90
Little Things You Do Together, The, 220
Local Call, *60-62*
Longer, 28
Look For the Silver Lining, 98
Losing My Mind, 63
Love Is a Game of Poker, 92
Luck, Be a Lady Tonight, 55, 78, 90, 91

Macon Love, 90
Mail Order Annie, 212
Make Your Own Kind of Music, 100
Man I Love, The, 27
Man Who Walked on the Water, The, 52, 65, *146-47*
Mandy, 66
Manhandled, 50, 55, 63, 67, *176-77*
Maniac, 8
Marcie, *89*
Material Girl, 5, 37, 55
Memory, 28
Menu of Men, *97-98*
Merrily We Roll Along, 92
Merry Little Minuet, 228
Michelle, 27
Midnight Mood, *28*, 50, 55, 63, *117*, 118
Miller's Son, The, 66
Miss Otis Regrets, 24
Mr. Bojangles, 52
Mr. Businessman, 50
Mr. Sandman, 90
Misty, 27
Mona Lisa, 50
Moody River, 152
Moon River, 20, 32, *90*
More Than Just the Two of Us, *37*
Mountain Greenery, 114
Move Out!, 55
Muscles, 10
Museum, *144-45*, 220
Mutual Surrender, 7
My Cup Runneth Over, 23
My New Celebrity, 220
My Old Yellow Car, 28, 55, 93
My Romance, 32
My Time of Day, 34
My Way, 48, 62, 120

Night and Day, 27
99 Miles from LA, 63, 67
Nitpick, *8*
No Reason to Stay, 55, *191*
Nobody, 8, 37
Nobody Does It Better, 5, 37, 44
Nobody's Chasing Me, 115
Not a Day Goes By, 34

Nothing Succeeds Like Excess, *247-50*
Nothing's Gonna Change My Love For You, 5
Nowhere Man, 53, 63, 197

Odds and Ends of a Beautiful Love Affair, 31
Ode to Billy Joe, 24, 48, 212
Old Friends, 32
Old Hippie, 52, 197
Old School, The, 63, 67, 153, 212
Old Songs, The, 90
On That Great Come and Get It Day, 66
On the Other Hand, 37, 91, 153
On the Road Again, 27
On the Sunny Side of the Street, 10, 27
One, 32
One For My Baby, 67
One Hundred Ways, 50, 171
One Less Bell to Answer, 120
One Man Woman, 41
Open Your Heart to Me, 41, 176
Operator, 63
Our Love Is on the Faultline, 38
Out Here On My Own, 28, 171
Out Of a Clear Blue Sky, 14
Out Of a Lemon Colored Sky, 14
Over and Over, 149
Over the Rainbow, 27, 110
Overboard, *96*

Papa, Can You Hear Me?, 50, 90
Papa, Don't Preach, 17, 50, 120
Partners, 32, *33*, 48
People That You Never Get to Love, The, 82
Piano Man, 63
Pina Colada Song, The, 43, 48, 141, 212
Please, Mister, Please, 53, 67
Portrait, The, 53
Pressure, 176
Pretty Girl Is Like a Melody, A, 94
Private Dancer, 38, 48, 55, 63, 212
Puff, the Magic Dragon, 23
Putting It Together, 91

Raindrops Keep Falling on My Head, 27, 86, 104
Rainy Day Woman, 99
Ready, *150-51*, 153
Red-eye Flight, 63, *64*, 67
Reunited, 48, 149
Rhinestone Cowboy, 48
Richard Cory, 52
Rose, The, 23, 92
Running on Ice, 92

Sam Stone, 52
Same Old Lang Syne, 14, 17, 65, 67, 212
Sandra, 152
Satisfaction, 48
Saving All My Love For You, 28, 63, 67, 119
Say You, Say Me, 44
Scarborough Fair, 23, 24
Search Is Over, The, 37
Send in the Clowns, 16, 27, 104
Separate Lives, 15, 37
September in the Rain, 78
September Song, 93
Shadow Knows, The, 24
Shadow of Your Smile, The, 32
Shall We Give It One More Try?, 95
She Believes in Me, 37, 57, 63
She Works Hard For the Money, 5
She's Got a Way, 28
She's Leaving Home, 10, 42, 52, 54, 65
She's Out of My Life, 27
16th Avenue, 15, 52, 63
Skylark, 78
Slow Hand, 67
Sly Like a Fox, 63, *206*
Smoke Gets in Your Eyes, 140
Sniper, 53, 58, 141
Snowbird, 50
Society's Child, 15
Softly, As I Leave You, 34
Solid (as a Rock), 41, 44
Soliloquy, 66
Someone to Watch Over Me, 7, 63
Something, 89
Sometimes I'm Happy, 32
Sometimes When We Touch, 38
Somewhere, 66
Somewhere Down the Line, 37
Somewhere Down the Road, 10, 38, 42
Song Sung Blue, 63
Spring Can Really Hang You Up the Most, 16
Still, 32
Stormy Weather, 97, 98
Stranger in My House, 38
Stuck Inside of Mobile with the Memphis Blues Again, 104
Sue and John, *24*, 52, 67, 83, *110*
Sugar Walls, 152
Suicide Solution, 152
Summer in the City Blues, 21
Summer Knows, The, 89
Sunny, 24, 25
Sunrise, Sunset, 10, 37, 42
Swanee, 50, 90

Take a Letter, Maria, 55, 63
Take Me Home, Country Roads, 50, 56
Taste of Honey, A, 23, 24
Taxi, 65, 67, 141
Tea for Two, 20, 32
Teach Me Tonight, 7
Tell Your Story Walkin', *39*, 42, 50
Tender Trap, The, 9
Thank God for Music, *43*
Thanks For the Memory, 86, 220
That's Entertainment, 220
That's What Friends Are For, 52
There Is Nothing Like a Dame, 41
There's a Song in My Heart, 32
These Fooling Things, 86, 220
They're Either Too Young or Too Old, 220
Things We Did Last Summer, The, 220
Three Coins in the Fountain, 27
Through the Years, 36
Tie a Yellow Ribbon Round the Ole Oak Tree, 5, 37, 53, 67, 141
Till the Clouds Roll By, 31
Time, Don't Run Out on Me, *90*
Time in a Bottle, 63
Times They Are A-Changin', The, 24, 82
Tired, *2*, 12
To Keep Our Love Alive, 220
To Me, 31
Tomorrow, 66
Too Young, 32
Touch Me in the Morning, 38, 41, 50, 59, 63, 67, 190
Toyland, 31
Traces, 86, 220
Try Getting Over You, 37
Try to Remember, 23, 50
Truly, 52

Up Where We Belong, 38, 42, 48

Valley Girl, 52, 197
Vincent, 55, 90, 176
Voyeur, 176

Wanted Dead or Alive, 23, 24
Way We Were, The, 67
We Are the World, 149
We Do Not Belong Together, 190
We Don't Have to Take Our Clothes Off, 153
We Shall Overcome, 48, 149
We're Off to See the Wizard, 111
We're Ready, *40*

Weren't We the Fools?, 183
What a Fool Believes, 67
What Are We Doing in Love?, 15, 55
What Do I Need?, 14
What Have You Done For Me Lately?, 185
What I Did For Love, 27
What Is This Thing Called Love?, 120, 183
What Kind of Fool Am I?, 32
What the World Needs Now, 27, 48
What's Forever For?, 26, 37
What's Love Got to Do With It?, 149
What's New?, 185
When I Marry Mr. Snow, 66
When I Need You, 28, 171
When October Goes, 33
When Sunny Gets Blue, 27, 169
When We're Together, 151
Where Have All the Flowers Gone?, 183
Where Is the Life That Late I Led?, 183

Where Were You?, *34*
White Christmas, 20, 32
Who Put the Bomp?, 183
Who Wants to be a Millionaire?, 183
Why Can't We Be Friends?, 183
Why Can't You Behave?, 183
Why Did I Choose You?, 17, 32
Why Don't We Do it in the Road?, 183
Wichita Lineman, 48, 90, 101, 212
Willie, Mickey, and the Duke, 52
Willow, Weep for Me, 50, 90
With a Little Help From My Friends, 149
With Pen in Hand, 63
Who Will Answer, 18, 84
W*O*L*D, 63
Woodstock, 48
Would Jesus Wear a Rolex?, 183
Wreck of the Edmund Fitzgerald, The, 65

Yesterday, 27, 48
Yesterday's Songs, 24

You and Me, 28
You Are Not My First Love, 16
You Can Get It If You Really Want It, 149
You Could've Heard a Heart Break, 10, 48
You Decorated My Life, 37
You Don't Bring Me Flowers, 17, 58, 104, 190
You'll Never Walk Alone, 20, 34, 50, 149
Young and Foolish, 32
Young Girl, 50
You're a Jerk, *16*, 223
You're Gonna Hear From Me, 50, *90*
You're Moving Out Today, 220
You're Only Human, 149
You're So Vain, 207
You're the Top, 15
You've Been Talkin' in Your Sleep, 190
You've Got a Good Love Comin', *60*
You've Lost That Lovin' Feelin', 41

SUBJECT INDEX

AAA (strophic) form, 22-26, 119, 197
  assignment in, 161-68
  refrain in, 23, 24, 25, 162-63
AABA form, 26-30, 35, 60, 119, 145, 197
  assignment in, 169-75
  bridge (release) in, 28, 170
ABAB form, 30-31
ABAC form, 31-34
ABCD form. *See* through composed form
abstractions, 81, 176
All About Eve, 88
All in the Family, 4
alliteration, 82, 85, 144, 163, 170, 192
allusions, 75, 84, 220, 248
ambiguity, 17-18, 75
anapest, 104, 111
anaphora. *See* echoes, start-of-line
antithesis, 177, 250
  poor example of, 134
antonyms, 9
apostrophe, 90
Aristotle, 13, 55, 101, 214
ASCAP (American Society of Composers, Authors, and Publishers), 258
assignments, ten lyric-writing, 156-236
assonance, 82, 116, 144, 163, 255
attitudinal songs, 11-12, 47

bars (measures) of music, 107, 108
Bassey, Shirley, 89
Berlin, Irving, 106
blue note, 21
blues form, 20-22
Blumenthal, Francesca, 144-46, 220-23
BMI (Broadcast Music Inc.), 258
borrowing, 84, 248
brain, the, 123-39
  brainstorming (free association), 124, 127, 136, 137, 183, 190, 204-05

clustering, 124-27, 131, 205
  switching sides of, 136-38
brainstorming. *See* brain, the
breakup theme, 190-96
bridge
  in AABA form, 26-30
  in verse/chorus form, 38-39

camera-eye lyric, 52-53, 231
  assignment in, 197-203
Chapin, Harry, 141
character, the song's, 2, 3, 4, 11, 52, 78, 86, 190, 212, 222, 242, 247
  becoming, 66, 141
  naming, 163, 197, 199
cheating theme, 86
chorus. *See* verse/chorus form
circular lyrics, 14-15
clarity, the principle of, 73-76, 215, 242
clichés, 77, 140-41
climb, the, 40-41, 176, 213, 215
clustering. *See* brain, the
Cohen, Noel, 214-15
coherence, the principle of, 79-81, 134, 242, 252, 253
collaboration, 159-60
collective we. *See* viewpoint
collective you. *See* viewpoint
colloquialisms, 9, 198, 250
comedy songs
  rhyme and, 118
  rhythm and, 105
  See also humor
common time, 107
Company, 220
Complete Lyrics of Cole Porter, The (Kimball), 183, 220
compression, the principle of, 76, 158, 242, 248-51, 254
Concise Oxford Dictionary of Proverbs (Simpson), 199
conflict, 15, 56
Connecticut Songwriters Association (CSA), 260
consistency, the principle of, 78-79, 100, 242
consonance. *See* rhyme

consonants, 116, 120, 198
Copyright notice, 159
cover record, 37, 42, 44
Coward, Noel, 141, 220
Craft of Lyric Writing, The (Davis), 13
critique session
  a guided, 246-55
  guidelines to conduct a, 240-45

dactyl, 104, 105
decisions. *See* key decisions, the
development techniques. *See* plot
dialogue. *See* voice, talking
diction (language style), 57, 78, 129, 158, 247
Dictionary of Catch Phrases, A (Partridge), 185
discovery, the, 15
double entendre, 91-92
Dramatists Guild, The, 259
dry ("scratch") lyrics, 115
duets, 40, 56

echoes, word
  end-of-line (epistrophe), 84
  start-of-line (anaphora), 83, 170, 250
emotional truth. *See* feeling, the principle of genuine
emphasis, the principle of, 77-78, 163, 184, 242, 249, 254
end-stopped line, 110, 192
epistrophe. *See* echoes, end-of-line

feeling, the principle of genuine, 86
femme fatale, 214, 223
figurative language, 88-102. *See also* figures of speech
figures of speech. *See* apostrophe; double entendre; metaphor; personification; pun; simile; symbol
first line(s), 10, 11, 69, 184, 191
flashback, 28
flashforward, 28

289

focusing, 68. *See also* key deci-
    sion, the
focus sheet, 130, 134, 240
Follies, 14, 220
foreshadowing, 14
format. *See* song forms
forms. *See* song forms
free association. *See* brain, the
fruit bars, 107
future tense, the. *See* time frame

genuine feeling, the principle
    of, 86
Gershwin, Ira, 7, 9, 118
Goethe, 241
Goffin, Gerry, 119
Great Songs of the Sixties
    (Okun), 161

Hammerstein, Oscar, 86, 92
*Handbook of Commonly Used
    American Idioms* (Makkai), 9
Holden, Stephen, 89
homonyms. *See* rhyme
hook ("hooky"), 41, 42
humor, 105, 221. *See also* come-
    dy songs
hyperbole. *See* overstatement

iamb(ic), 104, 105
iambic pentameter, 105
idea(s), song, 2-5
imagery, 13, 98, 198, 244
interior monologue. *See* voice,
    thinking
ironic tension, 16
irony, 16, 23, 143, 198, 214
"itosis," 73, 74, 80, 222

Johns Hopkins University, 151

key decisions, the, 128-29
Klee, Barbara, 162-64
Knee, Alan, 248-50
Kramer, Jan, 109, 250-55

language style. *See* diction
list song, 144-45
    assignment to write a, 220-23
Los Angeles Songwriters Show-
    case (LASS), 257
Love Song of J. Alfred Prufrock,
    (Eliot), 84
lyric assignments. *See* assign-
    ments
lyric forms. *See* song forms
lyric framework, 2-19
lyric sheet, 159
Lyrics of Noel Coward, 220

McBroom, Amanda, 40, 101

meaninful sequence, 13, 80,
    190, 220
measures. *See* bars of music
melody
    of an AAA, 25-26
    of an AABA, 26-28
    of an ABAB, 31
    of an ABAC, 31-32
    of a V/C, 24, 38, 40, 44
metaphor(s), 88, 89, 251, 252
    assignment using, 204-07
    guidelines for, 93-101
meter(s), 103, 104
moral dimension of lyric writ-
    ing, 149-53, 228, 231
Morgan, Jim, 146-47, 184-85,
    228-31
motif, word. *See* word motif
music forms. *See* song forms
music, writing words to. *See* set-
    ting the tune
Musical Theatre Works Inc., 259
My Fair Lady, 120

NARAS (National Academy of
    Recording Arts and Sci-
    ences), 258
narrative perspective, 12, 48-49,
    52
Nashville Songwriters Associa-
    tion International (NSAI),
    257
National Academy of Songwrit-
    ers (NAS), 257
nonce words, 115, 185
nonsense syllables, 250

opening line(s). *See* first line(s)
overstatement (hyperbole), 77,
    88, 145, 222
    See also humor; irony

parallelism, 83, 85
paraphrasing, 12
past tense. *See* time frame
payoff, the. *See* plot
performing rights societies,
    258-59
persona song, 48
    assignment to write a, 212-15
personification, 89-90
Phillips, Dr. Robert, 149
plot (scenario/script), 11-18, 29,
    47, 212, 222
    development (payoff) tech-
        niques for, 12-18
    pitfalls in, 2, 3, 4, 54-55, 57, 60-
        62, 96, 97-98, 132-33, 214,
        250-55
point of view. *See* viewpoint
polyptoton. *See* word deriva-
    tives

Porter, Cole, 15, 27, 104, 120,
    144, 220
post-first-draft quiz, 158-59
preachiness, 51-52, 158
prechorus. *See* climb, the
present tense. *See* time frame
principles, the top ten, of good
    writing, 72-87
    checklist synopsis of, 242
"private" lyrics, 243
pronouns, 73-76
prosodic symbols, 104
prosody, 77-78, 103, 254. *See
    also* word warping
protest song, assignment to
    write a, 228-31
pun, 90-91
purple patch, 95
pyrrhic, 104

question plot, 14

Radecki, Dr. Thomas, 152
redundancy, 76, 252
refrain. *See* AAA form
release. *See* AABA form
repetend. *See* word motif
repetition, the principle of, 82-
    85, 177, 192, 250
return, the, 14, 85
reversal, 13-14
rewriting, 132-36, 245-55
rhyme, 29, 113-21
    apocopated, 113, 192
    augmented, 116, 144
    broken, 114
    character and, 120
    consonance, 116
    contiguous, 114
    couplet, 40, 41, 171
    diminished, 117, 192
    emotion and, 185
    feminine, 113, 118
    homonyms, 113, 158
    identities, 113
    internal (inner), 3, 114, 118,
        207
    light (weakened), 114, 255
    linked, 114
    masculine, 113
    mirror image, 114
    mosaic, 114
    near, 116
    para, 116, 118
    perfect, 145, 220
    pop songs and, 116
    scheme of end, 117
    song forms and, 44, 119
    telegraphing, 117
    trailing, 114
    tricks of, 115
    triple, 113

unstressed, 115, 192
See also consonants; vowels
rhythm, 103-12, 185, 207
  pitfalls of, 105, 254
Richie, Lionel, 32
Rico, Gabriele Lusser, 125
Rogers, Carl, 244
Run-on line, 110, 192

scansion, 103
scenario. *See* plot
scene, the. *See* setting, the
"scratch" lyrics. *See* dry lyrics
script, the. *See* plot
SESAC, 258
"Sesame Street," 152
setting, the, 24, 46, 67-69
setting the tune, 77, 136, 159. *See also* prosody
Shelley, Percy Bysshe, 149
show, don't tell, 82
simile, 89, 92
  assignment using, 204-07
simplicity, the principle of, 72-73, 134
singability, 120-21, 249
singee, the, 8, 13, 42, 47, 56, 59
  addressing, 54, 62, 78, 79
  defined, 11
singer
  listener identification with, 4, 252
  over-particularizing, 4
  put, in attractive light, 3
  -singee connection, 53, 134, 252
situational song, 12
Sondheim, Stephen, 14, 15, 90, 91, 92, 104, 118, 220
song forms (format). *See* AAA form; AABA form; ABAB form; ABAC form; blues form; through composed form; verse/chorus form
song starters, 7, 236
Songwriters Guild of America, The, 256-57
Songwriting association(s), 256-59
  forming a, 259-60
songwriting workshop
  forming a, 239-45
See also critique session
specificity, the principle of, 81-82, 163, 184, 242
  assignment in, 220-23
spondee, 104, 110-11, 163
stanza. *See* verse

Starner, Carrie, 21-22
Stater, Sue, 82
Stevens, Wallace, 115
Stomping the Blues (Murray), 22
story songs, 11, 35, 47, 55, 72
strong start. *See* first lines
strophic form. *See* AAA form
structures. *See* song forms
Sugden, Maureen, 83, 198
Sunday in the Park With George, 112, 190
surprise, 15-16
Sweeney Todd, 89, 90
symbol, 92-93
syncopation, 109

talking lyric. *See* voice
telegraphing. *See* rhyme
theater songs, 4, 145
themes in songs. *See* breakup; cheating; *femme fatale;* friendship; protest
thinking lyric. *See* voice
through composed (ABCD) form, 34-35
time frame, 24, 46, 60-67
  assignment to write specific, 197
  future-tense, 66-67
  past-tense, 65-66
  present-tense, 62-65
title(s), 6-10
  assignment with a one-word, 176-82
  assignment with a question, 183-86
  brainstorming for, 136
  critique session and, 241, 242
  placement of, in AAA, 23
  placement of, in AABA, 27
  placement of, in verse/chorus, 37
  spotting the, in a tune, 136
  See also song starters
tone, emotional, 128, 158, 254, 255
triplets, 107
trochee, 104, 110
12-bar blues. *See* blues form
twist, the, 15

Udis, Arline, 83, 177-78
unity, the principle of, 85-86, 163
universality, 2, 5, 25
  importance of, 48, 53, 158, 212, 242, 252
Urback, Regine, 207

verbal echoes. *See* echoes, word
verbs, 5
  action, 77, 198, 214, 215
  active-voice, 77
  passive-voice, 77
  past-tense, 66, 163-64
  present-tense, 61, 222
verse (stanza)
  in AAA form, 22-23
  in AABA form, 26-28
  in verse/chorus form, 35
verse/chorus form, 24, 35-44, 119, 134, 171, 177, 213-14
  assignment in, 176-82, 204-11
viewpoint (point of view), the, 46, 47-54
  assignment in, 190-93, 212-15
  collective we, 48, 49, 50
  collective you, 50, 51, 134
  first-person, 48-50, 55
  mixed, 53
  second-person, 50-52, 55
  third-person, 52-54, 55, 59, 170
voice, the, 34-40, 46
  assignment in talking, 190-96
  talking (dialogue), 58, 60, 134, 158, 190, 192
  thinking (interior monologue), 58, 59, 68, 134, 158
  -viewpoint relationship, 55, 59, 134
voice, (finding) your own, 140-48
vowels, 119, 120

VVTS, the, 46-69, 77, 78, 97, 99, 128, 131
  defined, 47

Weil, Cynthia, 9, 100, 119
whistle test, 44
Wolfe, Tom, 163
word derivatives (polyptoton), 83
word echoes. *See* echoes
word fusion, 75, 241-42
word motif (repetend), 14, 83, 163, 170
word warping, 111. *See also* prosody
wordplay, 177, 221, 247
workshop. *See* songwriting workshop
writer's block, 18, 236
writing words to music. *See* setting the tune
Writings and Drawings (Dylan) 161